THIS SPORTING LIFE

David Storey

PENGUIN BOOKS

Penguin Books Ltd, Harmondsworth, Middlesex, England
Penguin Books, 625 Madison Avenue, New York, New York 10022, U.S.A.
Penguin Books Australia Ltd, Ringwood, Victoria, Australia
Penguin Books Canada Ltd, 2801 John Street, Markham, Ontario, Canada L3R 1B4
Penguin Books (N.Z.) Ltd, 182–190 Wairau Road, Auckland 10, New Zealand

—

First published by Longmans 1960
Published in Penguin Books 1962
Reprinted 1963 (twice), 1965, 1968, 1976, 1977, 1979

—

—

Made and printed in Great Britain
by Cox & Wyman Ltd,
London, Reading and Fakenham
Set in Monotype Baskerville

FOR HELEN

Part One

I

I HAD my head to Mellor's backside, waiting for the ball to come between his legs.

He was too slow. I was moving away when the leather shot back into my hands and, before I could pass, a shoulder came up to my jaw. It rammed my teeth together with a force that stunned me to blackness.

The first thing I see is Mellor's vaguely apologetic face alongside that of Dai – the trainer – who's bending down with the sponge, whipping water at me.

'Come off for a bit,' he says. 'You've cut your mouth.'

I stand up with his hands knotted in my armpits. I call Mellor a few things; the players watch unconcernedly, relieved at the interlude. I walk off with Dai shoving an ammonia phial up my nose.

I sit on the bench till he's finished shouting some advice on to the field, then he presses his fingers round my mouth and his thumbs roll back my lips. 'Christ, man,' he says. 'You've broke your front teeth.'

'That's good,' I tell him sibilantly. 'Blame me.'

He stares in at the damage, his eyes dodging round the end of my nose. 'Don't blame Mellor,' he says. 'Does it hurt? It looks as though you'll need a plate.' The reserves gather round him to peer at the scene over his shoulders.

'How d' I look?'

Dai's eyes move up to mine for a second to see just how anxious I might be. 'An old man. You don't want to see no girls for a week.'

'It feels numb,' I tell him when his thumbs drop the flap down. 'I'll go back on in a minute.'

There's no real need to go back. We've a twelve point lead over a tired side with less than ten minutes to go. The crowd have already accepted the decision, and are standing by to be entertained by incidents like mine. Perhaps it's for that reason I go on again, to show just how much I care. Already it's getting dark and that mist is rising from the valley to meet the low ceiling of cloud. One of those cynical cheers wafts over the ground and groans through the stands, as I trot on to the pitch in the gloom, waving my arm at the ref.

I've time for one burst. The effect of the benzedrine's already worn off. I run down the middle of the field swinging the ball between my hands to give the impression of a dummy that wouldn't deceive a boy. I go down with the tackle, play the ball, and stay away from trouble until the final whistle. We troop off in ones and twos. The crowd has parted down the middle like a black curtain, to trickle through the main exits either end of the ground. The lighted upper decks of the buses waiting in a row in the street outside show above the banking. It should be, in fact, the best hour of the week for me: the same time every Saturday when the match is over, the lights flickering up through the dusk and the air clean from a day of no work, and the prospect of a conqueror's leisure before me. Instead I watch Mellor's stinking back and pump into it every kind of revenge. He's got his head down as we go into the tunnel and he isn't looking at anybody as he breaks indifferently through a crowd of eager officials. He's always wise like that – affecting to feel nothing. It could explain the imbecile stillness of his face.

He's no different when we're sitting crowded in the bath, the hot water jerking at the broken skin. A thin seep of blood and mud darkens the surface. It breaks and coils round the slumped men. The heads stick above the water like protesting animals in a pool; I give over trying to think.

Behind us the reserves, helped by a hunch-backed grounds-man, are sorting out the jerseys and shorts, trying to avoid the muddied sweat by treating it only with their fingertips. Their raincoated figures look resentful. They move slowly. Overhead the tramp of the departing crowd still echoes through the metal joists of the stand. The air in the room – the yellow lamp swinging in a draught – is thick with the smell of sweat, sewage mud, liniment, grease, and leather, circulating in a coil of steam that hides one wall from the other.

Standing in the mist is George Wade. I almost knock him down as I clamber over the side of the bath and stagger to the massage table. I don't recognize him till I feel the paw of his dog under my bare foot and hear the whimper. He comes and stands over me as Dai greases and thumps my thigh.

'How d'you feel, Art?' he says, leaning on his stick and bending over the landscape of my body. He's careful to look only at my mouth.

I grin illustratively at his old retired face. He finds it funny and laughs. 'You won't be able to shoot your mouth as you used,' he says. 'Least, not for a few days.' He sees how amused I am. 'I'll fix up a dentist for you on Monday . . . no I can't, can I? Monday's Boxing Day. I'll see what I can do.' He peers at me a while, absorbing this new impression of me without teeth. I think it pleases him, for he asks me as though I'm a reasonable person, 'Will you be coming to Weaver's tonight? I thought he said you was.'

I've already thought about this. A Christmas Eve celebration, and the chance of meeting Slomer for the first time. I can't make up my mind. 'About my teeth,' I say. 'Can you get them fixed for me tonight? It's going to be a week before I get to a dentist otherwise.'

Wade chews his lips, and narrows his eyes in affected contemplation. 'Isn't there a dentist in the Supporters' Club?' I encourage him.

He shakes his head. 'I don't know, Arthur. I don't know at all. I could see.' He looks at me to see if it's going to be worth that trouble.

'Could you find out now, *sir*?'

He turns round, and dragging the dog stumbles through

9

the mounds of dirty clothing to the door. The animal staggers as it tries to get a hind leg over one of these piles of laundry.

'I'll see, old lad. I'll see. Leave it to me,' he calls through the yellow mist.

'I want it tonight,' I shout. He injects a cold stream of air as he goes out.

I get off the bench and sit under my clothes. There're a few screams from the bath: somebody's behaviour below the waterline is causing objection. One or two come shooting over the bath side and stand watching the water as they scratch themselves. 'Dirty frogs, man,' Dai's telling himself as he joins the inspection before laughing. I'm in the mood I'd have given anything to avoid this particular day.

Frank creaks the bench beside me, unconsciously pressing his great bulk against my arm. He looks at me understandingly, sensing my feeling in his slow miner's mind. It's with the same reluctant concentration that he rubs his shoulders: the nearest he can get to direct sympathy. I'm smiling at him; I'm always smiling at him – he has that humility professionals acquire after a life of hard grinding. It's the lack of arrogance I like most in Frank. I don't mind him being captain, and I don't begrudge him his age. Soon he'll have finished playing for good.

'Are you going to Weaver's tonight, Art?' He pats his huge thighs and makes them tremble. 'A've just been hearing about his feast from Maurice yon.' He nods towards Maurice's stocky figure, almost contorted by precocious muscle, and Maurice grins back at us, pointing out the argument in the bath.

'I'd been counting on going. How d'you think I look?' I say.

Frank stands up to dry his body; now it's his belly hanging and swaying like a sack. 'Maurice's been behaving like a pig again, Art,' he says, and watches soberly as Maurice doubles up with laughter. 'I'm wukking nights this week, did I tell thee? And I've the lad's stocking to fill.' He looks at me sideways and asks genially, 'How's thy Mrs Hammond?'

It's a big joke to mention me and Mrs Hammond. With

Frank it's sometimes a reproach. I grope under the bench and pull out a carrier. 'I've got something for her kids. A couple of dolls for the girl and a train for the nipper.'

'How old are they?'

'Lynda's around five. The kid's just over two. The bitch won't like it though. She doesn't like me interfering.' I pull a nigger doll out of its wrapper and make its eyes flash for him. He smiles.

'They say Slomer's going tonight,' I tell him.

He turns his eyes lazily to mine. 'I wouldn't press myself to get close to him.'

I laugh and he looks at my teeth. 'Any road,' he says, straining forward to pull on his socks, 'I can't see thee going up there solely on account of Slomer. What woman have you got lined up this time?'

Frank's one of those people who either don't hear or don't listen to what you say but just fire occasional questions to keep you occupied. If you do make contact it's usually with some subject you've finished dealing with. He stands up in his socks, pats his belly reflectively, and faces the coke fire across the room. He flicks the towel to me.

'Rub us me back, Art.' He sways with the massage and something he's saying is lost. 'If I were you I'd leave well alone,' he says when I hang the towel on his shoulder. He rubs at my back. 'It's dry. Did you hear what I said?' I nod, losing interest as a numb pain makes holes in my upper jaw. 'I'd get thy mouth seen to. It's more important.'

Cold air shoots into the room as the door opens. George Wade follows the dog in. 'How soon can you be ready, Arthur?' he calls through the steam.

'Have you got somebody?'

'Shut the door, George. That's a good old lad,' a voice shouts from the bath.

'A school dentist or something. Mr Weaver's arranging it if we hurry.'

'What a way to spend Christmas,' Frank says. 'Do you want me to come?'

Wade says something about: 'That's all right, Frank. Mr Weaver says he'll take him down in his car.'

'A nice piece of luck,' Frank decides. He's coughing in the steam, resting his inflamed body against the massage table, watching me dress.

Clutching the carrier, I shout 'Happy Christmas' from the door and follow Wade through the damp coldness of the tunnel beneath the stand. 'Of course,' he's saying, 'if you have to have dentures like Dai seems to think, the club'll pay. I'll tell Weaver. How do you feel? Your teeth, I mean.'

I give him a grunt as we climb the wooden steps to the tea room and bar. Standing just inside the door, as I expected, is old man Johnson. He takes hold of my arm as I come through. 'How are you, Arthur? Are you all right?' His eyes are small with anxiety. It's all up with him. I try to swing away without hurting him. 'I think Weaver's arranged a dentist,' he says.

'Leave him alone, Johnson,' Wade's telling him. 'We're in a hurry.'

Only we're not. I've already guessed, from seeing the back of Weaver's crombie coat, that a detour to a dentist at this time of the day's going to be a real nuisance. Wade jumps from one foot to another, trying to attract Weaver from his conversation. The dog stands still. Johnson watches from the door. Eventually Wade tires of his dance and rests his hand for a second on the plush material of Weaver's shoulder. The industrialist half turns, affecting his usual surprise at the incidents of life, and glances quickly at me before studying Wade's embarrassed gesture with severe amusement.

'Yes, George?'

'Arthur's ready to go, Mr Weaver,' Wade says, and adds after a moment, 'whenever you are.'

'Is that so? I shan't be a minute, George. How's it feel Arta boy?' He turns back to his conversation in time to miss what I say.

'Business,' Wade whispers, upping his thumb at the group in front of Weaver and, measuring his redundancy accurately, adds, 'I'll be at the bar if you want me. There's no point in me hanging on his coat tails.' He leads the dog to join the committee.

Johnson sees the chance to make a second approach, but just as his mind stumbles to the idea Weaver turns his baby face to me and says irritably, 'You ready, Arthur?'

When I say 'Yes', it's with an unavoidable sibilance that softens him.

'Let's have a look,' he says, unconsciously echoing my lisp, and I show him the scene. It soothes him a bit. He moves to one side casually so that his colleagues can accidentally see the view. 'You've copped a mouthful there, old son. I don't know how he's going to fix up mashers like those.'

Weaver has certain mannerisms, and not only of speech, which he thinks reflect his background of industrial democracy. Some people never get used to it. Wade, for instance, never calls him 'Charles' but always 'Mr Weaver'. I realize, seeing the blush deepen around the puffed-up encasements of Weaver's eyes, that he's just been talking about me. 'Do you mind waiting?' he says. 'Maurice hasn't come up yet. I want a chat with him before we go . . . was he nearly ready when you came up?'

'How long are we going to wait?'

'Oh, we'll have to wait until he comes,' he replies. 'Have a drink.' Then he suddenly looks at his nails as he remembers something. 'No, better not, in case the old boy wants to use gas. I'll send somebody down to hurry Morry up – he played a blinder today. What do you think?'

'It went his way.'

'It always does, old son.' He has a slight burst of excitement, then quietens down to say, 'You played well yourself, Arthur, until your accident. Why d'you go back on the field, hero?'

'I thought it was the best thing to do. I felt shaken.'

'Did you thump him?'

'Who?'

'The tree trunk who hit you.'

'Mellor played the ball too slow.'

'Aye – that might have been it. Never mind. It happens to the best of us. Not quite the present for Christmas.' One side of him raises itself to wave at Maurice who's just bounded through the door. 'Here we are, Morry!'

'How you feeling, Art?' Maurice says. He fidgets in his huge overcoat. The shoulders have collapsed either end because there's just no Maurice beneath them. 'Mellor,' he says. 'Did you ever see such a frog play a ball?' He looks at Weaver. 'I don't know why you have people like that on the books.'

'You think it was Mellor, then,' Weaver says, not much interested, but watching Maurice keenly.

'Aw,' Maurice pulls a face, drops the subject. 'Don't let it stop you coming tonight, Art,' he says. 'Though, Christ, are you going to a dentist? Dai said you'd gone.'

'We're just on our way,' Weaver tells him. 'Do you want to come in the car? I don't know how long we'll be, but we can go straight on up after Arthur boy's finished with his teeth.'

'Suits me. I wouldn't like to miss seeing Arthur in the chair. We might get a camera.'

'While we're about it, I think George Wade better come,' Weaver decides. 'He won't want to, but he can come all the same and see how much trouble we're going to.'

Through the rear window of the stand I can see Weaver's Bentley in the lane below. Frank suddenly appears beside it from the players' entrance, his head bowed, his throat muffled in a white scarf tucked into his dyed Service overcoat. The street light shows up the thinness of his hair.

'I might have to leave you at the dentist's if it takes too long,' Weaver says as he comes back towing Wade. 'You don't mind, do you Arthur? I've got Slomer and some other guests coming tonight so I want to be home in plenty of time. Are we all ready?' We all troop out. 'Do you mind much if we put the dog in the boot, George?' Weaver asks, leaning from the window of the Bentley after releasing the doors.

'That's all right,' Wade says uncertainly.

'It's unlocked. You can put it in yourself.' Then he says slowly, 'What about your dog, Arthur?'

'How d'you mean?'

14

He points at old Johnson standing at the players' entrance, his too-large flat cap hiding his face.

'That's not so funny,' I tell him. Wade and Maurice ignore my tone as though they hadn't heard.

Weaver pulls in his head and says from inside, 'Do you want him to come?'

I don't want him, but I give him a call and he comes lurching across preparing to show his gratitude. 'Get in,' I tell him. 'We're just going.'

'Where're you sitting, Arthur?' he asks. I pull him in the back.

'I only hope thy dog doesn't sup the ale, Mr Wade,' Maurice says from the front seat.

Weaver says, 'It'll have to have a mouth like a bottle-opener,' but nobody's laughing. The car slides past the visitors' bus. The three players inside stare out vacantly, and don't see us.

The lights of the town are splayed out below. We drop quickly to their level. The ridge across the valley at Sand-wood, where Weaver's house stands, is lost beyond the stone buildings. We reach the Bull Ring and turn up a one-way street where the car stops alongside a brick Victorian house.

'He's already there,' Weaver says. 'That's good.' He leans over the steering wheel to point out the lighted up-stairs window. 'Are you all going in, or will you wait in the car?'

'I'm off in,' Maurice answers. 'How about you, Mr Wade?'

'Oh, don't mind me.' He's lighted a cigar during the trip down from Primstone. 'I'll wait here with the dog.'

'There isn't much I can do either,' Weaver says, his usual coldness stimulated by the drive. 'I'll wait with George. If I'm needed let me know. I suppose Mr Johnson will go with you.'

The three of us get out. The front door of the house is open. 'Children's Dental Centre' is painted on the wood-work. Johnson has his hand pressed on my back as we climb the stairs. The dentist hears us coming; he's waiting on the first landing. 'Which of you is it?' he asks, and gives Maurice a preferential look.

Maurice's big coat gives him the passing appearance of an invalid. 'It's not me, old cock,' he answers. 'It's Arthur here.'

The dentist leads the way into his surgery. 'Sit in the chair,' he says. 'I've a member's ticket. That'll be how you traced me. Though I haven't seen a match this season.' He says this as though it should have disqualified him from helping. 'Where's Mr Weaver?'

'In the car. He's not in control of his knees. Isn't that right, Arthur?'

I nod, lying back in the chair and staring at the frosted glass covering the surgery light. The ether turns my belly over after the dank smell of the changing room and the plush warmth of the car. 'I won't be a minute,' the dentist says, and trots off down the stairs.

'You know what's the matter with him,' Maurice says. 'I reckon it might be up to me to remove those molars, Art.' He fingers the instruments, vibrating the wires on the drilling machine, and has just found the forceps in a drawer when the dentist starts pounding back up the stairs.

'He's coming,' Johnson says urgently from his corner.

'How much do you think he's touched Weaver for?' Maurice asks.

'A fiver.'

'Fiver at least. Remember whose birthday it is.'

The dentist's panting slightly; he glances at the forceps in Maurice's hand. 'You managing all right on your own?' he says. 'Or do you want my advice?'

'I wouldn't mind a bit of professional opinion,' Maurice says behind my head.

'Well it's this: don't meddle.' He sounds more than angry, and since Maurice doesn't answer I guess it might be serious. I half turn, but he's already holding my head. I open up and shut my eyes. His breath comes hot and fast, with an unprofessional smell. He makes a sound of irritation.

'It's a mess,' he says. 'Is it hurting?'

'Not much.' I hear noises of anxiety from Johnson; they correspond with a flow of blood from the gum.

'They might behave themselves for a few days yet without

giving serious trouble,' he suggests. 'You could go to your own dentist then – this is a children's clinic, you know.'

'What needs doing?'

'They'll have to come out, of course. Six of them. You might save one with a bit of trouble. In any case they should keep until Wednesday. You'll find a public dentist open by then.'

'Hasn't Weaver paid you enough?' I ask him.

I feel him draw back and I open my eyes. 'How do you mean?' He suddenly has a thick, natural Yorkshire accent. Maurice has moved up.

'If he hasn't paid the right fee we'll pay you the rest. I can get it out of him later. How much is it?'

'That's not the point,' he says. He hasn't yet, if he's ever going to, put on his white overall, and he looks something like a bank clerk caught with a threepenny default. 'It's the plate that's going to be the trouble. I presume you'll want a set of upper dentures.'

'Yes, he will,' Maurice says.

'Then it's going to make it a little awkward if he goes along with six recent extractions and asks a completely new dentist for dentures. Because I can't give him them myself.'

'Why not?' Maurice wonders, preferring an argument to nothing at all. 'You're just arsing around. Kids have false teeth. I know one who has myself.'

'Do you?' The dentist's nodding.

'You can fix it with one of your mates. You do the pulling and he does the plate.'

'I'm prepared to turn you out without even a sedative,' he says eventually. 'You're doing me no favour in coming here.'

I'm sweating, feeling sick. Johnson has now moved up to look at my face. 'It's no party here,' I tell them. 'Let's get it over with whatever the bloody price.'

'You see,' Maurice says. 'He's in pain.'

'It'll be five guineas,' the dentist says to me. I wonder whether to tell him what a mean stinking frog he is. I imagine some of the reprisals he could take. He asks, 'Do you want it?'

17

I tell him 'yes' and Maurice says he'll pay for the time being, and the dentist watches the money laid out. He puts it into an inside pocket. 'It's not as lucrative as you might think, working for a local council,' he says, pulling on a white smock. 'You won't find anybody else coming out at this time. It'll have to be gas. Have you eaten recently?'

'Not since dinner time.'

Maurice adds, 'And you'll fix it with a pal for the plate?'

'Yes,' he says. 'And would you mind waiting in the next room? You can leave the door open if you want to watch. But I don't want you in here.'

In a minute he's putting the mask over me. I begin to panic, and shout to Maurice. National Health, a stink of whisky. Let me out of here. Johnson's funny hollow face. And there's Johnson's sick face.

2

WHY worry about him? That's the first thought I had when I found myself wondering about Johnson. After I'd used him it seemed odd I should try to find out all I could about him. At first I'd relied on him entirely, so I didn't look too close in case I saw how fragile his support was. Yet when his usefulness had expired I began to wonder who he was. Perhaps I'd never come across a man who was quite as broken down as Johnson. I might have been a bit startled by his limitless simplicity. How small does a man get? I wondered every time I saw him stumping along.

I'd known of Johnson when I was a boy. He was fairly conspicuous to all the women and kids on Highfield estate because when all the men were at work Johnson would still be seen walking about the streets, the only man in sight. I suppose solitariness encouraged him to the idea of premature age – he pretended to be ten years older than he really was. This of course was added to the oddity of his persistent idleness. I think for a while, perhaps a couple of weeks, he'd been a park keeper.

When I was in my last year at school, and in the Rugby League team, Johnson got on to the committee of the City Rugby League Club up at Primstone. He wasn't there very long, yet it wasn't so short I didn't keep the impression of him as a person of some significance. This was a mistake, in every respect, yet it was to my advantage. How he got there, unless it was because he had more spare time than anyone else in town, I still don't know.

I didn't really get to know him until I was twenty. At that time I'd followed a newspaper advert to 15 Fairfax Street. Two years previous to this I'd been exempted National Service because of bad feet; my right ankle was misshapen from a football accident at school. I'd lost interest in the game. I'd got stuffed with living at home with my parents, and I'd been on the move from one Irish house to another.

Mrs Hammond could have been the four-eyed monster for all I cared. She was providing board and lodging for thirty-five bob a week, with a room to myself; it seemed *she* was wanting to keep *me*. I couldn't have made better conditions myself. I was the only lodger and she was a not-too-young widow and the house was in a terrace: it was natural that her reaction should be what it was, for she'd only recently been deprived of a fairly happy youth. Always standing in the hearth was a pair of brown working boots.

I'd been working at Weaver's for two years when I went to her place. She hated my guts, my parents hated her, the kids were yelling their nuts off all day. I didn't care. I'd just got my own lathe at Weaver's, and I spent most of my time watching Maurice Braithewaite who worked in the same shop. I found it interesting to see the sort of feelings he aroused. He was admired and he was detested. It wasn't difficult to decide who felt what. He'd given up using the works' canteen and went to a nearby transport cafe with a couple of pals. He looked pretty special, I thought. And he was only my age.

By playing Rugby League he kept his head above the general level of crap, and that to me was the main thing. I could barely keep myself afloat. It was he who explained the need for a backer or a talent scout when I suggested I'd like a trial at Primstone. I didn't seem to know anyone, and he made it clear he wouldn't push me, so I mentioned Johnson. 'Never heard of him,' he said. 'But you ask him. You'll have to have somebody to vouch for you.'

So I went to see Johnson. I didn't go thinking he'd be able to help me. I just went to see what'd happen if I asked him. When I knocked on the door he came out and peered at me, and I was in no doubt at all that his wife was right behind the door. When I began to explain what I wanted he blurted out, 'But you can't come knocking at my door!' It struck me as being right funny and I laughed. He didn't know what I was laughing at, but he came one step down and whispered something about the 'King William'. I went away holding myself up. I leant against hedges, gates, and lamp-posts. I felt I'd never seen a funnier man than Johnson. I met him in the pub. It was the only time I did laugh at him.

I was soon discouraged by the start I made. The year of waiting while Johnson made his devious, laborious efforts to get me started at Primstone benefited him a lot more than it did me. He knew it too. I wouldn't be surprised if he spoilt his own efforts so's to postpone the time when I could act on my own. He began to show signs of relying on me that I wasn't sure I liked. His footsteps seemed to follow me down every street. Why not find some other means of getting in at Primstone? I'd been hoping Maurice Braithewaite might change his mind and give me the little push I needed. But he gave no indication of wanting to help. There was a long queue of prospective forwards demanding trials; I had to rely on Johnson exclusively to take me to the head of it.

When I ran on to the field it was almost dark. A heavy mist hung over the valley and enclosed the ground in a tight grey wall of drizzle. It was bitterly cold. The players ran around in groups, small and unreal beneath the half empty flanks of the terraces; insects released in a space. I felt sick and frightened, uncertain why I'd come up to Primstone at all, why I'd spent a year getting there. Everything outside the dark wreath of the crowd and the wooden pinnacles of the stadium was hidden. We were isolated; all that was familiar, encouraging, had vanished, leaving us in the shell of the stands. I wasn't sure any longer what the performance was for.

Johnson had been at the tunnel mouth as I ran on to the field. How he'd fixed up the four trial games I didn't know. But this was supposed to be his hour of triumph. He stood sullen and dejected when I passed him. I could still see him, as we waited for the emergence of the other team, climbing slowly up the centre steps of the main stand. Then the tunnel mouth erupted with a stream of white jerseys flooding on to the field.

I'd asked Mrs Hammond to come, but she'd refused and made it plain she didn't want to be pestered about it.

'Aw, it's my first game. I need somebody there to cheer me.'

'You can cheer yourself. You won't catch me up there in the cold, freezing to death for an hour.'

When I tried to soften her up she said, 'You don't have to do it.' Her whole face glistened with animosity.

'It's only a job. If I play well I might collect three or four hundred quid.'

She laughed. 'I don't doubt they'll give you all that.'

'That's just the sort of encouragement I need. But I'd still like you to come.'

'I'm not going,' she moaned. 'If I wanted to I would. I've said it. I don't want to go.'

'Wish me luck then.'

'All that's coming your way. I don't wish you my luck.'

I jumped up and down on the spot, restless, trying to re-collect her face as I left the house. There'd been a look of suspicious interest, clouded by a lot of self-pity. I was glad she hadn't come. In any case it didn't look very impressive: a couple of hundred people, two reserve teams playing, Johnson now waving his spider arms. But her aggressive sort of indifference roused in me a kind of anger, a savageness, that suited the game very well. I lost all sense of caution. By half-time in the first game, as we filed off the pitch, I'd realized this wildness was essential to the way I played. Although it seemed to correspond to my personality, it didn't please me to admit that this slower, unskilful way of playing, the use of my advantage in size and weight, were the only assets I had to offer.

We lined up for the second half under a thin persistent drizzle, shrouding one end of the ground from the other. I was suddenly happy, relieved, full of air. I didn't put it down to anything at that moment; I used it to encourage myself. Afterwards, I recognized it as a preliminary feeling of power. I was big, strong, and could make people realize it. I could tackle hard and, with the kind of deliberation I took a pride in later, really hurt someone. I was big. Big! It was no mean elation.

I listened to the tune of the crowd, a sound I'd never heard before. I tried to conduct it, for a minute, for two minutes; for quite a while I raised noises from them as I might have done from a tamed animal. I was big!

In the last quarter of an hour the elation gave way to a weariness I'd never imagined before. I never wanted to play again. The cold and dampness reached the very centre of my body; my hands and feet disappeared. Now a wall had been built between me and the crowd: I couldn't hear them. The field had grown, its limits disappeared into that suffocating mist. The ground continually surged up to absorb me. I listened to the thud of my vanished feet as they pushed automatically against the earth. I hated the crowd making me suffer like this. My eyes hung out, my mouth hung open, the air dropped down my throat like lumps of filed lead.

All this was unnecessary. I was running round the field like a big tart, dropping my guts out with every stride I took, when I could have been ambling along easily. Even in the space of four trial games I learnt to save energy just for those moments when I could use it most effectively. But I never felt so exhausted and relieved as after that first match. I didn't care if I never played again. Just to get on my backside was enough. I never wanted to move again. I lay soaking and gasping in the bath, the water clinging to my chest in a suffocating grip, my skin convulsed as the heat burnt at its broken surface. Behind me I could hear Johnson's excited

22

voice; around me the laughter and chatter of communal relief.

Somebody held a towel and rubbed my back, then the trainer was dabbing yellow liniment on my arms and legs. Johnson was standing by the door, his eyes glowing and fixed on me with pride and fascination. He was making signs of approval. When I was half dressed he found the excuse to rush over.

'You played a blinder,' he stated quietly, waiting for me to license his delight.

'You enjoyed it.'

'Aw now, Arthur,' he said softly, shaking. 'Arthur, it was the best game I ever saw. They'll be all over you.'

'You think so?'

'I know so.' His eyes widened as he encouraged himself. 'I was sitting right in the middle of the committee,' he lied. 'I know them, the way they think. You played just right, just the right game. Didn't I tell you?' He started off on several incidents I never knew occurred.

'Don't make it sound too good,' I told him, because his voice was beginning to carry, and several people were smiling too openly.

'Too good!' He pulled his hand away in feigned injury. 'They looked like schoolboys the way you played.'

'They didn't feel that young. Don't get so excited, Dad. We're still in the dressing room. How d'you get in here, anyway?'

'They don't mind me,' he said. Then he whispered, 'There'll be no holding you, Arthur. You'll be able to ask any price you like.' He looked at me carefully. 'But don't I know? Wasn't I on this committee here before you could even hold a football? You know – you've been able to take my word for it so far. Don't you think so, Arthur?' He took hold of my arm.

'They won't all feel the same way as you do, Dad. Try and see it from their view.'

'You'll find them no different from me.' He looked sick. 'Maybe they won't show it. Naturally – they won't show it like me.'

23

He let go of my arm and waited for me to dress. He looked round the room and made a few obvious comparisons between me and the other players, looking at their legs and their chests, and then at mine. I joined them round the fire for a while to make sure Johnson hadn't lost me anything by his loud mouth. Then he showed me up to the tearoom.

'There's nobody important here,' he said. He sounded confident.

'Aren't any of the committee you mentioned?'

'No. In any case George Wade, the chairman, 's with the first team at St Helens.'

We helped ourselves to some tea and sandwiches. 'What's Wade like?' I asked.

'He'll be the one who decides. I've seen him about you. He's hard but he knows his business. He's been in the game for as long as you've lived.'

I felt tired of Johnson. I wanted to talk to the other players, to find out how hard they were, what the layout was, how well I'd played. I was already tired of the old man and his big looks at my body. I watched his little mouth opening and closing and wondered what it was made him do that. Why go on talking, little man? I meant to ask him. And all this froth, too. Instead I said, 'What about Weaver – or Slomer?'

'How do you mean?' He looked puzzled, slightly worried.

'Don't they have a say?'

He shook his head. 'They provide the money. Wade provides the football. You don't want to think about them.'

'What's Weaver like?'

I don't think he heard. I shouldn't think he'd have understood if he saw me more interested in Weaver than in playing football. The tearoom filled, and after ten minutes emptied again. No one was interested in staying. I waited on my own while Johnson wandered round the room distributing opinions and confidences that raised a few eyes in my direction and even more eyebrows in his. He had little black boots on that made his feet look like stubs.

We left together and caught a bus outside the ground. An early winter darkness had already settled. The lights of the town glowed hazily in the valley. We sat at the front of the bus and watched the grey stone walls and buildings slip away either side. I took out the paper book I'd been trying to read on the way up before the match. Johnson's elation was beginning to drain now it was all over. He made occasional comments, glancing at me with a new type of possessiveness. In the same mood we got off the bus in the Bull Ring and caught the 10 bus along West Street to Highfield.

'I've read that,' he said, touching the book, then laying his finger across the page to stop me reading.

'What's it about?' I asked him.

'A boxer.' He coughed, and blew his nose through his fingers.

'You can tell that from the cover,' I said, showing him the picture on the front. He stared at the painted face and the two big red gloves.

'Do you like the book?' he asked.

I shrugged, said something casual: I didn't want to show him I was impressed by this tough hero. Eventually, as if he'd got fingers clamped round his throat, he let out what had been occupying him since the match. 'Do you want me to come home with you?'

He looked at me with a bewildered sort of anxiety; acting.

'It's no trouble – no trouble to me,' he added.

'If you like. Come and have some tea. Mrs Hammond won't mind.'

He didn't say anything else. We rattled on through the pools of lamplight, past the estate, to the more isolated extremity of the town below the hospital ridge.

There was no one in the house. Mrs Hammond was out with the two kids. Probably on purpose. We sat in the kitchen at the back and waited. Johnson started off about the match again, glancing now and again at the pair of brown boots in the hearth, digging at the fire with the poker, and adding more coal. He tried to make himself at home.

It was at the fire, and its now huge blaze, that Mrs Hammond's eyes flashed the moment she was in the room. She stared angrily at me and one of the kids said, 'I'n it warm, Mam?'

'Warm!' she said, then caught sight of Johnson struggling to his feet in the corner of the room. 'It's like an oven,' she added bitterly. 'You know we can't use all that coal, Mr Machin.' She ignored Johnson and waited for me. Her resentment turned from the fire to Johnson: I shouldn't have brought him in.

'Mr Johnson came home with me,' I told her aimlessly. 'We've just got back from the match. This's Mrs Hammond,' I told him. They said something to each other. Johnson stayed by his chair.

'We haven't much in for tea,' she said.

'Don't boast about it,' I told her. 'Mr Johnson might get the idea we're poor.'

She was close to tears or to breaking out in threats. She'd no feeling left for anything. I helped her to empty her bag. I saw it was a big mistake bringing Johnson back, and I found I wasn't blaming her. I was blaming him. I put the few packets on the table, and wondered why she'd bothered buying them.

'I've just been shopping,' she said. 'It's awful weather.'

'It is,' Johnson said. 'Nowt but drizzle and mist.'

She fussed round the table, content I should help her, wanting Johnson to see that I did. She filled the kettle. The kids were still standing by the door. They sensed their mother's resentment and glowered at Johnson's figure.

'You sit down,' I told him.

He slid into the chair and sat upright, alert, watching me. Mrs Hammond said, 'How did the match go? Did you win?'

There was no need for her to hide her interest; she wasn't at all concerned. I made some reply, then Johnson almost cried out, 'He played a blinder, missis!'

'Did he?' She looked at me for a second. 'And how much have they signed him on for?'

'It's not as quick as that. He's another three matches to play afore they settle ought like that.'

'I'd have thought', she said, lighting up at Johnson's concern, 'if he was as good as that they'd have signed him, right off.'

'Oh, no,' He sounded pompous. 'They've to have a safe-guard – you know, where so much money's bound up.'

'He's another three matches to play for nothing then.'

'Not for nothing. He gets thirty bob; amateur pay. It's a sort of safeguard.'

'That's very good,' she said. 'Thirty shillings.'

'It's nowt really,' he told her. 'He'll be able to ask for anything he likes after four matches like today's. It won't pay them to refuse him, Mrs Hammond. I'nt that right, Arthur?'

'I don't know.'

'I'm sure they'll give *him* it, Mr Johnson.'

'Yes,' he said, his eyes watering in the heat. 'He'll sail away.'

'You'll be very pleased,' she said with even greater tart-ness, and looked at Johnson with increased surprise.

We were outside the front door, in the street, when John-son suddenly touched my arm and whispered, 'I forgot to tell thee. Slomer was there today.'

I pulled away from him. 'Why didn't you tell me before?'

'I forgot. He left before the end. It's not often he comes to watch an "A" team match.'

'What did he think?'

He smiled. 'Nay, he didn't talk to *me*.'

'Couldn't you tell by his face? He's a cripple, isn't he? Where was he sitting?'

'Behind me. A few rows back.'

He suddenly regretted having mentioned Slomer.

'Where are you going now, Arthur?' he said, and looked behind me into the lighted passage distastefully. 'Come on out. We can go down to the King.'

'I feel tired.'

'We can be down there in a minute. We can catch a bus.'

When I moved aside the light showed up his small anxious face; an irritated mask in the darkness. Behind me I heard Mrs Hammond in the passage. 'I'll come tomorrow, maybe. Around dinner-time,' I told him, and stepped back inside the door. 'I'll see you then, Dad.'

'You don't mind me helping you? Do you, Arthur?'

'Why d'you say that?' His face disappeared, replaced by the worn top of his flat cap, as though he'd scraped under many roofs with it on.

'I was hoping . . . you know, that you didn't think I was pushing in, interfering,' his hidden face said.

'No. . . .' I began uncertainly.

'Because I want to help you – you know what I mean? If I'm in a position to help I think it's only right. . . .'

'Yeh. That's right, Dad.'

'You don't mind?'

'No,' I emphasized. 'I don't know what you're talking about. I'll see you tomorrow, then.'

'Tomorrow,' he said. 'Eleven o'clock.'

'Thanks for everything.'

'That's all right, Arthur. Any time. Any time at all.'

He waited for me to close the door on him.

Mrs Hammond was clearing up in the kitchen. I remembered that particular look on her face for a long time afterwards. 'Since the fire's so high we don't want a light,' she said.

'I only want a rest,' I told her. 'It's all right by me.' I sat by the fire and didn't make a sound.

'Why don't you go to your room if you're tired?' she said when she saw me getting out *Blood on the Canvas*. Her voice was half strangled. The flames moved about on her.

'I couldn't rest there. I don't feel like sleeping.'

'Aren't you going out? I'd have thought you'd be wanting to enjoy your fame.'

I gave a big sigh to show how really tired I was.

'You could do something then, to help out.'

'As you like.' Ted Williams was telling his woman about the fight. She was stroking his hair, laying it on thick, making him feel it was worth it, for her. He was wincing with pain. But he was tough. 'What do you want?'

'You could wash up. Everything seems to have piled up today. One thing and another.' Her voice had no tone –

that is, it had only one tone, dull, as if she were suppressing some big internal pain.

I went to the sink and put the tea things in the bowl, then the dinner things, then the breakfast things, then the plates from last night's supper. 'Leave that Johnson's cup on one side,' she said. 'I'll wash it out later myself – scald it. There's some water in the kettle for washing.'

I poured it out, steaming, but when I had to cool it from the tap she said, 'Don't put too much cold water in. You might as well not have used the water from the kettle.'

'Where's Lynda and the kid?'

'They're upstairs. I'm putting them to bed in a minute.'

'It's early for them.'

'They always go early on Saturdays.'

I clinked a few cups and wiped the mist off the mirror so I could see myself, and she added, 'If they don't they're kept awake by the drunks, and they never settle down.' She watched me wash the first cup. She waited for the second, then said, 'If you rinse the cup under the tap after you've washed it you get the soap out – it's cleaner. I don't want to keep bothering.'

When she came down from shoving the kids to bed the pots were standing on the table ready to put away. I was sitting by the fire, getting a dose of what Williams's domestic routine was like after a big fight. I wondered why they didn't put a picture of his blonde sample on the front cover. Say in the background, behind one of those big red gloves, just to the right of his ear. She could be draped on this sofa she had in her flat. It'd look pretty neat, him stuck out front, taking the knocks, and she waiting behind, all ready with a big load of comfort. What it must be like to be Williams! All those samples to choose from. Nobody to beat his left chop and that killing right hook. His left chop –

'You can smoke if you like,' Mrs Hammond said, and after examining the plates to see how much grease I might have left on them, she began carrying them to the cupboard.

'How d'you mean?'

'I say – you can smoke.'

'But what's all the fussing, the telling, about?'

'Now the children are out of the way. I don't like smoking when they're down here.'

'You never mentioned that before.'

'Well, now you know.' She messed about in the cupboard, making some noise. Then she said, 'It's hardly a wage.'

'You mean this afternoon?'

She didn't say anything.

'They make it one when they sign you on,' I told her.

'And will they?'

'I don't know.'

'The old man seemed pretty sure . . . He treats you like a son.'

I turned to look at her. 'I wouldn't say that.' I thought about what she'd said. 'I only call him Dad because he's old.'

'I don't mean that.'

'What do you mean?'

'The way he treats you – ogles you. He looks at you like a girl.'

'Aw, don't come with that. He's interested that's all.'

'I'd say excited.'

'Excited then. What's the matter with that? There isn't much for him to get excited about at his age. He's done a lot for me.'

'That's what I mean – it's unusual.' She hung the cups on their respective hooks in the cupboard as if her argument fell into place in the same easy way.

'If you don't take an interest in football yourself, just how do you know what way it affects other people? Most of them that do get excited over it are his age.'

'Not personal, though. It's personal with him.' She'd come to stand with her hands flat on the table.

'Look – I know you're tired and I shouldn't have brought him back here. I'm sorry. I won't do it again.'

'I'm not tired. I don't care if you bring him back or not.'

'What are you getting at, then?'

'Nothing.'

'He hasn't a son of his own. Do you know him or something?'

'I might do.' She'd tensed across the table, with the fire-light flickering on her. 'How much would he get if you did sign on?'

I tried to act hurt. But she wasn't noticing. It seemed to me she was trying to keep up with me, and ahead of Johnson. I put the hurt tone into my voice. 'He'd get nothing. I've never even thought of it.'

'I bet *he* has.'

I suddenly felt there might be something in Johnson's friendship I ought to protect.

'He's not like that,' I told her.

'Isn't he. He's never had a job in his life.'

She was really bitter. I wondered how Williams would have handled her. Beaten her up? Slapped her down – he'd at least have done that. That could be the smart way a tiger acted. Rough. 'And how do you know he's never worked?' I said.

'I've got eyes. Just look at his hands. He's never done a day's work. He's got awful hands. They're all soft.'

'What the hell have his hands got to do with it?' I took a quick look at my own. 'He's got awful hands. I've got awful hands. We're not all women. I don't even know if I will be signed on. He doesn't know either.'

'He seems to have a good idea.' She sounded casual. 'I heard him mention Slomer.'

'What does that mean?'

'I heard him mention Slomer.'

'So you heard him mention Slomer. You're talking like a kid. What're you talking *about*? That's what I'd like to know. Slomer helps to pay for the club. In fact, he probably *is* the club. At least a good half of it. He's got a lot of money.'

'And you're satisfied with that sort of money? He's a Catholic.'

I wondered how far that should affect me. After all, in this street, in the next street, in all the streets, the battalions of them you could see from the hospital ridge over the valley, a Catholic more or less represented a foreign agent. They might be on your side. On the other hand they might not. It was better to treat them all as enemies, then you could be sure. If you made every one of them a tiger then you couldn't go far wrong. With Slomer I felt somehow it should be different. He had money. He was a punter. I'd have thought that'd cancel out any other affiliations he might have had.

'From what I hear,' I told her, 'I don't approve of Weaver. But I still work at his factory. You think I should change my job?'

'It's nothing to do with me.' She seemed pretty pleased at having provoked me. The fire had sunk too low to read by, and she wasn't having the light on. She even began to polish the boots in the hearth with a little yellow duster, kneeling in the fire-glow.

'I gather your husband worked at Weaver's,' I said, and sounded formal, as if making an important announcement about some trouble with which I wasn't personally concerned.

'Who told you that?' she said, but didn't look up. She had her forefinger inside the duster and was rubbing in the creases round the lace-holes.

'This bloke. He happened to ask where I was living. And I told him. He said your husband used to work there.'

'He must have told you something else besides. You wouldn't be bringing it up if he hadn't . . . I suppose you told him how you were living for next to nothing with old Hammond's widow.'

'No. But I told him what I paid, and said I made up the rest by helping round the house.'

'I bet he thought that was very . . . chivalrous. Helping round the house – is that what you told him? What did he say?'

'You reckoned it was nothing to you what people said.'

'It isn't.' The fire'd subsided to a fierce knot of glowing coal. It made red streaks on the brown leather of the boot in which she'd buried her hand. 'It's bringing Eric's name into it I don't like,' she said.

'I shouldn't have mentioned it.'

'I don't mind them talking about me. They always have

done. When he died they said . . . well it doesn't matter. I don't like anybody dragging his name in like that.'

There were kids playing over the backs. Their feet crunched on the ashes outside the door. They cried and screamed in the dark. Young Farrer in the next yard was revving his motor-bike engine, making it splutter and cough, then die. It was a circus going on out there. I stood up to go out.

'What do they say about him at Weaver's?' she said.

'I've only heard him mentioned that once.'

'You must have been talking about him – bringing it up like that.'

'No. I've never mentioned him. . . .'

She took her hand out of the boot, and put it down beside its partner. 'You see when Eric died . . . well, all my world went out.' Her silhouette was framed against the glow, bowed. 'He used to say he didn't know why he was living. He used to say – why was *I* ever made alive? When he went like that, I felt I hadn't been proper to him. I hadn't made him feel that he belonged. . . .' She looked up. 'I shouldn't tell you this, should I?' she said.

'I don't mind. . . .'

'No, I mean with you being what you are. Self-reliant. I suppose that's what you'd call it. All that cockiness. You don't seem worried like Eric was.'

'I only mentioned it because you started polishing them boots.'

'Is anything the matter with me polishing them? Don't you like to see me do it?'

'No . . . as I said, I don't mind.'

I saw she was crying. I got out before anything started.

*

I found the second trial game easier than the first. For one thing I hadn't a great deal to do: this big character comes round the blind side every time there's a scrum. He carries the ball loose. All I do is stand in his way, and he's never looking. I get my shoulder under his jaw and he goes down like a child. I start counting the times he comes round this way. Fourteen. I've hit every part of his face. The fifteenth time they carry him off. How thick can you get? This shows I'm good at defensive play.

I felt cold towards Johnson. For some reason I couldn't stick the sight of him standing up there against the Batley skyline. I spent some time in the bath and even longer dressing, but he was still waiting when I got outside. He thought I'd been injured, and his anxiety only added to the general effect.

'We're just going,' I told him. 'I didn't think you'd wait.'

'Just to see if you were all right, Arthur.' He looked me up and down to see if I was all there.

'Where're you going now?' I tried to hide how I felt.

He shrugged, but when I got hold of the door handle to swing myself into the bus he caught my arm. 'The bus isn't going yet,' he said. 'Come and have some tea.'

'They're only waiting for me. The lads want to get back to town.' I nodded at the row of dazed faces behind the bus windows. Everybody was tired, aching, wanting to get away.

'Are you coming to the King tonight?'

'I can't get.'

'You can't?'

'I'm going out.'

He began to measure some of my feeling towards him. He pushed the tuft of grey hair that always stuck out from his cap back under the peak. 'When'll I see you then?' He tried to push in some reproach by looking up sullenly from beneath his cap, giving his eyes a half-dazed look. 'Just say a day, Arthur. You know me. I'll be there.' I got into the bus.

'If I don't see you before,' he calls out, 'I'll see you up at Primstone. That's honest. That's a bet. After training. Tuesday night.'

As the bus pulled out of the yard I waved and bent down to see how he'd taken it. He was by himself in the middle of the dusty area. Programmes were blown in the wind. The pitch was grey-green flat mud. He was waving hard.

'He asked me if he could come in the coach,' the trainer said over my shoulder. 'But you know how it is. One starts and they all want to come.'

34

'It's all right by me, Dicky. He's a bit of a nuisance.' I felt Johnson should keep his age to himself.

'Okay then, Art.' He slapped my back and we sat down. The bus swept through the early evening back to town. The sky glowed with the last daylight; the limestone hills stood out purple and bare.

Six of us played brag on the back seats. I lost three quid, and a bit of silver.

It was almost twelve when I got back, and the house was in darkness. I tapped lightly on the front door. Within a minute I heard her on the stairs. The passage light went on and she unlocked the door. She didn't say anything as I came in. She fastened the door and started back up the stairs.

'Sorry I'm late,' I told her.

'That's all right.'

'That's all right, then.'

She had her coat on over her nightgown, and held her hands with cold. 'You've been drinking,' she said quietly, and stopped where the stairs merged into darkness.

'Aren't you going to ask me how I got on at Batley?'

'Do you play until this time?'

'It's some way. We didn't get back till late. I went dancing with some of the lads.'

'I didn't know you liked dancing so much.'

'I don't. Not that much. But we go to the Mecca now'n again.'

'Do you like it?'

'Pretty fair.' I didn't want to sound too enthusiastic. As it was I leant against the wall with the strain of looking up at her.

'You're drunk!' she said. 'You've come back here drunk!'

'That's no bloody crime. You're not my mother, my . . . something or other. What're you getting at me for? I tell you – I'd like it a lot if you'd let me call you sunshine . . . Valerie.'

She'd started up the stairs. But she stopped, and half-turned as if she wasn't sure what I'd said. 'Sunshine.' I told her, and belched.

She shot upstairs and I heard her door close.

Johnson was waiting outside the changing room, in the tunnel, so I couldn't miss him. He'd been on the touchline all evening watching the training and making his usual signs of encouragement. 'Is he your dad or uncle like?' one of the players said as we came out together.

'No. He got me a trial here, that's all.'

'Good neighbours? It's all right if you can get it.' He winked, slapped my shoulder, and went off chewing his gum.

'You were in good shape tonight, Arthur,' the old man said. 'How d'you feel after last Saturday?' He was looking at me carefully to see if I was in the same mood.

'Just getting used to it,' I said, and felt myself shaping up to encourage him.

'That's right, son. That's right.' He was concentrating on detecting a note of friendliness. 'It's keeping at it regular: that's the secret. Training and more training. You can't do too much, Arthur. You know what I mean? You'll never beat it. After that you can take it all in your stride.' Now he was looking me up and down to see any change that might have taken place since he last saw me. 'There's many a good player been ruined . . . really ruined, because he was too damn lazy to train. You know what I mean? Because he could play a couple a blinders in a row he thought he needn't train. It goes to their heads. You see them walking about as if they owned the place. . . .' He went on pleading, his old tired body hurrying and lurching as it kept up with mine, until we'd reached the bus stop. 'I was wondering', he said, his voice loud enough for the other gum-chewing player to hear, 'if we couldn't go up to your place. We could take some fish and chips. It'd be no bother to your Mrs Hammond – I'd like to meet her again.'

I looked at him to see why he'd like to meet her again. What did he want to see *her* for? 'She's busy tonight, Dad. And she's a bit touchy at the moment about bringing things on without notice. She likes to be told.'

'We'd be no trouble, Arthur. We could all buckle in. . . . We'd have a little party. Take along some ale and a drop of stout. She drinks stout, doesn't she?'

'Some other night, Dad. She's on edge at the moment. Has been for the past week. We'll try some other time.'

I sounded pretty definite, but we'd no sooner got on the 10 bus than he started again like a small boy. 'I can't see what harm it can do.'

'Why're you so keen all of a sudden?' I asked him.

'Why? Well, we're sort of related. I didn't think she liked me the last time.'

He looked at me to tell him the truth.

'She's not keen on having people in, that's all.'

'But she didn't like me.'

'It wasn't that. It was the fire. We put too much bloody coal on or something. She's touchy.'

We passed those squat rows of houses before the bus goes over the river. Little black hutches nailed together by those big pegs of chimney. A barge had been hauled up out of the river and the kids slid down its sloping deck: a lazy, stupid animal, with its gaping, vacant hold. Two coal lorries were parked by the coal slip, ready for the morning. The lights were sucked down into the river, until they disappeared in a quick thin dribble. Johnson said, 'Do you like staying there?'

'Like it? I don't mind. It's cheap. Why?'

'She struck me, you know – as being a bit peculiar. That sort of moony look she has on her face. What were them boots in the hearth? They're not yours, are they?'

'They belong to her old man. That's why she's a bit queer. He was killed not long ago, at Weaver's.'

He was still not satisfied. He tried to say one or two things about feeling sorry. But he was more uncertain than before: he couldn't make out why I stayed there. When it came to it, neither could I. I spent an hour with him in the King William.

At Thursday night training I was told George Wade wouldn't be travelling on Saturday with the first team to Wakefield, but was saving himself the journey and watching the 'A' team. I took this to mean he was watching me, though there were four other trialists in the team. In the changing room before the match I acted like the Big Frog around the place. I rubbed on other people's vaseline, tied other people's shoulder pads and bandages, did a lot of shadow boxing in the corner. There was no doubt what I was aiming for. And for the first time the weather was fine.

I heard my name go out over the loudspeaker, then the roar of the crowd as the visiting team went out first. Dicky, the trainer, gave us his last instructions, we lined up, and moved down the tunnel. The front of the line broke into a trot. The boots clacked on the concrete, then slurred, and were suddenly silent as they prodded into the bare earth just inside the tunnel mouth.

The darkness broke away. The light blinded for a second, mingled with the shock of the crowd's roar. I seemed to inflate as I ran on to the field. The loudspeakers blared 'The Entrance of the Gladiators' as we ran quickly, importantly, to the middle of the field, and swerved aside to make a circle. The tune changed to a crackly fanfare as the captains tossed up.

The teams spread out, filtered across the pitch, and stood still, red and blue in the worn brown and dusty green patches of the field. We waited, quiet, for the whistle. It blasted. The ball rose into the air.

Fifteen minutes of the first half passed and I'd never even touched the ball. I was aching with activity, and blowing hard. It took me most of the first half to realize I was being starved of the ball by my own team.

It was the hooker, Taff Gower, who was organizing it, I decided; a quiet little frog working out his last days in the game with the 'A' team. With his scarred, toothless face, his short bow-legged figure stumped alongside me in each movement and casually diverted the ball whenever it came my way. I gathered he mustn't like me. I might be keeping one of his mates out of the team, stopping a wage. I didn't worry about this. I just saw an early end to my ambitions. As we folded down for the next scrum his face was further forward than mine. 'Why're you keeping the ball from me?' I asked him. His head was upside down, waiting for the ball to come in, but he was grinning, fairly politely. I could see the back of his throat. When he spat I couldn't move my head. I didn't think he could like me.

I waited three scrums, to make him feel relaxed and also to get the best opportunity. I kept my right arm loose. His face was upside down, his eyes straining, loose in their sockets, to catch a glimpse of the ball as it came in. I watched it leave the scrum-half's hands and his head buckled under the forwards' heaving. I swung my right fist into the middle of his face. He cried out loud. I hit him again and saw the red pulp of his nose and lips as my hand came away. He was crying out really loud now, partly affected, professional pain, but most of it real. His language echoed all over the ground.

The scrum broke up with the ref blowing his nut off on the whistle. 'I saw that! I saw that!' he shouted, urged on to violent mimes of justice by the crowd's tremendous booing. They were all on their feet demonstrating and screaming. Gower had covered his face with his hands, but blood seeped between his fingers, as the trainer and two players directed his blind steps off the field.

'You'll be nailed for good for this, you dirty little swine. You'll never play again,' and all that, the ref was shouting. He pointed with real drama at the opposing hooker. The crowd's response reached a crescendo – far more than it would provide for, say, the burning of a church.

The young hooker shook his head. 'I ne'er touched him,' he said, looking round for support from his own team. 'I swear to God I never touched him.'

'You can tell that to the league chairman!'

The hooker was beside himself with innocence. 'Nay, look at my bloody fist,' he said. 'Look, there's no blood on it.'

'I'm not arguing.'

The ref took his name and sent him off.

I'd never seen such a parade before. The whole ground throbbed with rage as the young figure in his little boy's costume passed in front of the main stand.

'They're not fit to be on a football field,' the ref said to me, since I happened to be standing nearest. I didn't know

39

whether he meant the crowd or men like the hooker. The free kick put us two points ahead.

We stood around the tunnel mouth at half-time, drinking from the bottles and listening to Dicky tell us a few yards of mistakes. We were quiet. It was a fact that since Gower had gone off I'd been getting the ball just as I liked it, and as often as not in openings. I was looking up, trying to pick George Wade's homburg out in the committee box, when Dicky came over to me. He took hold of my hand and looked at the knuckles.

'Got some nice bruises there, owd lad,' he said. 'What got into you?' He didn't look at me, but at the other players.

'How d'you mean?'

'Taff Gower – you could see it plain as day from the bench.'

'He was keeping the ball from me.'

'Come off it, owd cock. Nobody lakes that game here.'

'Not now they don't.'

He grimaced, annoyed I should try to be smart. 'You'll do just fine at this club,' he said. 'Any rate, I'm not saying a word about it, 'less Wade asks me in private.'

'You're on my side,' I told him.

'Get this, lad. I'm on my own side.' He winked, importantly, and banged my shoulder. 'Keep it up, Art,' he said in a loud voice, and went over to advise the full-back.

As we stood on the field waiting for the second half kick-off, I examined everything with real care, telling myself I ought to savour every second of this feeling. I had my eyes fixed on the twin buds of the power station's cooling towers, and watched a cloud of white steam escape across the valley and come over the pitch. The ball rose towards it, and in a slow curve fell towards me. I gathered it cleanly and, beating two men, ran to the centre of the field. Somebody shouted for the ball. I kept it. I found myself in an opening and suddenly thought I might even reach the line. I went straight for the full-back, and when he came in I gave him the base of my wrist on his nose. The crack, the groan, the release of his arms, all coincided with a soaring of my guts.

40

I moved in between the posts keeping my eye on the delight of the crowd as I put the ball down.

Everything was luminous, sparkling. The houses beyond the stadium turrets, the silhouetted trees at Sandwood, the ice-blue sky, the mass of people – they were all there intent on seeing me. I was carried along in a bag full of energy, no longer aware of effort, ready to tear anybody into postage stamps and at the same time smile for the crowd. I came off the field fresher than when I went on, and still waiting for some damn thing to tire me.

Although George Wade wasn't in the tearoom, Johnson was. He devoured me with a rapturous gaze and slipped his little arm round me, swaying and chanting, and bringing a lot of eyes in our direction. 'What a game, Arthur! What a blind!' He talked so much wind I'd to take him to the bar to try and quieten him down. He immediately danced off to the lavatory: he'd been holding himself till he saw me. I ordered two beers.

'Allow me,' a voice said over my shoulder. I turned round to see the soft features of a smiling face. 'No, allow me. I really do insist,' the man went on, and although I wasn't supposed to know I knew this was Weaver. He held my money away from the barman and slid a quid note in its place. He took off his hat and ordered a beer for himself.

'You had a good game today, Arthur,' he said, intimately – as if we were good friends. 'How do you like the City?' His little protruding lips parted to small, even teeth, which weren't, yet looked, artificial.

'It's my third game. It's going all right, I reckon.'

'Yes,' he said. 'So I gathered. You seem to have made a good start. If you don't mind me saying so.' He nodded towards the frosted glass of the committee room. 'Wade's been talking about you in there. I imagine it was just the day for it.' He nodded this time to the window overlooking the pitch. 'Do you like a firm going?'

'I must do.'

He laughed extravagantly. I saw Johnson emerge from the lavatory and stand some distance away. I beckoned to him but he didn't come.

41

'Have you played for any other club . . . any of the Inter-mediate League?' Weaver asked, and took no notice of my attempt to attract Johnson. I shook my head.

'I didn't think I'd heard your name before – Machin.' He made it sound fairly common. We stared at one another with an instinctive sort of reaction. 'It's a great pity about Taffy Gower.'

'What's happened? I didn't see him after the match.'

'You wouldn't. They've taken him for an X-ray. Gone to hospital. I heard it was a broken nose. For a little fellow . . . their hooker's got quite a punch.' He was smiling, almost laughing, and blinking his blue eyes.

'Bad luck.'

'It is.' He picked up his hat and left his beer undrunk. 'I better be pushing along. You're not signed on here yet?'

'I've another game before they make up their minds.'

'I don't think they'll have much difficulty there, do you?' He blinked his baby eyes again, folding them up in those fleshy encasements. ''Bye, Arthur.'

As soon as he'd gone, I turned to Johnson.

'Who was it?' I asked him.

'You should know, Arthur.' He knew I knew.

'Who was it?'

'Guess. . . . Go on, have a guess.' The grin on his face showed he was enjoying the game.

I got hold of his hand, just above his thumb, and squeezed it hard.

'Who was it, Dad?' I was surprised myself that Weaver made me act like this. It seemed the only way I could control my excitement.

'That's mean, Arthur. That's mean.'

I squeezed it harder, and the old stump of his hand went white. 'That's mean,' he groaned.

I let go and he rubbed his wrist slowly, watching me.

'Why d'you do that, Arthur?'

'I don't know.'

He couldn't cope with all his mounting reproach. 'Why d'you squeeze my wrist like that?'

I shook my head. 'Was it Weaver?' I said.

'You hurt me. Is that why you squeezed my wrist?' He bandaged it with his other hand. 'Just because it was Weaver?'

I found it odd that he, Johnson, should resent being hurt; should resent my hurting him. He seemed to be somebody who always had been hurt, and who was always going to be hurt, whatever he might or might not do. I didn't like hearing him complain to me. If I didn't hurt him somebody else would. Why should he blame me for it – making me out to be a bully?

'You're too excited,' he said, tired, stroking the inflamed skin. 'I thought you knew it was Weaver.'

'I was surprised him talking to me like that. Isn't that something – when he comes up to you and starts talking just like that. He must have been impressed.'

Johnson was sulking. He wanted to quarrel but he didn't know how. By hurting him I'd cut him out of the afternoon's success: that's what he felt. I left him and set off to walk into town. Lights were springing up with silent explosions. It was the time of the evening when everybody starts pressing the switch. I could trace the lights up the valley as far as High-field estate, row after row of them, like a big army camp, stretching up to the confused mass of the Riding hospital on the ridge above it. A mist was spreading from the river and covering the valley, beyond the park, whose central hill stood up in isolation, its thick bushes and trees dark shapes squatting like animals on its slopes. When I turned round I saw Johnson following me fifty yards behind.

I couldn't make up my mind where to go. I hadn't a book on me: I'd left *Toreador* at home. I fancied a car ride out in the country. I bought a sports paper, and after a lot of searching found a small report of the match on an inside column and sure enough, only an hour or so after the final whistle, my name printed in capital letters. Going by lathe standards they'd be a sixteenth of an inch high. Not very big. But I could make them grow.

When I got into town the only thing I could do was catch the 10 bus.

She was in the kitchen, bent over the sink. Lynda and Ian

43

were playing on a chair near the fire. They were making a big noise. Ian had no pants on. I gave his bare arse a spank and sat down, annoyed, like a visiting inspector, to find her still stuck in her den of unventilated air, cluttered spaces, unused rows of crockery, completely unaware of the success I brought into the room. 'Have you had some tea?' she asked.

'I had some after the match.'

'How did it go?'

'Are you interested?'

'Not really . . . now what is it?' she said as Lynda broke into a wail. She dried her hands to settle the fight, and gave them both a little pat. They both looked at me a minute; then, sensing a drop of sympathy in my stare, started a double wail of unhappiness. 'Now what are you laughing at?' she asked.

'Don't you find them funny?' I said.

She went back to the sink where she was washing a pair of Ian's peculiar home-made trousers. No doubt she was thinking of all the time she spent with them, every day and all day, and why she couldn't find them funny. 'Sometimes I do,' she said.

I dug myself a seat from the newspapers, dolls, torn books, washing, frayed cushions, bricks, and tin cars. 'I met my employer half an hour ago,' I told her.

'And who may that be?' She turned on a tap. 'Who do you mean?'

I called Weaver's name over the running water. She nodded as if the word meant nothing to her.

'Where d'you meet him?' she asked eventually.

'At the match. He seems to think I won't have any trouble signing on.'

'That's good of him. He's a man you can trust, I suppose.'

'Nay, he was impressed. I could tell. And he bought me a drink.'

'What happened to your other friend today – Mr Johnson?'

'He bought him a drink too.'

'He knows who his friends are, then.'

44

'I've been thinking – on the way back here – why don't we go for a walk? We can take the kids if you can't dump them.'

She stopped the tap, and for some reason Ian stopped shouting, then Lynda. 'What on earth for?' She looked at me in amazement. 'What do you want us to go walking about in the bloody pitch dark for?'

'You never seem to get out of here. I thought some fresh air might do you good. I like to talk to somebody when I'm walking. Your problems sort of. . . .'

'I can look after my own health, thank you very much,' she said.

The fact was I felt like walking, but not alone, and she was the only person I felt like walking with. I couldn't explain that to her. I just wanted to talk to somebody. She waited for an explanation. She might even have been glad of this opportunity to show her independence. When nothing else came from me, she said, 'You must be mad to think I'd go out there . . . walking with you.' She was thinking what those two rows of people would say, lining both sides of the street for every action that went on in it. 'I think we ought to get it clear once and for all, Mr Machin. Whatever private lives we have, we keep. I don't want you poking your nose into my affairs. And you won't find me poking into yours. I don't want you mixing with us – in that way. I've got some pride left, in case you didn't know.'

There was nothing to say. I wanted to tell her about the afternoon, about Gower, about what I thought my chances were; show her the bit in the paper where I'd scored.

'What's the matter, don't you want to be happy?' I said.

'Happy – 'course I want to be happy. You must think I'm miserable just because. . . . If I'm left alone I'm happy. I can settle my own affairs. I don't need you pushing in.'

'I'm not pushing in. I'm just trying to be friendly. The other night you seemed pretty glad you could talk to me.'

'You've got plenty of friends. You don't have to be friendly here. Why don't you pester them?'

'But how can you be happy here? Just look at it. You never go out. You've no women friends with the neighbours.

45

Not what you'd call friends. What sort of pleasure do you get, stuffed up here all day? Don't tell me you're happy.'

'I'm happy.'

'You say that. You *say* you're happy. I don't believe you.'

'I'm not asking you to believe me. Remember who you are, pray. You're not running this place like you run that little man Johnson. I'm not your servant. I'm not running round all day with a grin over my face just to make you think I'm happy.'

'I don't mean laughing all the time. I mean just looking happy. You: you don't look happy. It's not a question of laughing.'

'You make me sick. Aren't you going out?'

'Yeh, I'm going out. I'm sick of living here, that's all.'

'Oh, well that's easy settled. Don't. Just don't live here. You must think . . . I'd go down on my knees to make you stay. That's the easiest thing I ever heard of. Just stop living here. We'll be better off without you.'

I banged the door on the way out. The house trembled. I could imagine how she felt when all her house trembled. I crashed it twice, and walked round till late evening, then went and filled in time at the Mecca, and tried to pick up a sample.

It wasn't difficult to see during the next week that she was in two minds to ask me to leave. For once I wasn't sure which side she'd choose. When I got back from work on Wednesday she'd put on her grey wool dress. The table was set for tea, and Lynda and Ian had already been fed.

'Are you going out tonight?' I asked her.

'We've just got back from the park,' she said, and making a point of it added, 'We've been for a walk and we haven't had time to change. They're tired.' She nodded at the kids half asleep under a blanket on the couch. She watched me eat. Probably she wasn't aware how closely she did it, and I tried to be natural.

'I'd been meaning to ask you,' she said.

'About me leaving?'

'You know – making things work out here.'

'You've been thinking of asking me to leave?'

'I don't think I want that,' she said, as though she still hadn't made up her mind. 'One or two things want clearing up. Don't you think so?' She looked at me openly, self-absorbed; a healthy sign for her. The dome of her forehead gleamed with the same intensity as her eyes, like an Italian mother in an American film. 'I mean, do you know why I asked you to pay so little board at the beginning?'

'I've helped in the house. I thought I had.'

'I'd no experience of running lodgers. I had a woman in mind, you know. But what woman would come here? Until you came all the callers had been Irish. But don't think I'm grumbling about the way you've helped.'

'How much does it cost you to keep me?'

'I wasn't thinking of that. It doesn't come into it.'

'Aw now, you know you ought to charge more rent. You can't keep me on less than three quid.' Her face turned hard at the actual mention of money. 'Some landladies charge up to five quid a week. I might as well tell you when I first came here I thought I'd fallen easy.'

'I don't want a list of my shortcomings.'

'I wasn't giving you one, I'm trying to show you where you're hurting yourself most. Can't I talk to you as a person for once? If you listen to what I'm saying I can put you right.'

She stood up to control herself. We were both trying to be kind, sympathetic, and at the same time careful we didn't give too much away too soon. Her feelings always looked like poses to me. So I could never tell how deep each one went.

'I wish you wouldn't always try and work me into a fit,' she said. 'I've asked you, over and over again, to leave me alone that way. I can't *stand* it.'

'I'll go out,' I told her.

*

The pitch alone depressed me. It formed the centre of a dog track. The club was one of those that had difficulty paying its 'A' team, with the result that most of its players were

47

drafted up for the afternoon from the next door colliery. The atmosphere of neglect was dictated by this condition. Some kids had collected for autographs as we stepped off the coach. Their eyes followed our gaze as we took in the crumbling stadium, the uncut grass, the worn track, the uneven pitch. Nothing of the town was visible over the low unambitious terraces, since the pitch was on the summit of a slight rise created by a denuded slag heap.

As I gave my autograph I found the signature of Charles Weaver already scrawled in the corner.

'Where d'you get this?' I asked the kid.

'Off a chap on the stand. We asked him.'

'How long ago was that?'

'Just now. A few minutes sin'.'

It wouldn't be unlike Weaver to give autographs. I put my name below his and took a look along the stand. It was empty; the crowd wouldn't collect for another twenty minutes. What did *he* want to come here for? I couldn't think of any reason, other than I was the hero. I followed the others into the small unheated dressing-room at the back of the bookies' row. They were already stamping about, knotting their hands in their armpits, arguing, waiting for the names to be read out by Dicky.

'Can't we ever cancel this match?' somebody said. 'It's the same every bleedin' year. They freeze you solid, then they knock your head off. It's like coming to a mortuary.'

'You should know, yer dead-head,' Dicky said.

He has a right sharp wit, Dicky.

'I'd give 'em winning pay just not to come.'

'Hear thy herald angel sing.'

'When you've come here as many blinding years as I have, owd lad. . . .'

'Why not lake in the first team then?'

'Oh Christ, kid. Give over.'

Even Dicky looked sad. Once we were on the field we jumped about, ran round the posts, passed the ball, and got no warmer. There was no sign of Weaver on the stand. The only place he might have been was in the starter's box. But it was in shadow and I couldn't see inside.

The game started with a brawl and didn't develop. I was more or less all right, but for the 'backs, in spite of their padding, it wasn't anything I'd have done for the same money. Miners if nothing else are strong. Trying to miss their fists and boots was dancing in between raindrops.

Towards the end of the game I was short-arm tackled, right on the bridge of my nose. The ball was torn from my hands and I lay on the ground, smelling the slag, waiting for Dicky to run on with the sponge.

'What're you playing at?' he said. He was more than angry.

'Bloody football.'

'You walked right into it. Now you know what it feels like, maybe you'll be satisfied. Reckon to be hurt and walk off with me.' There wasn't much else I could do. As it was he'd to hold me up and I walked as if I'd got five legs. 'It's your special day today. You want to take care of yourself.'

'How d'you mean, Dicky?' I tried to look at him.

'Keep out of trouble, and keep your fists down,' was all he'd say. 'They can see you swinging a mile away.'

'I'm not the only one. There're twenty-five others.'

'If the ref catches you then you will be the only one. He can stop you three matches. Take my advice. Just fill in time till the whistle and keep out of trouble.' He shoved my head in the bucket, gave me an ammonia sniff, and I went back on.

I took a lot of care to keep out of the way, to make sure I was second man into the tackle, and never under the ball when it came down. For the first time I was frightened of being hurt. My whole face ached and throbbed, as if the bones were riddled with pins.

'I've ne'er yet seen a game of football on this ground,' Dicky said as we dragged back into the changing room. 'Am I glad that load's over. It's the same every year. They just come up to fight.'

'If you ask me, Dicky, they don't know the bloody Romans 've left.'

We had tea in the hut overlooking the track. Nobody was speaking. Faces, hot and red and gleaming from the bath, peered silently out of the streaked windows. Everyone wanted to get back to town, to the Mecca, to feel civilized.

Before the winter sun had set we were on the forty-mile journey back, across the flat plain, to the valleys, our guts gradually rising. I'd seen no sign of Weaver.

Most of the players got out in the Bull Ring.

'Can you stay on, Arthur?' Dicky said. 'We're taking the kit back to Primstone. They want to see you up there.'

'What about?'

'I reckon you know more than me. Stick tight. We won't be long.'

I was shown into the committee room by one of the groundsmen who'd been waiting for the bus. The first person I recognized was Weaver, though he was at the back, staring at a gallery of photos of City teams. Then I saw the dog, and George Wade. The dog slept by the fire.

'I hear you'd quite a rough passage this afternoon,' Wade said. He considered a smile, and held his hand out. 'I expect you know why we asked you up here, Arthur.'

'I didn't think it'd be so quick,' I told him.

Wade thought about this, then said, 'Quite. That's right, lad,' and we shook hands. 'Won't you sit down?'

There were five men. Apart from Wade and Weaver there was red-faced Riley, the secretary, and two committee men I hadn't seen before. We sat round the polished oak table. Weaver turned from the photos and started smiling right away, at me and at Wade, at the dog, the wall, and the table.

'You've met Mr Weaver before, or so I gather,' Wade said. 'And this is Mr Riley the club secretary. These two gentlemen, Mr Glover and Mr Thorpe, they represent the committee's interest.'

I looked at Weaver for some sort of reassurance. He stared back familiarly. 'How have these four matches suited you, Arthur?' he asked.

'I've enjoyed them.'

Wade said, 'You won't be used to the professional game. I suppose you find a bit of difference.' He was out to minimize my position and sounded confident about it. 'You've never played the game reg'lar.' When I hesitated he looked shrewd and added quickly, 'We've been looking up your records. You know – past stuff. You haven't played regular since you left school. That's six or seven year back.'

Weaver gazed at me as if he could be slightly bored, perhaps interested in how I'd answer rather than in Wade's criticism. I didn't answer and Wade said, 'Course, you won't mind us laying the facts down, Arthur, so we can see our meal afore we eat it. So to speak. We've checked up on you, just as you've had four week to check up on us. I hope you don't think we've gone behind your back or ought. You see that, don't you lad?'

They were expecting some sort of performance from me to begin any minute, and I was looking round my mind to find one I could use. All I had was what Maurice had told me when he heard I'd got a trial: keep your hole shut and just say how much you want. 'That's all right,' I said.

'We see you're not married.'

'No.'

'And where do you live?'

'In Fairfax Street at the moment.'

'Isn't that near the works?' Weaver asked.

'Yes. I work at your place, Mr Weaver.'

He looked at me carefully. 'Do you? I'd like to have known that before.'

'Aye. That'll be convenient,' Wade said round the table. 'Braithewaite works there as well. You're in lodgings, then, in Fairfax Street?'

'Yes.'

'Are they all right?' I nodded. 'I mean, you can tell us. We can always fix you up with good accommodation. If you were married, for example, you'd be eligible for a club house. Do I make myself clear, Arthur?'

'I'm settled,' I said, and wondered how much they knew about me already.

'And you've no legal ties with anyone – home or anything thing?'

'No, I've nothing.'

'Do you enjoy working at Weaver's?' Wade said this

51

importantly, as if in this capacity he'd superseded Weaver himself. 'You needn't mind Mr Weaver if you're not satisfied, you know. He'll be only too glad to know if anything's wrong.' Weaver smiled to confirm it.

'I get on fine.'

'You've got the job you want? We could fix you up elsewhere if you're not content.'

'It suits me fine.'

'He sounds a very happy man – easily pleased,' Weaver said casually.

They all looked at me as though I was a very happy man – either that or thick.

'I suppose you've decided in your mind', Wade said, 'whether you'd like to carry on playing at Primstone.'

'Yes, I'd like to carry on.'

In the tearoom and bar somebody was laughing loud; shadows crossed on the frosted panels of the door.

'You'd like to sign professional forms with us?'

'Yes.'

'Would you prefer to sign amateur forms? I mean. . . .'

'No.'

'You've thought about it and you're sure? You see, we don't want to rush you into anything you're not fully prepared for. That's our concern, Arthur. The City's a big club – any mistake here is a big one. I want to make that clear before anyone or anything is committed.'

'Yes, I know.'

We all suddenly looked casual. Riley, the secretary, hunched his shoulders over the table and concealed the huge club emblem on his blazer. His face had sunk a deeper red, as if his skin had been turned inside out. His teeth were vivid. 'Don't mind my briskness, Arthur,' he said as this red ball swung into action. 'But the sooner settled the better. Had you any signing-on fee in mind?'

'Five hundred pounds,' I told him.

No one's face had altered. As if to conceal any embarrassment the sound of money might cause, Wade played hard with it.

'Five hundred. Five hundred. That's decent.' He

hummed, and put a few looks round the table. He'd probably been thinking he was playing me along for a couple of hundred. 'Five hundred.'

Riley stepped in briskly as soon as he saw Wade surprised by the weight on the line. 'What about three hundred down, and one fifty for county honours and one fifty if you play for Britain?'

'Great Britain,' Weaver said to himself.

'I'd want county and international honours on top of that,' I said, seeing myself saving them three hundred quid by being just a good club player. 'Five hundred down.'

'You'd want', Riley began, gathering up late surprise himself, 'five hundred down, *plus* one hundred and fifty for county and international honours respectively?'

'Yes.'

'And that's quite definite?' he said.

When I nodded he turned to Wade who took over the lead weight again. 'That's a lot for somebody just coming into the game. Tha's no experience at all of the professional code, you know.'

'You saw me play last week.'

'That's one match, lad. And an "A" team one at that. There's at least thirty-six matches a season – you see what I'm getting at? I'm not suggesting you didn't play well last Sat'day.'

'And impressed us all,' Weaver said archly.

They were going strong. They'd all got a hold and were pulling. They seemed to take a big breath before Riley said, 'Would you consider this? We pay you six hundred pounds – six hundred – three hundred now, three hundred after completing a full season with us, that's this time next year, and one hundred pound bonuses for county and international honours respectively.'

'Yes,' Wade said, making a big fuss of his breathing. 'By Christ, that's very fair.'

Weaver was wondering whether he should smile at Wade's faked enthusiasm.

'I want five hundred down, and two bonuses of one fifty.'

'But you'd get the same amount this way, exactly the

53

same,' Riley said. 'Either way it's eight hundred pounds. Our way you'd actually get your money quicker. You'd have six hundred in hand. You can see that? As a safeguard three hundred of it is retained for a year – it's purely as a safeguard.'

'But more of a safeguard to you than to me.'

'Now Arthur,' Wade said, 'you're putting us in the position of a gambler. If we accepted your way we'd have no guarantee that we'd see adequate returns for our investment. I'm not saying it isn't a good gamble, and that, but on principle alone we try and avoid circumstances like that. You see, you're not dealing with us as individuals. Personally we might think you're worth every penny of what you're asking. But it's not our money we'd be paying you. You see – that's the point,' he added after discovering it. 'This is a company. We've responsibilities stretching beyond this football ground. By Mr Riley's suggestion we have a safeguard that covers both our interests – yours and ours.'

'It's still a gamble, whichever way you look at it,' I said. He watched me rub my head as I tried to keep awake in the mellow light. 'I might be injured and not play again this season, or ever. I wouldn't be able to put in a full season's play and I'd lose my three hundred.'

'Oh, we'd cover that. We'd have a clause to cover that,' Wade said with a return of confidence. 'Available to play, would be the actual phrase used.'

'I wouldn't be available if I was injured.'

'We'd waive injury incurred while playing football: that's always understood. We're not providing a comprehensive insurance, tha knows.' He tapped his fingers on the table; his hand pranced on the polished surface like a nervous horse. He waited for me to give way, his head slightly on one side, his eyes fixed on me.

'I can't change my mind,' I told him. 'I feel I'm worth it.'

He sighed, maybe rudely. 'We're not trying to put anything over on you, Arthur,' he said. 'I wish you'd try and get that into your head. It's in our interests to satisfy you with the conditions of employment here. But we're representing other people. We're responsible for investing their money soundly. What will they say when I tell them I've handed over five hundred of their money to somebody who, as far as we know, has played one good "A" team game in his life? I mean, all the arguing we're doing is only over *how* the money's to be paid. We've agreed on the sum: six hundred pounds and bonuses.'

'Five hundred.'

'How d'you feel?' he said. 'You keep rubbing your head. Did you get it knocked today?'

'It aches a bit. I got it banged.'

'Do you want a drink?' I shook my head. 'Well, what do you say?'

'Five hundred down,' I told him mechanically.

He looked cold. 'If you're certain on that,' he said, 'can you wait outside a minute?'

Riley was already holding the door. I went out into the bar and came up for air.

'How goes it, Arthur?' A paunchy character, in a rain-coat and trilby get-up, came across to the counter. 'Have they made up their minds?'

'About what?'

'Whether there's gonna be a war – you know, fixing you up with a lining.' He laughed a bit to show he'd got humour.

'They're talking about it now.'

'Do you want a drink? Let me get you one.' He ordered a beer. 'They drive you hard, I imagine,' he said, with no imagination, and clenched his fist to show what he meant. 'They're tight-fisted.'

'I'll soon know.'

At the other end of the bar Dicky and a few of the committee were drinking, waiting for the result, looking to see how I looked.

'By the way, I'm Philips, from the *City Guardian*. You might tell me about yourself. You know – if the need arises.'

The beer numbed my head, comfortable. Philips looked into my face and said, 'You needn't take it seriously.'

I didn't know whether this was advice or criticism.

'Why shouldn't I take it seriously?'

'It's only a game, old sport.' He caught hold of my sleeve

in a confidential way. 'It's all a game,' he said. 'For Weaver's benefit.'

'They act like that just for Weaver?'

'It's his cash they're dishing out. He likes to see them behave properly. I see you've got a bruise coming. They wouldn't have you up here just to say ta-ta.' He examined my bruise again.

'We'd quite a fight this afternoon,' I told him.

'So I've been hearing from Dicky. It's always the same out there in the wild provinces. U-uh, it's that man again.' We both looked round to see Weaver standing at the committee room door. 'Careful how you tread on *his* toes,' Philips added.

'Could you come in now?' Weaver said as conversation in the bar stopped.

I didn't sit down; they didn't seem to expect it.

'What d'you aim to do, Arthur, if we don't sign you?' Wade said. His dog was awake now, as if it'd just been consulted, and it watched me with red upturned eyes.

'I don't know. Carry on as I am. I hadn't thought.'

'You mean you'd planned on signing with the City?'

I nodded, wondering if I'd done the right thing in sticking.

'Would you be very disappointed if we said we couldn't accept your offer?'

'Are you turning me down?'

'Can't you change your mind about splitting the payment? It's only a matter of procedure when all's said and done.'

I almost said 'Yes'. But I shook my head, and before I could say 'No', Wade stretched out his hands hopelessly saying, 'Well – I'm afraid there's nothing for it, Arthur, then.'

Weaver was still smiling, narrowly, as though he might be astonished with himself.

'You're not signing me,' I said.

'That's it.' Wade breathed in heavily. 'We'll have to.' He swung his hand across the table, the dog lead attached to his wrist, and smiled cheekily. 'Congratulations, Arthur.'

They broke out with confirmations. Weaver shook my hand softly and looked right into my eye with a kid's delight at a new toy.

'Who put you up to it?' Wade said.

'To what?'

'To asking so much and not talking about it.'

'Maurice.'

'Braithewaite? I thought so.' He slapped his thigh. 'I thought I could see his stubborn attitude behind everything you said – or rather didn't say.'

It was a game then.

I listened to Wade go on about, 'If you play football as hard as you've played us you'll be collecting your international cap by next year. I mean that.'

Riley was silent, slightly purple, staring concernedly at Weaver. After a while he said, 'If you'll just read and sign these forms, Arthur, then that's all there is to do.'

We finished the forms and went into the bar. Wade stamped beside me with his stick, pulling the dog after him. I began to wonder when I was going to see the money. Perhaps they wanted me to ask for it. I didn't like playing their sort of crap game.

'A round on the club,' Wade said to the barman with cauliflower lugs, and when we were served he brought out the toast, 'Here's to the future and every success, Arthur.'

They drank, Dicky and Philips drank, a small crowd drank, I drank, and Wade put his glass down.

'And here's that piece of damned paper we argued over. I might as well tell you, Riley here signed it while you were out of the room. We were that sure.' He clenched my right hand in his and we both got a grip on the paper. 'Hold it,' he whispered with an urgency he hadn't mustered till now. 'Hold it a second while he gets in his flash.' His teeth almost shot out, stayed there for the time it took Philips's photographer to take a picture, then disappeared once more as his figure melted.

I wasn't sure which pocket I should put the cheque in. It was like the pre-title weigh-in, with all the fans and backers milling round. They watched me switch the cheque about, then Weaver said, 'Aren't you going to read it?'

'Oh yes,' I told him, and glanced at the words and numbers, and put it in my inside pocket. I could see Dicky asking Thorpe how much it was, and when the committee man whispered the answer, the little 'A' team trainer's face broke out in angry surprise. Weaver wasn't rubbing his hands, but he was smiling as if that fragile skin might crack. 'Don't spend it all at once,' he said, and laughed. For a minute I hated the stinking money. It burnt a hole in my pocket. Then I remembered it was mine, and I was smiling.

'About that gentleman there,' Wade said, taking the dog's lead off his wrist and pointing at Philips. 'You say nothing to Ed Philips. I'll tell him all he needs to know. It's on his contract, Ed. No statements to the press.'

'What's *he* got to state?' Ed said.

Wade didn't hear him. He was nodding at me. 'That's the procedure, you see, Arthur.'

Then he saw me looking hard at Philips and taking me by the elbow walked me away. 'You won't be playing next Sat'day,' he said. 'But the week after that we've two First team games on the Sat'day and the Monday. You'll be playing in both. Two games close together like – that'll give you a chance of settling into the second row more quickly. I'll tell you now, Arthur, we've got two or three good second row forwards – ' and he goes off into how it's essential I play better than anybody else, good faith and a lot of other bull. I don't wake up till he says, 'You'll find one or two bonuses cropping up. A week Monday night it'll be worth twenty quid for a win, unless Weaver or Slomer or somebody are extra satisfied and put up a personal bonus. Over Christmas and the New Year week-ends you should collect fifty quid for each if it's a winning run. So you see we treat you fair from our end. It's up to you to give your very best – and remember with me it's good football that counts, not big fists. You know what I mean?'

I saw by the way he was talking that he wasn't at all sure he'd picked a winner. He was worried. 'Come to the first team changing room Tuesday, of course,' he finished, gave a round of good-nights, and went off home with the dog.

I left soon after. I'd reached the bottom of the steps behind the stand when a figure shouted from the bar-room door, 'You going already, lad? Hang on minute and I'll be with you.'

I waited by the players' entrance wondering what else Weaver could want now. 'That friend of yours was here an hour or so back,' he said. 'Johnson. We told him some blind and he went away. We didn't want him hanging around at a time like this. You don't mind, do you? How are you feeling now?'

'Pretty tired. I was just going home.'

'That's why I came after you. I thought you were. Come on, I'll give you a lift. You've got that cheque to look after. We'd better see you home safe with it.'

He said this as though he was talking to about fifty of me, to a load of tree trunks, to a long brick wall, and all the time he was looking at one or two things in the air or down at his feet, and feeling in his trouser pocket.

Standing under the lamp was the Bentley. It had a blue gleam. I could smell it twenty yards away. I walked round the other side and waited for him to open the door. A pale hand reached out to release the catch. 'Jump in, lad,' he invited. 'I've got the heater on.' It was warm, soft, and scented: a cinema armchair.

We slid down the lane and turned into the road. 'Fairfax Street, you said?'

It sounded a new place, maybe a dirtier, scruffier place, now that it was coated with his voice. 'Yes,' I replied.

I didn't say anything for a while, then I told him, 'I thought I saw you at the "A" team match this afternoon.' I looked at his rubber outline and felt hat. It seemed he was concentrating on the road.

'This afternoon,' he said with faint interest. 'Yes, I came to watch.' He smiled with quiet reproval. 'You didn't play too well.'

'Did anybody?'

'That's a point.'

59

He moved the wheel a bit, flashed a few lights, changed a gear, switched the dashboard glow on a second, squinted at the dials: everything as if I wasn't there. He knew the town well. Cutting out the city centre he took the road round the park and came out opposite Highfield estate.

'What do you think of Wade's bargaining powers?' he asked. 'Did you find him "tough opposition"?'

'I don't think I found him anything. I just kept saying five hundred and hoping the result'd turn out right.'

He shot round a couple of cars, dimmed his lights, and said, 'And has it?'

'Turned out right? I think so. I hadn't expected it to be done so quickly.' He must have thought, with the five hundred now in my pocket, I was trying to be naïve. He glanced across. 'I don't really know what I think,' I said.

'What's it feel like to be five hundred up in one day?'

How much of me did he want? I could feel him polishing me and putting me on the shelf as his latest exhibit. He came and breathed over me and gave me a gentle rub of his cuff.

'I don't feel anything yet.'

'It's all a bit quick,' he suggested vaguely.

'Yes.'

'I'm afraid that's my fault. I like to get these things settled. I don't suppose you mind an awful lot.'

'Not now I don't.'

He laughed. 'The fact is, one or two clubs were after you. They had somebody watching last Saturday. So perhaps I'm not altogether to blame for rushing you. Did you have any other offers?'

'No. I haven't heard anything.'

'Well, if you do you'll know what to say now: property of the City.' He gave a bigger laugh and slapped my thigh. Then he squeezed my knee. 'Best to make sure, Arthur.'

We passed Highfield and he said, 'Riley – he looked a bit sick, I thought. What do you think? He likes to manage these affairs rather smartly, you know. Make them look like big business. These crumby accountants, I find they always like to do that. Dress the money up to disguise the filth it is. What do you think?'

'Maybe it's filth I like.'

He was laughing again. It was like turning a little knob. He wanted me to feel a good chap, so he laughed. I laughed with him. I couldn't say I disliked him. He was giving me all these confidences, if they were that. 'One of the family' business. I just felt a bit shy, being the newest member. His elbow gave me a slow nudge as he turned the wheel.

'Fairfax Street,' he said. 'You know, that rings a bell. Who lives down there that I know?' He scratched the side of his nostril with the tip of his little finger.

'A bloke called Hammond used to live there. He was killed at your place.' I was surprised at the way I said 'your place'. It sounded big, communal. 'At Weaver's,' I told him, to show there was a difference between him and the factory. 'I've digs with his widow.'

'That's the name,' he said quietly. 'Hammond. Wasn't it Eric Hammond? I remember the funeral.'

'How'd he get killed?'

'On a lathe in "D" shop. Quite nasty.' The car'd slowed down and he switched on a headlight, as if the thought reminded him of the inevitability of accidents. 'He was facing the boss of one of those vee-belt pulleys – with a hand file. One without a wooden handle. To a large extent it was his own fault. Anybody knows you don't use those files on a bloody lathe. Naturally as soon as he touched the pulley rim the damn file shoots off. Stuck half-way through him. We've had all those files removed, even from the benches. But you'd have thought people could see a plain thing like that.' He switched off the headlight. We were going slowly. 'Not only that, his clothing got caught up in the lathe, and that didn't help. . . . There were one or two other complications too.'

He didn't say any more so I asked him, 'What were they?'

He shrugged. 'Nothing. What's his wife, or rather his widow, like? He'd a couple of kids if I remember properly.'

'She's all right.'

He looked at me a second. I don't know why. Then he said, 'She didn't get any compensation. The case went against her. We gave her a bit, not much.'

'Shouldn't she have got compensation?'

'I don't know, lad. It wasn't going to do us any good to admit liability. Still, it's not for me to say, is it? Where do you want me to drop you? At the end or at the front door?'

'End of the street'll do.'

'Bit of a coincidence you living there.'

'So it seems.'

'Yes, quite a coincidence I call that. Eric Hammond. It's amazing how these dead people keep popping up.'

He stopped the car as if he knew the street. I slipped the catch and opened the door.

'Well, you shouldn't lose your money between here and home,' he said. 'I can't see any great temptations down that street.' I stood on the pavement and looked down at him, a fish in an aquarium. A three thousand quid aquarium. 'Good night, Arthur, and my best wishes.'

I told him good night, and waited till he'd backed and turned the car. I watched the Bentley head back along City Road.

I'd no thoughts at all because I was no sooner in the street than it began to spin upwards at a terrific rate, and very shortly took off on a long staggering flight, careering about the darkened landscape in great leaps and jumps. I leant against somebody's door. Something ran down my nose and I tasted the bitterness on my upper lip.

The next thing I saw was Johnson.

He was calling my name and telling me he's my friend. 'What've you been doing?' he said. 'What've they done to you?'

'I'm tired. Jesus I'm tired.'

'You've been drinking. It's not wise.' He laid his arms round me as if I needed all his protection.

'Did you see me get out of Weaver's car, Dad? Did you see me get out? He brought me home in it.'

The nearest thing to acting shrewd came into Johnson's movements. 'What happened tonight? Have you been celebrating?' he said, and prodded me like a fellow drunk. 'Did you sign? Have they signed you on?'

I felt pretty chuffed with myself. I straightened up so I

could see him better. The street had landed. It was heaving, but it was resting.

'Aw they won't have me, Dad. They won't have me. I told 'em what to do with their stinking no-good filthy money.'

'You haven't done that!' he cried out. It seemed to explain to him why I was acting like I was. He still thought I was drunk.

'You're not crying about it?' I asked him. I looked into his face. 'You're not crying?'

'No,' he said, leaning against the lamp-post and shielding his face like a kid.

'It's not worth that trouble,' I told him. 'It's not that important.'

My head was splitting open and everything was dripping on to the pavement, my clothes, the road. There was a big pain over my eyes. I prodded Johnson, but he wasn't moving.

'Weaver just brought me back in his car, Dad.'

'I've been waiting here two hours, Arthur,' he said.

'Two hours. But why'd you do that?'

'I wanted to hear what'd happened. So it was all for nothing.'

'Aye. . . . That's right.'

'Ah, well,' he said, and kept his face shielded.

'Are you disappointed?' I asked him. He didn't answer. But a moment later he turned his head down the street and I thought he was going to walk off for the last time.

He said, 'They told me they were coming down here to sign you on. That it was no good waiting around up yonder. Weaver: it was him who told me. He said they'd be calling on you. I've waited two hours.'

'I'd have seen you tomorrow. There's no need to have waited all that time. Why d'you wait all that time? You could have called later on tonight.'

'I wanted to see,' he mumbled.

'Wanted to see what? Me sign a bit of paper? There's nothing to see. You know I've been kidding you, don't you?'

'I was waiting.'

'I've just been pulling your leg about signing on.'

He didn't say anything.

'How much do you think it is, Dad?'

'You *tell* me about it, Arthur,' he warned. He looked numb.

'Well – how much do you think it is? How much do you think they paid for Arthur Machin?'

'You *tell* me.'

'Aren't you going to guess? Try and guess how much I got.'

'You squeezed my wrist when I said the same thing to you. You've to tell me, Arthur.'

'Five hundred – five hundred quid. I'm just beginning to feel what it means. Five hundred pounds. Do you want to see the cheque?'

He stared at the lamp-post. His face glistened as it turned round in the street light and faced up the street, looking at me. 'Could I see it?' he said. His eyes were in shadow. I took the cheque out and held it under the lamp. He put both hands round the paper, like it was a delicate moth, and studied it carefully.

He looked at me then. 'You and me, Arthur,' he said.

'You think I'm worth it?'

'You and me. That's us.' He held the cheque up.

'I had to argue.'

He didn't seem to hear.

'We did it together,' he said.

'Old Wade – and that mean stinking Riley. If you'd only seen his face. It was red. It was as red as ... well anything you care to think of. They were all for cutting it down. They wanted me to take half or something, a measly few quid. I might be dead in a year. There might be a war. They're not sure what hit 'em even now. Weaver said that. He reckoned Riley was hurt real bad.'

Johnson hadn't been listening as all this flooded my head and took the pain away. He'd started a little dance round the lamp-post. He looked the funniest little frog I'd ever seen. His stubby little boots shuffled in the gutter, then on the pavement, then on the road, as he circled the light. He wasn't listening at all. But when I said, 'How much of it do you want?' he stopped dead. I'd shot him.

'What d'you mean, Arthur?'

'How much of it do you want? Five hundred quid. You put me in the way of it. How much do you think you should have?'

'Oh, no, Arthur.'

'How d'you mean, "Oh, no"?'

'You know I didn't do it for that.'

'I don't know at all,' I said, irritated, thinking he was trying to be modest before he took a big cut. 'What did you do it for?'

'Not for that.'

'For something, then?'

'No.'

'Look – you must have done it for something. You spent a year greasing round Wade, and that committee. What do you mean, you did that for nothing? Nobody'd do that for nothing. Greasing round all those fat frogs. Don't tell me you enjoyed doing that.'

'I didn't do it for that.'

'I don't mind splitting it, if that's what you're worrying about. There's a lot more for me from where that's come from. I know how to treat those frogs. I don't mind clipping some off. I think you deserve it. I honestly think you do.'

He'd stopped dancing, and he'd stopped talking. It looked as if he'd stopped breathing. He just drooped there.

'What did you do it for, then? . . . Aren't you going to tell me? Come on, come on. Have I hurt you in some way?'

'It's not any of that.'

'What is it then?'

'I wanted – you know. You know what it was.'

'I don't know,' I insisted, and tried to think of what it was he wanted if it wasn't *all* the five hundred.

'I wanted to do something on my own, something by myself. I wanted to.'

'You don't sound convinced,' I told him.

'You hurt me, Arthur. You press yourself on people. You try and make me think like you want me to. You shouldn't have thought I'd want money – paying for it. You spoil it.'

'Well, I don't reckon I wanted to do that. But you know it's been a money proposition for me from the word go. I haven't been pressing hard on you.'

'Let's leave it at that, then.' His face was a hard little mask.

'No, I want you to listen. I don't want you to start on this again. Let's get it settled. I want to pay you something. Call it a present, whatever you like. But I want you to take something. I don't want the thought of your stooging always lying over me. Because let me tell you straight, I don't enjoy getting knocked around a field for people's amusement. You see what I mean, Dad? I only enjoy it if I'm getting paid a lot for it. That's the bit I enjoy. So I want to see you share some of it.'

'I don't want any of it, Arthur. If that's what you want out of it, well and good. I've got what I want.'

'I never guessed you took it so seriously. Look – do you know what Mrs Hammond said?'

'What about?' he asked quickly.

'About this – what we've been just talking about. *She* says you did it for money.'

'She would ... she would,' he said, trying to think of something *he* could say. 'She would say that. I don't like that woman. I don't know why you stay there, Arthur. She doesn't like me.'

'That's not what I meant. I'm only telling you this to show you it's not much for me to drop you a few quid. I know you haven't done it for money – aw Christ, I'm not arguing any more. I'll send you something. Here, give us the cheque.'

'When'll I see you?' he said. He looked cold now, and lost.

'I don't know.' I took the paper off him and folded it up.

'What about tomorrow, Sunday?' he said.

'Sunday? The way I feel I won't be up by next Sunday. I feel sick.'

'You go in and rest,' he advised. 'I'll call down tomorrow and see how you are. . . . Have you been drinking?'

'Yes,' I told him. 'I'm blind drunk.'

He watched me sway down the street to the front door. There were one or two parties in the front windows. Hers was in darkness, its usual gloom.

'Who's that?' she called after I'd knocked.

'It's me. The King of England.'

'Is that you?' she said.

'No. It's me.'

'Is that you . . . ?'

'For Christ get the door open. There's not a bloody war on.'

I heard the bolt slide back, then I was inside leaning against the wall.

'What's the matter with everybody tonight?'

'You're drunk,' she said. She was quiet while she tried to look at me with disgust. I got into the kitchen under my own steam and lay down in a chair.

'Your eyes are all red,' she said. 'They're full of blood.'

'It's concussion, lady.'

'Have you been fighting? You've a mark on your forehead as well.' She watched me a while, maybe hoping I'd sprout other symptoms to give her a clue. She wasn't sure how she should respond. 'There's a blue mark between your eyes.'

'You don't have to tell me these things. I can feel it. Have you got any codeine or something?'

She banged around a bit, opened a few drawers, a cupboard, then came back and slipped a cup into my hand. I held out the other hand, felt her fingers, then the tablets. 'Aw come on. At least four.'

'Two'll do for now,' she said primly. 'You can have another later if it doesn't go off.'

'That's just like you: if it doesn't go off. Why can't you give me four now and make sure it'll go off?'

'You sound very brave and manly all at once – just because you've got a knock on your head.'

I didn't answer. She waited while I drank, then took the cup and rinsed it under the tap. The water roared. She sat down opposite me.

67

'That Johnson was here. That friend of yours.'

'I've just seen him outside. He's got the idea for some reason you don't like him. That's odd, isn't it?'

'He seemed to think I was hiding you somewhere. He said he'd been told you were down here.'

'He was. How long ago did he call?'

'Over an hour . . . There must be something the matter with him waiting all this time for you. Don't you honestly think so? I don't know why you encourage him.'

'That's just about what he said about you. He didn't know why I stayed here.'

She had nothing to say for a minute.

'You should have friends your own age,' she decided.

'I have.'

'He ought to be at work. He's not too old to work.'

'They've signed me on.' My voice sounded dead. She lifted her head at the tone. There was a late-night, worn look about her. Her eyes, usually vague in any case, were now almost completely absent. Empty holes.

'Do you want some tea?' she asked.

'Didn't you hear what I said?'

'Yes. Are you glad?'

'Tell for yourself when you guess how much it is.'

'I don't know anything about it . . . going by the way your Johnson was worked up it must be thousands. I couldn't tell what he was saying. Perhaps it's just as well.'

'Forget him. Guess how much much I'm worth.'

'I don't know. I don't know anything about football.'

'I know you don't. So just guess how much you think I'm *worth*. How much solid cash do you think *I* am?'

'I honestly couldn't say – if I'd anything to do with it you'd probably have to pay them.'

I rolled my head across the back of the chair so I could see her, then I laughed. 'You made a joke,' I told her.

'I know.'

'I knew you were like that under that mask.'

She smiled seriously.

I looked at her afresh. I'd never seen her much as a person. She didn't want to be seen. Her life, while I'd known her, had been taken up with making herself as small, as negligible as possible. So small that she didn't exist. That was her aim. And it was exactly opposite to mine. It was mainly this I resented. I wanted the real Mrs Hammond to come popping out, as it almost seemed to do then. Living had turned up so many bad cards for her that she was refusing any more deals. She was withdrawing and lying down. I hated her for it. For not seeing me: how I could help her. Everything was bad. Even me. Nothing counted any more. Not even me.

'Aren't you going to have a guess?' I asked her, wanting to impress it upon her.

'No,' she shook her head.

I waited for her to change her mind. 'I'd better tell you since you're so keen. Five hundred pounds.'

She laughed suddenly and lightly. I'd never heard the sound from her before. 'You don't believe me,' I said.

'No.'

'If you come here I'll show you the cheque, signed, crossed, and dated.'

I held it out and she reached for it.

'You see,' I told her as she read it. 'Five hundred in letters and in numbers.'

She held it briefly then handed it back.

'What d'you think?'

She thought I sounded eager. 'It's very good.'

'You don't sound excited.'

'I wouldn't get up and dance about it.'

'You shouldn't say that. It's not like you.'

'You haven't had to do anything for it.'

'As you like. If we're going to be that happy about it let's forget it. I'm going to try and get upstairs. I'll feel better lying in the dark – what with those kids screaming about out there. . . . You ought to be glad about it,' I couldn't help adding.

'They don't care – their parents. They let them play all night so long as they don't come in the house.'

'They'll miss me at the Mecca tonight. They'll be expecting me to buy the place. Old Dicky – you should have seen his face go green when that Thorpe told him how much I'd got. Don't wake me in the morning, Mrs Hammond. I might be dead.' I made a big effort to the stairs to see if she was tempted to help me. She stood uncertainly in the middle of the kitchen. I wasn't sure whether she'd mind me dropping down or not. 'That reminds me,' I said. 'Weaver was talking about your husband tonight. Told me how he got killed.'

'Did he?'

'I just mentioned it – sorry if it was the wrong thing.'

I'd been lying in bed some time, unable to sleep for the aching, having a glance at *Toreador*, how he could make the crowd follow every little sneeze he made, waiting for her to stop crying downstairs. She must have hated me getting this money, as easy as that. And Eric had to die to get perhaps a couple of hundred out of the firm. This toreador used to shout at the crowd. He'd make them crazy just by shouting at them, then he'd do something so spectacular they'd be ready to kiss his arse the next minute. The next thing I heard was her voice the other side of the door.

'Does it mean you won't be staying?' she said.

I hadn't thought about it. When I didn't say anything she went on, 'The money – does it mean you'll be moving?'

'I don't think so,' I called to her, then I heard her door shut. I put the cheque on the chair beside the bed so that it'd be the first thing I saw when I woke up.

3

'TATA-RUM, tata-rum, see the conquering 'eroes cum.'

I can see Weaver's crombie-coated arm wrapped round Maurice's shoulders. Maurice is shouting his song. Their heads are close together; between them the lights are picking out a tunnel through the foliage. We're travelling uphill at high speed, somewhere in Sandwood. Beside me I can smell George Wade's cigar, and on the other side feel Johnson's body pressed close to mine. The old man reaches forward and carefully touches the back of Maurice's head.

'What is it, Dad?' Maurice turns round. Then he sees my open eyes. 'Oh . . . the patient's awake, Doctor.'

He presses Weaver to have a look. For a moment I'm the only person looking through the windscreen.

'Doesn't he look a picture? You've behaved right well, you have, Arthur,' Maurice says and breaks into a scream of laughter. 'Hasn't he though?' he says to Weaver, and glances over at George Wade. 'We've heard all his subconscious what-nots, haven't we, George?'

I can see but not hear Weaver suppressing his laughter. 'It's the best turn I've heard, Art. I hope to Christ nobody's there when I have my teeth out. I wouldn't have a friend left in the world.'

'And have I?'

Maurice laughs a bit more, and says, 'Did you hear what he said, Mr Wade?' He chokes and gurgles. 'You've one friend, Art, and that's me. I can't vouch for anybody else.'

He's looking straight at Wade whose face I can't see. Then it's Weaver's turn. 'I had my doubts about psychology and that,' he says. 'But from now on I think I'll look into it, the deep subconscious and all that load as Morry says – you know: what we keep under the counter.'

'It's the ramblings of an unconscious man,' Wade protests. 'Why make it out to be anything more?'

'Ramblings or not, George,' Weaver says, 'he seemed to have a path to tread and he trod it.'

'A bloody stampede,' Maurice says. 'Tata-rum, tata-rum . . . see the conquering 'eroes come.'

'Well, I don't hold anything against Arthur,' Wade says. 'He's a sick man. I still think we ought to have taken him home as the dentist suggested. Or at least, have waited there until he came round properly. How do you feel, Arthur?'

'He wanted to come. Didn't you, Art?' Maurice says. 'It's Christmas Eve – he doesn't want to be locked up in a bloody room for the night. Isn't that right, Arthur?'

'I don't know.'

'How d'you feel?' Wade says. He gives the impression

71

I've done him some harm while I've been out. His voice's tired and hurt, his concern too showy.

'Have I been letting my mouth off?'

'They brought you out into the fresh air before they should. Mr Weaver couldn't wait any longer, and Maurice decided to bring you with them. The dentist gave you a heavy dose, it seems.'

'You didn't want us to leave you there, did you, Arthur?' Maurice says. 'You should have seen yourself when we lugged you out that dentist's. You thought you were swimming. Your arms were going . . .'

'You could have gone ahead,' Wade says. 'We could have got a taxi.'

'And taken him home? What sort of a bloody Christmas would he have had there? Aren't I right, Art? You wanted to come.'

'I've got this far. There's no point going back.'

'That's the spirit, Art. Show 'em you can take it.'

'The best thing to do', Wade says, 'is to phone a taxi as soon as we get to Mr Weaver's house, and get him home to bed.'

'Oh, I'm not going to bed now,' I tell him.

'That's it, Art. Let's have some criping fun while we've got the chance. We might be in Russia tomorrow.'

We all lean back and watch the leaves flicking past the windscreen. I've to pay some attention to Johnson, who's been nudging me for some time. But he only wants me to look at him. In the reflection from the headlights I see him smile, a dumb sort of pleasure.

'We'll be there in a few minutes,' Weaver says. 'I've come round the back way from town. Less traffic. If you look to your right, George, round this bend, you'll be able to see across to Primstone.'

I swallow some blood and rest the tip of my tongue on the empty front sockets. They're soft. Jelly. There's a dull ache, not too unpleasant, across the top of my mouth.

The car swings out of a cutting that brings us over the lip of the valley. We see the town lit up below, the string of lights coiling up to the darkness round Primstone. The flanks of the cooling towers in the valley reflect the light with diminishing strength until their summits are hidden in the darkness of the sky. They're two columns holding up some mysterious weight.

'It's a right cake hole,' Maurice says. He spits out of the window. Weaver takes his arm away.

'Some of that got me, Morry,' he says, wiping his hand across his cheek. 'Where're your manners?'

I don't think Maurice hears. Any rate he spits again and Weaver calls back to Wade, 'There's no holding him, George. What do you think?' He's annoyed with his boy but keen not to show it. Wade doesn't answer; he's staring down at the view with a submerged expression. He might be going back over his life for reassurance.

The headlights show up a white gate in a high hedge. Maurice gets out and after a lot of complaining and shouting he opens it and we drive through. He clambers in and we manoeuvre up the drive.

Every window of Linga Longa is alight. A full-scale party's already under way. Half of it comes hooting and screaming to escort us to the glass porch. Maurice lolls out of the window hollering back.

'Like Rome in the ancient days,' Weaver says with a quiet, patronizing satisfaction. He restrains himself from lavishly knocking a couple down.

'Run them over, they don't mind,' Maurice says. 'It's Christmas.'

For a while they can't get anything open to get out. Then Maurice gets the sun-roof back and climbs up. Both his feet rest on Weaver's crombie shoulders, then suddenly disappear as he falls into the arms outside.

'That's the most expensive doormat that lad's ever had,' Weaver says, still polite, but looking pale and strained in the glow from the dashboard. The engine stops. I can see a vast Christmas tree inside the porch. Its lights tremble as people fight by.

'I think the best policy is to drive straight on out,' Wade says.

'You might be right there, George. Only I'd never get

ten yards.' He's trying to open his door with some show of dignity, but the weight of bodies gleefully presses it shut whenever he gets it free. 'I never invited all this lot. Half the bloody town's here. It looks as though we'll have to leave by the sun-roof ourselves. What do you think?' He collapses back into his seat.

'I say drive straight out,' Wade tells him. 'I can't imagine any civilized person, let alone Slomer or the like, wanting to mix with this lot. They're absolute imbeciles.'

'I never invited these. Thank God for one thing: we've an hour before Slomer's likely to turn up, or the M.P.'

'What time is it?' I ask. It seems weeks since we were at the dentist's. Wade fumbles in his waistcoat.

'It's not yet eight o'clock.'

Another ten minutes pass before the door's opened beside Johnson and the old man suddenly vanishes. Maurice's grabbing my arm and shouting, 'Be careful with the sod. He might pass out again before we can see his lovely baby smile.'

I get to my feet outside and lean against the car. Bodies and faces and glasses wrapped with fingers press against me, laughing and shouting and clinking, yet I can hear George's voice distinctly in the car saying, 'I'm not moving from here until this mob clears. You can leave me.'

'Go on. Smile, Art,' Maurice's shouting.

Quite a crowd's collected, stretching to and filling the porch. There're faces like masks dangling in every window. Maurice is compère. I make puzzled faces at him to encourage him to come close. When he's right up and shouting all over my face, 'Go on, smile for 'em, Arta,' I push off from the car and belt him in the belly. I hold him up with my left hand. 'Don't get so excited, Maurice,' I tell him.

He twists away. 'I forgot to mention,' he's saying to those near him, 'there's a couple of crates of beer in the boot.'

They move round with him to the back of the car. Weaver's already there, pressing the handle. The women scream and clap when the dog comes into sight coiled between the crates. It's enough to get Wade out of the car, and he forces his way to the front. 'I'll get the dog,' he says.

74

''s all right,' Maurice tells him. 'I'll get it out for you.'
He looks round at Weaver who simpers. 'Come on doggie.
Come on little doggie, then.'

It whines and slides to the back of the boot. He grabs it
and pulls it out, one hand on its tail, one round its thick,
silver-studded collar. The body arches and twists, then it's
wrapped in Maurice's arms. The women take the opportunity to show how human they can be, and give it a few
pats and nice words. The dog lowers its head and Wade
smiles.

'Whoops,' Maurice says as it slips from his hands. 'I've
dropped it.'

'Don't let it get away,' Wade's shouting.

'I'll get it,' Maurice says, but in trying to pick it up he
seems to give it an accidental kick. It whirls round in the
forest of legs and, suddenly finding a gap, rushes off into the
bushes.

'Oh hell fire,' Wade says.

Maurice's covered his face with his hands; his shoulders
are shaking inside his big coat. 'It's got away,' he manages
to say.

'Come here, Toby! Heel, Toby boy! Heel!' Wade's
calling in a voice divided, contorted between anger and
encouragement.

It's the first time most people have heard the name of the
dog – the first time I'd heard it – and a lot of laughing marks
the event. One or two turn away.

'We'll soon find it, George,' Weaver says, looking a bit
happier for the diversion. 'It can't get out of the garden.
We'd better get these crates in before the air gets to them.
Come on girls, show the warriors where to put them.'

Maurice passes me carrying a crate and still giggling.
'Come on in, George,' Weaver calls to Wade, still standing
at the back of the car looking hopefully at the bushes.

'I'll have to find the dog first, Mr Weaver. I can't leave
the damn thing out here.' He begins calling and whistling
to show Weaver what he means.

'Right you are, George. We'll be out with you in a minute when we've sorted things out inside. It can't get out of

75

the garden, I tell you, there's wire fencing in all the hedges. So don't start worrying.'

Wade answers by disappearing into the bushes, prodding his way with his stick: a doggie hunter. Weaver has a consoling grin when he turns inside. 'Can you manage on your own, Arthur?' he says, and walks by without waiting for an answer.

I know my way around Weaver's house as well as I do around any other public building, although it's the first time I've seen a party here this size, even on Christmas Eve. The only feeling I have is to find a quiet corner somewhere and lie down. The place I have in mind is a small bedroom tucked under the eaves, the summit of one of the pyramid roofs. It's a place where I usually end up when I come to Weaver's football parties. But I only get half-way up the stairs when Johnson comes into the hall like Wade's lost dog itself. I get up to the landing without him seeing me. I'm dizzy.

The door's locked. I can hear some grunting inside. I bang on it. 'Come on. Come on. You've had your time.'

There's a lot of creaking and scurrying, then I hear the voice of Tommy Clinton, one of the City reserves.

'Get knobbed, we've only just come in.'

'Come on Clinton,' I tell him. 'Your father's downstairs.'

'If you don't go away,' he says evenly, 'I'll come out there and jump you, whoever you are.'

'You're too young for this sort of thing, Clinton. And jus' be fair. You've got all night for your cocoa.'

'Is that Arthur?' he says suspiciously, with a big drop in his voice.

'Yes. How long you going to be?'

'Give us five minutes, Art. We'll be out by then, honest.'

'Five minutes. I'll wait on the landing and count.'

I go back and wait by a large aspidistra in a brass can one of Mrs Weaver's fads. It smells as though somebody' watered it recently, and not from a tap. From behind it I can see the stairs and part of the hall. The noise down there' deafening, thudding through the wall by my ear, and sending ing my head buzzing. I've been here no more than a coupl

76

of minutes when Johnson comes into sight again, this time trailing Maurice. They argue a while, then start to come up.

I nip down the landing and get into the bathroom. The light's out and I lock the door.

'If he's anywhere, Dad, he'll be here,' Maurice's saying. 'He won't have gone home, you can count on that. He's just shy with having no teeth.' He bangs on the bedroom door opposite but gets no answer. 'Come on Art. It's me. Maurice. I know you're in there, you frog. What's the matter? Sulking?'

'For Christ's sake!' I hear Clinton's faint voice. 'Can't we get a minute's peace in this bloody house!'

There's a moment's silence, then Maurice says, 'Sorry, Tommy. I thought Arthur might be there.'

'I'm not that kind,' Tommy says. 'Go stuff yourself, Maurice.'

'He's not here,' Maurice whispers to Johnson. 'Why don't you look in the other bedrooms? I'm off down.'

When they've gone I fill the basin with cold water and stick my head in for a minute. I find some aspirin on the shelf, by a tin of Mrs Weaver's talcum. Or is it Weaver's? I take four tablets. Then two more to make sure. The bedroom door's just opening as I come out of the bathroom, and Tommy steps on to the landing with his sample.

'Where's your sweetie?' he says.

'She's coming.' I nod at the bathroom. He winks.

'Fixing things up,' he says. Tommy fancies himself a pretty smart frog with women. 'Maurice's been looking for you.'

'Tell him you haven't seen me.'

'That's for sure, Art. Good hunting.'

He's not left the key in the lock. I bolt the door, then straighten the bed. There's a thick stink of scent. I turn off the light, pull back the curtains, take off my coat and shoes. I get under the blankets and start thinking why Weaver hates me so much nowadays. Where have I gone wrong?

4

THAT first week-end of first team football brought me in six quid more than George Wade forecast. From the two games I made fifty-six quid: being Christmas, they were heavily bonused. It gave me quite an impression of the future and I bought a car which Weaver put in my way. It was a Humber from the County Hall garage which I got for just over three hundred – half the price I'd have had to pay if Weaver hadn't been around. I got its real market value when I sold it for a Jaguar a few months later.

It took me three weeks to get Mrs Hammond to sit inside it. It was only the second time she'd been in a car; the first was at Eric's funeral. She couldn't make up her mind what attitude to take. It was a Sunday morning, and Lynda had been fretting to go out. She didn't mention the car, but Ian did. Mrs Hammond fussed but didn't tell them off as she might have done. She kept smiling at me, as if I'd already made the offer. The car was shining in the street – I'd been cleaning it at eight that morning, and now it was surrounded by a gang of kids who'd never seen anything like it on the premises.

'All right,' she said. 'I'll take you in the park in a few minutes.'

'Aw mam!' Lynda bawled, looking at her with an adult disappointment.

'Well, I thought you'd been shouting all morning to go out,' she said.

Some of her reluctance to accept the car was because she associated it with Weaver, and all of a sudden she hated Weaver, perhaps finding it convenient to blame him personally for Eric's death. She didn't know how he'd got it for me, but she'd heard he'd been teaching me to drive. I'd taken good care he didn't come further than the end of the street.

'You know what we mean, mam – go in Uncle Arthur's car,' Lynda said.

'That's not for me to say. It's not your motor-car, young miss.'

'I'll take you', I told Lyn, 'so long as your mother comes.'

The kid jumped up and down, assuming that now there was no barrier.

'I don't know whether I can,' Mrs Hammond said. 'I've all this to clear up.' She looked round at the room – a junk shop. There was a pool of soap flakes and water where Ian had been cleaning his car, and a pile of empty tins and corn-flake packets Lyn used for a shop. 'What would you say', she asked the kid, 'if there was no dinner for you? There's all that to get ready yet.'

'I wouldn't care,' Lyn said.

'And we can't go without your mam,' I warned her. The kid tugged at her mother's skirt uncertainly.

'Just for a few minutes then,' she said, and took off her apron. 'Round the houses.'

'Aren't you going to put your grey dress on?' I asked her.

'What, for two minutes?' She looked at me dumbly.

'It's Sunday. Lyn and me, we've got our Sunday clothes on. Haven't we, Lyn?'

She wasn't in a mood to argue. She probably knew what I wanted, and she went upstairs without a word.

I waited in the kitchen for her while Lyn and Ian hung around outside blowing the horn, kicking the tyres, rubbing the windows. She spent some time getting ready, and when she came down she was right on edge. She'd been crying. She'd been crying a lot recently: a lot more than usual. She brought the kids back in and polished their faces with a flannel till they both started wailing. I put on my sports coat and went out into the street. She locked the front door care-fully and held the key in her hand.

It was a sunny winter morning. There were a few spec-tators at the front doors. Mrs Hammond kept her eyes down, not wanting to look concerned. She was worried. She knew what they were thinking, and was frightened of them be-cause of it. As I held the door I told her, 'They'll think you're quite a lady now.'

'Yes,' she said. 'But do you mind if I sit in the back? I

don't want it to seem. . . .' She saw my look and added, 'Lynda and Ian'll want to be in front.'

'We'll all be in front. There's plenty of room. The car's usually carried those big fat frogs from the County Hall, so it won't complain at us.' She got straight in.

I drove slowly down the street to give the neighbours the benefit of the carnival. I talked to Mrs Hammond in a way conspicuous enough to show how independent I was, that I didn't really need to notice people any more.

I turned left along City Road and headed away from town, stepping up the speed. She was nervous. She held Ian tightly between her knees, and had her arm round Lynda. She watched the huge bonnet of the car as if it was some giant reptile nosing its way through the landscape.

'How far are we going?' she asked, when the last houses had shot past and we were skimming between high banks of sooted hedges.

'I thought we might make a day of it.' I couldn't use Lyn to argue this, so I said, 'You've locked the house. We'll take a run in the country. You don't mind, do you?'

'We can't very well get out now.'

'If you're going to be like that I'll turn back.'

She didn't answer. 'Even if it's only for the kids' sake it'll be worth it. Don't you reckon?'

I could wait a long time for the answer I turned north and headed over the ridge into the next valley. We by-passed the big towns, spending half an hour weaving through the suburbs. The kids got restless seeing so many damned houses. I took the road over the next moors and we came out at the top of a huge limestone ridge which gave a view over ten or fifteen miles of wooded countryside. We all woke up a bit and I parked the car on a grass plot. We got out, eased our legs, and sent Lyn and Ian behind the bushes. There was another party already parked; they waved at us pretty cheerfully and Mrs Hammond smiled and waved back, shyly. 'I've been here once before,' she said. 'We came on the bus. Just before we got married.'

'I suppose it looks even better in summer. We'll come and see.' She was still smiling. We pottered around for a while amongst the rocks and birches; I chased the kids until they were bored and wanted to be moving.

We followed the road into the valley and drove alongside the river, passing through a couple of bare empty woods and a village. Turning a bend we came on Markham Abbey standing in meadows by the river. Mrs Hammond made a sound of surprise. Lyn almost bounded through the windscreen at the 'fairy castle'. I headed the car up a narrow lane and we stopped at the foot of the ruins, just beside a flock of sheep. They moved round the car as if it was just another part of the ruins, shoving their black faces under the wheels to get at the grass.

'You'd never think anything like this existed,' Mrs Hammond said. We stood by the car and looked up at the shell of the building, its great window empty to the sky. Ian stayed near us, afraid, but we could hear Lynda's shouts echoing inside.

We strolled round after her. She kept nipping back to tell us some discovery she'd made. We only caught her up at the side of the river where she was watching the water for a fish to splash again. The river'd been widened there centuries ago and a dam put across. All that was left was a line of stepping stones round which the water, like a smooth sheet of flecked marble, crumbled. Lynda jumped on to the first stone, swayed, and said, 'They've got fish in this water. Shall we go across, Mam?'

Her mother shook her head. 'It's too dangerous, Lyn. And it'd take too long in any case.'

I picked Lynda up.

Her mother knew what I was going to do. She didn't say anything. She started to make a move, then stopped, and stood frozen to the spot. She watched us on to the first, then the second stone, and turned away. She looked towards the ruins, stiff, small, and erect.

The river was high, running smooth and fast with its winter rain; the bottom couldn't be seen because of the water's sheen. The foam gurgled and splashed over the stones but slipped like glass over the unseen submerged ones. Lynda was frightened. She stared around her disbelievingly, as if the water was new, something she'd never seen or reckoned with before. She was heavy, and striding from stone to stone it seemed that any minute she might panic and pitch us both into the river. We got half-way before I found some of the stones were insecure, and when I tried to turn round none of them were broad enough to take my splayed feet. I'd given up hope of keeping my feet dry. I splashed about in the water as I fought for each stone and having reached it, stopped to regain my balance. The last stones had been pushed together to fish from, and once we were on this tiny pier I told Lynda to wave back.

'Ma . . . am!' she called in a loud bleat.

'Do you want to look round, Lyn?' I said. 'Or go straight back?'

She didn't know. She looked at me, then at the water. The bank this side was low and soggy, and my feet were beginning to sink. I thought about trying to find a bridge, but downstream the river disappeared into a wood, which seemed an unlikely place to accommodate one, and upstream it tumbled down by the side of a rocky escarpment, fringed and surrounded by heath and moor. Lynda went behind a bush or two. She found a bird's nest, and we both looked at it nervously, more intently than we might ordinarily have done. I held her up so she could push her hand into the middle of the bush and feel in the cup of the nest. She brought out a small wet feather.

'Do you want to go back now, Lyn?' I said.

She shook her head slowly, and stared at the bushes in the hope of finding some other diversion. She was pale. After a while she went and stood on the low bank and stared across at her mother, fifty or more yards away. I could see the car, sticking up out of the flock of sheep, and the red blobs of paint on the sheep's backs. I tried to imagine how I'd feel if I was responsible for Lynda's drowning, then forgot the idea as I picked her up again. 'Here we go,' I said, so cheerfully that she laughed.

She began to moan as we got nearer the middle and she heard me panting hard, breathing in gasps as I balanced from stone to stone. I stopped to rest. The water drowned

every other noise. Mrs Hammond waved and shouted sound-
lessly, her small figure almost standing in the water itself.
Lynda watched carefully where I put my feet on the next
stone, then seeing them slide on the green, mossy weed, she
lifted her head and stared at the tiny figure on the other
bank. I felt her trembling between my hands as she clung
there patiently, her fingers digging in my arms, waiting for
me to make several attempts to get my feet on to a loose,
green boulder. 'There Lyn! Did you see that fish?' I said.
But she couldn't hear what I was saying.

The closer we got to the bank the tenser she became.

'Ma . . . am! Mam!' She waved stiffly.

Her mother shouted, 'Give over waving – you'll have Mr
Machin in the water.' Her voice sounded peculiar, uninterested.

When I stepped on to the last stone Lynda struggled to
get down. I dropped her on to the close cropped grass and
she flung herself on her mother. 'We did it!' she said. 'Did
you see us?' Her fear had completely disappeared with
relief. Her mother folded herself round her, and didn't look
my way. 'We soon got back, didn't we?' Lynda said,
muffled.

My feet were sodden. When I put on a pair of football
boots I had in the back of the car Mrs Hammond gave a
shy laugh.

'You're not driving in them?' she said.

'I've nothing else. Gonna lend me yours?'

She blushed, and watched me lace them up. She had been
flushed altogether since the moment Lynda had jumped
down from me to her, as if the excitement had brought the
blood up in her, and made it surge in parts she'd thought
or felt dead. Her face was relaxed with broken strain, and
tanned red as if it'd been exposed to the weather for a long
time.

'We'll see what difference they make when the car sets
off,' I said.

'Is it safe?' She looked serious. 'Can you steer as well with
them on?'

When I laughed she smiled back nervously.

'I thought you'd have noticed I don't steer with my feet.'

'I meant those things you press.'

We looked at each other coyly, realizing we were both playing. Then she glanced down at the sheep, and stamped her foot at them.

We felt the security of the car more than ever. With the heater on, the smoothness of the running added to the cosiness. 'It makes a big difference having a car,' I said, and she pulled a face of restrained, dubious agreement.

'Did a king live there?' Lynda asked, flushed like her mother, and looking at the ruins as we climbed out of the valley.

'I should think so, dear,' Mrs Hammond said. She probably didn't know it had been a monastery. Lynda watched till the last stone summit had disappeared amongst the bare trees.

'Where're we going now?' Mrs Hammond said. We had a long run downhill and were travelling fast. I put my foot to the floor and the car rocked and swayed, and the air screamed past a hole somewhere.

'It's a place I've heard of. We'll go there and get some dinner. It's not far.'

We drove in silence, but as we passed the next village, its grey stone houses like sombre banks to a stream, she asked, 'Does that mean we'll have to eat with other people?'

'Depends if anybody else is there. It shouldn't be crowded this time of the year. Do you mind eating with other people or something?'

'No, I don't mind,' she said uneasily. 'I just wondered if we were dressed right.'

'I reckon so long as we've got sommat on they won't chuck us out.'

Howton Hall's an old country house converted into a hotel and an eating place for the sort of client who can afford to drive out there for an evening, or a week-end. It's an equal distance from three large industrial towns, and approachable from two more. This distance used to act as a kind of social sieve. But with the bigger hand-out of cars and other crap propaganda since the war it's stepped down a peg or two. A couple of Rugby League clubs have their annual dinners there, and at the week-ends you find school-teachers and an occasional clerk who's sweated on his bike all the way from town. Because of this increase of trade and general lowering of standard the place's been cut into two. On one side, overlooking a deep wooded valley and a lake, is the residential sector and the restaurant, and on the other is a car park, a bicycle rack, and a café.

I took them to the restaurant. It was after one o'clock and not very crowded. I tried to get Mrs Hammond to go in the cocktail bar, but one look at the plush interior and the Riding cloth merchants, and she wouldn't budge past the door. The restaurant was the same: people who couldn't be bothered with cooking a Sunday dinner. They lounged around eating and drinking and making too much noise. But they were more dispersed and it wasn't quite so over-bearing.

Along one side the wall had been knocked out and glass put in its place, which gave the impression as you sat down of the room's being suspended over the valley: an exclusive sensation for which you had to pay.

She was frightened – more frightened than when I'd carried Lynda over the river. And she was worried that both Lynda and Ian were going to behave like pigs. I tried to give her the feeling that nobody'd mind my keeping my football boots on.

I did all the talking with the waiter, who made no attempt to hide his feeling we'd strayed over to the wrong side of the hotel. He coughed a lot, and pointed out the big prices with the tip of his smart pencil. He underlined one or two prices to emphasize the dearness of everything. I ordered every-thing that cost the most. He wasn't sure whether he should be pleased. He wanted to get quickly to the point where we paid for it all. Mrs Hammond was quiet, terrified of him, looking at him as if he was responsible for a peculiar odour.

But it didn't prevent us, when this marmoset wasn't there, from enjoying the meal. Mrs Hammond's eyes widened as she ate the juicy food. It made her feel that the indignity of coming to the place was somehow worth it.

'Is it one of those places where they have coffee after the sweet?' she said, as if she knew all such places backwards. She'd just finished stuffing the last potato down Ian's gullet. When I said 'Yes' she nodded significantly.

'Now you're here, do you want some?' I asked her, because I'd been aiming to miss the coffee out. I'd no socks on, and one or two smart frogs had been pointing at my football boots under the table. One of them had already directed the waiter's attention to them.

'Well,' she said, her confidence restored by the fact we hadn't been flung out, and looking at me to see if it was money that held us back. I ordered two coffees.

When they came Lynda wanted some; in a cup of her own. I got her an orange juice instead, which the waiter made clear was no end of trouble. We sat back and looked at the view for less than five minutes when the kids got restless. Lynda had wandered off on a tour of the tables and was watching a quiet-looking man eating his chicken. I told Mrs Hammond to take Ian and catch her and I'd join them at the car.

The waiter was out to make me wait for the bill. I gave him three minutes. Then I made quickly for the door.

He intercepted me with a prolonged stumble down the long room, swaying and diving between tables as if his rear was on fire. 'Have you got your bill – sir?' he panted.

I tried to think of something very smart to say, but all I gave out was, 'No.'

He grimaced with some sort of politeness and held it out on a plate. It came to around two pound sixteen. I asked him how it had arrived at that. He explained it carefully, feeling justified at last, checking each item we'd eaten, marking it with his fine pencil on the menu, keeping at the back of his mind the pleasure of calling the manager. I asked him if he'd made a mistake in the addition.

He trilled up the penny column and down the shillings, and stabbed quickly at the pounds. The pennies, I suggested, I think you've gone wrong there. He added them again, a bit more slowly, having a look at me for each shilling he ticked off. I thought we ought to check the prices with those

86

on the menu. He did that. The figures on the bill were thickened in now like a kid's drawing with the number of times he'd run over them. His pencil was blunt. He was in a can of a temper. I still wasn't sure he hadn't made a mistake. He went over it all again, and he couldn't read some of the numbers.

I counted the money out carefully, and put a sixpenny tip on top of the pile, 'Thank you,' he said, his eyes like charcoal.

They were waiting by the car. Lynda was crying and Ian leant sleepily against the mudguard. He scowled at me as I came up as if I was responsible for all his troubles.

'What's the matter with our little girl?' I asked her.

'She's been smacked for running round those tables,' her mother said. I nodded wisely at Lynda and unlocked the doors. We came away from Howton Hall with a sense of achievement.

I drove a circular way back, through countryside I'd only visited as a boy on a bicycle. It was something of a triumphal tour. Lyn fell asleep. We stopped to lay her on the back seat and Mrs Hammond sat beside her. We got back to Fairfax Street with the sunset.

*

I was too busy the next few weeks to think about what effect the trip might have had. Mrs Hammond was quieter. I wasn't in the house much, and we hardly spoke. I stepped up my rent and she didn't complain. It meant I didn't do any washing up and didn't help her any more with the washing. I got the coal in now'n again.

I spent most of the time getting to know the new bunch of people I'd moved into, and the car was the biggest asset I had. One thing, it meant I could avoid Johnson more easily, a really difficult thing when there'd only been the bus to travel on and the park to walk through. The only times I saw him were after home matches and on one or two training nights. With a lot of new friends pushing round I soon got the technique of slipping away.

The great thing with Weaver was that he couldn't do

enough for me. I was in with the mob; and him and me got fairly close. He put me in the way of a Jaguar after I'd got five hundred and eighty for the Humber, and he lent me the extra hundred and fifty so that I wouldn't break into my bank balance. What amazed him was I paid him back within five weeks. The reason was some weeks I was making up to twenty quid on the dogs at Stokeley, a mining village down the valley where Frank Miles, captain of the City, lived.

With the confidence a car and no worry over money can give, and with being stuffed up there in the public eye, I found I'd a knack of getting close to some important people, from local industrialists and area managers to soccer stars from nearby towns and the local M.P. It usually lasted a short time. Taff Gower was about the only friend, apart from Maurice, who I stuck with. Ever since I'd flattened his nose – it'd been permanently bent from that day – we'd been friendly in an unambitious sort of way. We never did anything great for each other. Whatever there was it must have been something to do with his nose and me hitting it. I saw him fairly often, even when he gave up the game and took over a pub near Primstone – he helped to train the youngsters on Thursday nights.

I wasn't so close to Weaver that I didn't see he was as good an example of the come-and-go type as any I knew. He'd never got past the stage of treating friendship as a kind of patronage. I gathered he'd once been really ambitious – more than I could have seen or imagined – and he was still very particular where his only rival, Slomer, was concerned. They were supposed to be the most dangerous people in town – if you could have dangerous people in this town – and Primstone was their mutual toy. They bought and sold players, built them up and dropped them, like a couple of kids with lead soldiers. But that seemed to be the way with any professional sport. I just found it important to keep up close to Weaver.

When I first started with him, or rather he with me, I hadn't appreciated how potent he could be. I thought I deserved somebody like Weaver to be always hanging over me. I didn't realize how much people could hate till I met a few who didn't like him, or who didn't like Slomer. Weaver was supposed to be a fairy, which could mean he was just sensitive to other people's opinion. He might have been a bit that way inclined but he didn't do anything about it. He watched us getting bathed a lot, but he only got round to patting and arms-on-your-shoulder stuff. His likes and dislikes were a bit keener than most folks'. Any objection I had I put right outside for the simple reason Weaver liked me a lot. He was rich, and I'd never met a rich man before.

I'd been with Weaver some time before I met his wife. She never showed her face at the Saturday night parties, and he never mentioned her. From what I gathered she was a holy lady, patronizing the Bishop and his social whirl next door, and making herself responsible for most of the official charity to old folks in town. A picture like that made me think she and Weaver didn't get on well.

I was in the cocktail bar of the Woolpacks in Victoria Street one Saturday afternoon during the close season – the first summer after I'd signed on – when I saw Ed Philips come in. I'd just come up to town to collect the car from the garage, and since it was after closing time, I reckoned it was probably that waiting outside that brought *him* inside. He saw me with that shudder of late recognition which some men and more women adopt to make them look preoccupied.

'Hiya Arthur. Us athletes stoking up?'

It was the thing with him to look and act athletic – the brim of his trilby slightly bevelled, his yellow gloves slightly turned back, his coat collar just slightly raised round the back. His athletic activities, apart from golf, were confined to his head – which didn't restrict their effect in any way. I always found it difficult to decide from which particular achievement he'd lately returned. Perhaps when he was in the lavatory that morning he'd won the final Test, maybe on the way to the office he'd won the 1500 metres. It was difficult to tell. But he was certainly winning something as he came strutting up. 'Are you busy?' he said casually as he sat down.

'How're you keeping, Ed?'

'Fair. You know how it is, this summer heat. Can I get you a drink?' he asked safely. 'I wondered whether you were busy.'

'I just might be, if you pressed me.'

'If you weren't I thought you could run me up to Weaver's place,' he suggested.

'Why me?'

'The car's laid up, old sport, and I don't want to take a taxi. It might made a bad impression – it's the lady I'm seeing, not the old man.'

'What's wrong with the bus?'

'Aw, Arthur.' He brightened up. 'How could I go knocking on her door after I'd just stepped off a damn bus? Your County Hall car'll fit the programme fine.'

'I've sold the Humber. It's a Jag now. And it won't impress her. Weaver got it for me in the first place.'

'Ah, pity about the Humber. It had a glass partition, hadn't it? No? Anyway she won't notice the difference. Cars all look alike below a Daimler to her. We can go when you're ready.'

As we got nearer Ling Longa I felt that bit nervous, then curious. And feeling nervous and curious I noticed a change come over Ed too. Weaver wasn't there – only his wife. He was right on edge by the time we reached the white gate. 'Shall I come in with you?' I said.

He looked at me in half surprise. 'Oh, I don't know if I should drag you in, Arthur.' He continued to treat me simply, like a trained animal he had to pacify. 'You only came for the ride, old son. It's no good thrusting things unexpected on you, like.'

'It's private business and you don't want me to hear?' I suggested.

'There's nothing private, Arthur. . . .' He shrugged stiffly. 'I come up here on and off – purely in the way of duty. Just for chats, you might say. She's got various connexions and tells me the news. It saves a lot of walking around. You come in if you like, old sport. It's a lot of parochial chatter. Come in if you really want to.'

He talked so much about it he convinced me he didn't want me around: I was the chauffeur. I thought his bloody cheek was funny and I could only grin. 'You go in,' I said. '*I*'ll wait.'

'You're sure? You don't mind?' But he was already up the steps and ringing the bell.

May, the Weavers' Irish maid, appeared. He leered at her and made a few sly motions with his hands as if he was advertising the car and himself at the same time. He'd lost some of his confidence by asking me to wait.

'Hello, Arthur,' May called over his shoulder.

'Is Mrs Weaver in?' Ed asked. 'It's Mr Philips from the *Guardian* calling,' and he disappeared into the hall.

I sat and tapped the wheel, and wondered how long Ed would see fit to keep me waiting. After all, he couldn't be sure I wouldn't drive off and leave him to walk away down that long garden. I stared up at the windows in the hope of catching sight of Mr Weaver, but there was only May. She held her nose as if there was a peculiar smell about the place, and smiled down at me.

I'd got out to sit on the front mudguard, in the sun, and I hadn't been there ten minutes when the front door re-opened and Mrs Weaver came out, followed by a displeased Ed. I must have looked too independent a chauffeur for his liking, sitting on, not in, the car.

'Arthur Machin,' Mrs Weaver said, staying on the top step. 'He's one of the stalwarts of the City team according to my husband ... we've been watching you from the window.'

'Yeh,' I said, standing up awkwardly, putting my hands in, then taking them out of, my pockets.

'I must say', she turned to Philips, 'he doesn't seem a very sociable giant.'

Ed brought out a smile, and tried hard to change his mood. 'He's probably shy,' he said, almost harshly.

Mrs Weaver seemed to enjoy playing him along. She came down the steps slowly, and we shook hands. 'Oh, don't tell me he's shy,' she said. 'He comes up here often, don't you, Machin? But then on slightly livelier occasions.' She laughed pleasantly, and I couldn't help comparing her with other women I knew, and liking her. She seemed glad she was winning me over, and that Ed could see her do it.

He put a polite hand on the door handle to show he was calling it a day. Ed counted the whole incident a mistake. 'I asked Mr Philips to bring me out and introduce you,' she said. 'But he's such a slowcoach . . . and I rather think he wanted to keep me inside talking.' She raised her eyebrows, and we laughed.

'Well that's what he came for,' I said, pressing the intimate advantage. Ed tried to smile too.

'Ah now, don't go making me just a gossip-talker,' he said, and opened the car door, pointedly. 'Sometimes I can be a very busy man.'

'I come out for a word with Machin, and you immediately want to rush him off,' Mrs Weaver complained. 'We were watching you pulling faces,' she said to me. 'Sitting on that mudguard and looking bored to tears. I might have known Mr Philips wouldn't have the gumption to ask you inside.'

'Oh, I don't like intruding as it is . . .' Ed began.

'No matter,' Mrs Weaver said, as if remembering herself. 'If you must appear the busy executive, you must. Still, I do like meeting Mr Weaver's protégés now and again. He keeps them to himself too much, I sometimes think.'

They shook hands, and after Ed had eased himself into the car she said, 'You must come again, Machin. We might be able to have a longer chat . . . and I might even find out why Mr Weaver spends so much time at that club of yours!' She raised her eyebrows and again we laughed. She moved back on to the step as I started the car. 'Drop me a line if you're not too busy,' she called to either one or both of us.

'She means you,' Ed said sulkily as we moved down the drive.

'Or is she just being funny?' I asked him. He didn't answer.

As we went through the cutting into town I said, 'Is Weaver really rich?'

Ed thought about it, then said, 'No.'

'You don't think he is?'

'I know he isn't. His father was. . . . But then again, Weaver's not a poor boy either. What money he's got he lets lie. Slomer, now . . . he's a different case. He makes his money work.' He was pleased to be able to tell me something: to point out the situation.

'So Weaver's – the factory – it's just a name?'

'Weaver's a director, and all that. But he's not in the position his father was. If he had been the place would've dropped in the river long ago.'

He didn't say anything else till I'd stopped the car outside the *Guardian* offices. But he didn't get out: he put his arm round the back of the seat. 'You know, old sport. The way Mrs Weaver was talking to you back there . . . you don't want to let it mislead you. She was just being polite. Not friendly.'

'Oh I know. Treating me as an equal, and that.'

I felt his breath on my cheek. He must have been looking at me intently. 'You don't need me to tell you how things are up at Primstone. Weaver and Slomer split fifty-fifty. Neither of them likes the other. You know what I mean, old sport?'

'No.'

'Well,' he shifted in his seat, 'they notice who's on whose side.'

'You think I ought to float about in the middle?' I said.

'Take it or leave it, sport. But you know as well as I do that Primstone, as far as those two old . . . gents are concerned, is a hobby. And people can get real mean about hobbies. Just suppose Weaver had to withdraw his support from the club. There was a bust-up, say. *You'd* be out in the cold. And so would Wade, just to mention one other. . . . You see what you're doing? Identifying yourself with Weaver. Riley, the secretary, he's with Slomer. You see how these things are fixed?'

'I reckon it's not as crude as that.'

'There's only one player at Primstone who's played consistently in that team. For nearly twelve years as well. That's Frank Miles. And why? Because nobody knows whose side

93

he's on. When all these squabbles blow up on the selection committee each week Frank's is the name nobody argues about. He's neither one side nor the other. He *floats*, boy. And that's the only way with those wolves. It's as crude as that.'

'What makes you think there's going to be a bust-up?'

'Now, now. . . . Don't put words into my mouth. I said *if*. You're a relative newcomer on the scene. I'm just giving you a glimpse of the layout. I've seen a lot of the history of this place. You might think I'm a bit of a tart with all this "old sport – old boy" business. But I'm in the trade, Arthur. I've had to manage with these people, and I've learnt to do it. Don't take me as you might think you see me. If you want to go on having a nice car, lots of friends, and the kind of suit you've got on – well just keep your eyes skinned. And here's a tip for nothing – Weaver's likely to retire soon. He mightn't be around much longer.'

He got out in easy stages and stood on the pavement. 'Course, you don't go talking about this, old sport. I've your word on that.' He ambled up the steps to his office and didn't look back.

*

After that first Sunday drive to Markham Abbey and Howton Hall the feeling between Mrs Hammond and me was more relaxed. While I was getting used to new surroundings and to Weaver's patronage, and while I was still playing football, she never shoved her nose in my affairs as she'd been prone to. I took her and the kids out almost every other Sunday. It became a habit; we visited every historical monument, every hill and lake in the county.

Beginning of the close season I was bored, restless. It'd been one of the reasons I'd accepted to drive Ed up to Weaver's. There was no training, no playing. I even began to take some interest in work, surprising a few people.

But I was really bored. It dried me up. There wasn't a moment when I was relaxed or satisfied. I even thought about killing somebody, holding a bank clerk up, chasing an old tart across the park. I felt like a big lion with a big appetite which had suddenly stopped being fed.

94

It was a cloudy, heavy day, a Saturday afternoon at the beginning of July. I came in the house about three o'clock, already feeling that way and hoping a sleep'd get rid of it. Mrs Hammond was out in the backs hanging some washing. Ian was in an old hen-run on the ashes so he couldn't run away, and Lynda was across the backs with the other kids, whose shouts filled the area. The bed wasn't made. I covered it up, lay down, and tried to sleep.

The next sound I heard was her footsteps in her front bedroom, pacing up and down. She must have been making the bed. I lay still, and watched a couple of flies dancing round the bulb, and a bee droning on the pane outside. The two flies made one shape. I was hoping one minute she'd go down and the next that she'd come in. When her footsteps sounded along the landing I couldn't stop trembling. I looked at my hands in surprise: they were actually shaking. The moment she opened the door I was really fighting. I was two people on the bed.

She gave a cry.

'Oh – I didn't know you were here,' she said. She held her hand to her throat. 'I didn't hear you come in. I've come up to make the bed.'

'I just covered it up. I felt like sleeping,' I said, and rolled off and stood up.

'I'll make it while I'm here. I haven't had a chance so far today. I've had the washing, and Ian kept running off. How long have you been in?'

'An hour or so.'

'It must have been when I was putting the clothes out. I won't be a minute.' She had her back to me as she bent over the bed, tucking in the sheets.

'You're not playing cricket or ought,' she said, stretching right over the bed to push her hand under the far side of the mattress. She seemed too busy to need an answer.

One minute I was calm, the next my neck and ears prickled with heat. I waited until she'd made the bed and was tucking in the sheet, hoping she'd sense the atmosphere and do something to break it. But she carried on with what she was doing, until disbelievingly I had to put my hands

95

out and touch her hips. She relaxed for an instant, then suddenly stiffened. I pulled her back from the bed and folded my hands round the front of her body. I'd never felt such a loose jointed shape before. She jumped about and shouted something particular. I held her tight and didn't make a sound. All the time I reminded myself of the ugliness of her face, of her terror. I was half stunned by her lack of excitement.

Her head twisted every way as she went on yelling something I didn't understand. I seemed to be fighting the bed itself. I couldn't understand why she hadn't expected it, why she didn't give in.

Then suddenly I felt sick, retching, put off by the sight of that shabby underwear. I wanted to get out. I pulled back to free myself, and saw Lynda just inside the door watching us, uncertain whether to laugh or cry.

'Ma . . . am?' the kid gave a long wail. It seemed she was crossing the river again.

'Go away, Lyn!' Mrs Hammond said. 'Go away. Go away!'

The kid stood undecided, but her mother didn't move. She looked carefully at what we were doing, her eyes moving from one end of the bed to the other, as if she looked from one bank to the other. 'Are you fighting, Mam?'

'Go away, Lynda!' her mother shouted. 'Go away, Lyn. We're only having a game.'

She looked doubtful. 'Can't I play, Mam?'

'Go away, Lynda! Go on. . . .'

The girl lurched round and went banging down the stairs.

Mrs Hammond lay with her head turned to the wall. Her body began to mount in a slow fit – of rage and bewilderment. Surprise. 'You're a man!' she screamed. 'You're a bleeding man!' Her fists were knotted and rose on the thin stems of her arms. Her eyes slid about in her head. She smelt of soap powder, steam, and damp cloth. She was singing out loud at the end.

She got off the bed and went straight down. I thought it was to find Lynda. Only I was wrong. As I grabbed my coat and rushed out I saw she'd gone back to the washing. Just

96

as if nothing had happened. She had her peggy stick in the tub, and was beating slowly, almost as if it was empty.

I drove round for an hour, then went to the Mecca as soon as it opened. The place was deserted. I sat at the bar and got out *Tropical Orgy* – a moonlit night on a calm tropical sea, and Capt. Summers had just come on deck after leaving his sample 'fully satisfied and utterly contented' in his cabin down below. A boat came alongside to collect the contraband, and Capt. Summers took out his dark little .38. I found I wasn't blaming myself. I wasn't all that responsible, I told myself. Don't tell me she's *that* innocent. She's been married. I wouldn't have tumbled like that if I hadn't thought. . . . Still, I didn't feel safe till I saw Maurice and the girls come through the door.

'Tarzan's been fighting again,' Judith, the Mayor's blonde secretary, said. 'Won't he fight me?' She pulled my coat back and found my shirt wet and flushed with blood. She grimaced.

'Oh well, you've got to be brave about these things,' she said. I laughed with some sort of relief: I'd been frightened they'd run away at the sight of me.

*

We didn't do it very often. I preferred to go upstairs with her in the middle of the afternoon when it came to me more easily than at any other time of the day. So it was usually a Sunday. We had a routine. She'd go upstairs and get on her grey wool dress, and if I didn't come up in time she'd call or come down and sit quietly by the fire till I stood up. She made sure I went with her. The routine continued in the bedroom, always mine she insisted, as if she'd made up rules at the beginning and keeping them was the most important part. She was always quiet about it. She never spoke. When it was over she'd put on her working clothes again. She suffered it. She thought, I imagine, there was no alternative. She didn't care. It normally happened once a fortnight.

She became cleaner in her habits. The boots disappeared from the hearth.

Pre-season training had been under way a few weeks when

I eventually decided to get in touch with Mrs Weaver. Her suggestion that I might see her again had me thinking a while as to what my advantage might be. I wasn't so sure that she didn't indicate the boundary: Deep water. Keep out.

Then I was suddenly worried that I'd left it too late. Why I should bother at all when I could cruise along without it was beyond me. I'd been asked to pass some charity tickets on to her, and I gave them to Weaver himself to deliver. If *he* forgot, that'd be all right. I'd just drop the affair. The tickets were for a Darby and Joan Whist Drive at the Co-operative Rooms, 7.30–9.30 p.m., and I'd written my name on the back. If anything as vague as this could interest her I felt there might then be something in it for me. Weaver told me she'd be pleased for news of any other charity event I might pass on. 'It's her hobby,' he said, digging me for a laugh which I gave him.

I was surprised when she did turn up at the Co-op Rooms and played her rounds of whist. Admittedly she looked a bit out of place – like a battleship racing yachts. Perhaps a bit foolish. To some extent it was her usual routine, except the drives she attended were vetted by the Inner Circle and took place at the Town Hall. I wasn't sure what I should do. Better to leave it to her, I decided, and went through the drive as though she'd never existed.

At a quarter past nine she caught my eye. She looked impatient, bored, a bit sick with the smell. I went over. 'I thought we might have spoken before now,' she said. 'I'm being collected in fifteen minutes.'

She was angry, realistic.

'I thought you wanted to be formal,' I told her, fitting in.

'Formal, here?' Her voice whined off round a bend. 'Nobody knows us.'

'They know me.'

'Perhaps that's as it should be,' she said, and gave a critical look round the room.

'They're going to die soon. I shouldn't let them see you look like that.' We both seemed surprised at the way we were talking.

She got up and made for the door. I waited some time before following. I'd seldom been so excited. I reached the entrance downstairs in time to see someone opening the door of her Morris Minor. I backed inside and watched them drive away.

A week later, when I'd just got over worrying about it, I got a letter from her amongst my little pile of fan mail at Primstone.

Dear Arthur Machin, I'm sorry if I appeared rude and abrupt the other day, but my nerves were a little stretched by a recent event and I was feeling out of sorts. I hope you will forgive me. Perhaps you could come to tea some day this week? Wednesday might be suitable. As you know, Mr Weaver is away and I should like a little company. Best wishes, Diane W.

On the bottom, as if she wasn't sure how thick I was, she'd added, 'This does not mean bring any of Mr Weaver's rowdy friends who visit him at week-ends!'

It was the only letter from an adult amongst my pile.

I took Wednesday afternoon off work. I wasn't sure that she knew or remembered I worked at Weaver's, but it seemed the best excuse possible to play an afternoon – to see the boss's wife. I went home and changed into my suit.

'Has somebody died?' Mrs Hammond said.

'No. I'm going out. I've got the afternoon off.'

'It must be important – you only wear your suit on Sat'day. Are you going somewhere with Maurice?'

'No. It's all private business.'

'What private business have you got, pray?'

'Private private-business.'

She came to the front door to see me drive off. She'd begun to take some pride in what I did and how I looked.

I spent a couple of hours in the billiard hall, played three games of snooker, then felt it might be around her teatime. I was so nervous I'd to stop the car twice on the way up for a slash. Funnily, the only person in sight when I got there was Johnson. I'd heard some weeks before he'd found a part-time job at Weaver's, probably on the strength of my name.

But I got a shock seeing him there, large as life. He was weeding a flower bed at the side of the drive. I pulled up beside him.

'How are you, Dad?'

He dropped the little shovel he'd got and opened his eyes.

'We're starting on Saturday – a friendly with Leeds. Are you coming?'

'Yes,' he said. He looked at the car, then back at me. 'Mr Weaver's away this week,' he said.

'I know.'

'What've you come up for then?'

'It's the lady I'm seeing.'

'Are you off work?' He looked worried.

'Only for the afternoon . . . I'll see you, Dad.' I ran the car up to the glass porch. He watched me get out. May opened the door when I knocked, and I went in.

'Hello, Arthur. You're a stranger at this time of the day . . . and week. I thought you knew Mr Weaver was away.'

'I came to see Mrs Weaver,' I told her, and like Johnson began to worry. 'Hasn't she told you?'

May shook her head thoughtfully. 'She's said nothing to me. I'll just nip in and see.'

Whereas on Saturday nights I ran through the house like a dog, now I stood frozen in the hall, my feet moulded in the carpet which was taken up at week-ends. I saw it was a mistake coming here. She might have expected me to reply to her note. Perhaps she didn't even expect me to come at all.

'This is a surprise, Mr Machin,' she said coming through the lounge doorway, and I could see by her neckline she was expecting me. 'I'm very sorry, but I must have mislaid your letter . . . or did you phone? It's all very naughty of me. . . .' She looked at me expectantly. May was standing just behind her.

'I mentioned it to Mr Weaver,' I told her heavily. 'He said Wednesday afternoon would be your free day. He must have forgotten to tell you about this charity. . . .'

'Well. At least his information is correct,' she sighed. 'You had better come in the lounge and let me hear all about it.'

This sounded so rough I thought May must be hiding a laugh. She said to Mrs Weaver, 'What shall I do for tea?'

'Tea,' she said. 'You'll stay to tea, Mr Machin? It won't be much for a big man like you, I'm afraid, but May will rustle up something . . . won't you, dear?'

We went into the lounge and she shut the door. There was a green-leaved wallpaper that had me quietly scratching. The french windows were open. I could see Johnson busy with the effect of weeding, and when he occasionally looked up he could see me. It was a bit of consolation. She might have placed him there deliberately.

Mrs Weaver was about twelve years older than Mrs Hammond, and I was the same distance the other, younger, side. The general effect of all these years on Mrs Weaver was to make her a bit fat round the ankles, and to give the overall impression, outside her tight, brown dress, of the very best sort of seal. As she sat down she added to this the idea that she was a good sport. She crossed her legs.

The first thing I could say was, 'The gardener – he's new here.' I meant to sound casual, but she laughed.

'Yes,' she said. 'Do you know him?'

I didn't answer, and she stepped in with, 'Edward Philips – how's he keeping these days? I haven't seen *him* since that Saturday you were up here.'

I was about to say, 'Neither have I,' when I told her, 'He's all right. He's getting his pencil sharpened for the beginning of the season.'

'Oh – the beginning of the season! That's something I'd forgotten about. It makes the summer seem very short when we're talking about football again. Are you glad to be playing again?'

'Yes – I get a bit bored over the close season.'

'A bit bored! But I can't imagine you being bored. Tell me, what do you do when you're bored? Go off drinking?'

'I'm just bored. Do nothing, I reckon.'

'Don't you go out a great deal?'

'I try to. It runs up the petrol with the car though.'

'Oh. . . .' She thought about it and recrossed her legs. 'So you aren't paid over the summer – for football, I mean.'

'No.'

'I suppose that's one of the reasons you'll be glad it's started again.' She smiled to herself, and said, 'What I was really wanting to know is why you came up that Saturday afternoon with Philips.' She was smiling broadly now, and had her fingers stretched over her knee.

'He wanted to use my car,' I said.

'To use your car.' She hadn't expected this. 'Why was that?'

'His car was laid up – he thought it might make a bad impression if he came up on the bus.'

'Oh . . . if that isn't just like him. I might have known. . . So he dragged you all the way up here just because he needed your car. Still, that's not surprising. . . .'

She got up and went to the french window and shut one side, then folded her arms. 'What do you think of our flowers?' she asked.

I thought about whether I should get up, and when she turned her head my way I did, and went to stand beside her. 'They look smart,' I told her.

She had a kind of resigned stance. 'That's Johnson,' she said, as we both watched him look up. I suddenly realized there was no reason why she should know I was pally with him, and I decided it might be better if she didn't know. Johnson saw us watching and started trowelling a bit faster than usual.

'Do you do any gardening yourself?' she asked.

'No.'

She found that funny, and turned to laugh with me. Then she put her hand on my arm. 'Oh, Arthur,' she said lightly, casually, and I heated up.

We'd both got back to our seats and she was saying something about not being much interested in flowers herself, when there was a knock on the door and May wheeled in a tea trolley. 'Thank you, May,' she said.

'I'll be going now, Mrs Weaver, if there's nothing else to do.'

Mrs Weaver looked surprised. 'So soon?' She glanced at a clock shaped like a ship's wheel.

'You said I could go an hour early today, Mrs Weaver.'

We seemed to be back with the bad-memory act again, and both Mrs Weaver and May played their parts seriously, though they must have known it was something of a flop. 'I'll stack the washing up for you to do in the morning,' she finally told May, and saw her to the door.

She fastened it with some care I thought, and came back to pour out the tea. I started to balance things around me, unused to eating so primitively, and I glanced at her to see how I was doing. She was balancing things herself so she hadn't much time to notice, but when she did look up she saw how I was fixed and said, 'You won't be used to eating as delicately as this, I suppose. Do you think we ought to set a table?'

'That's all right,' I told her. 'I'm not so hungry.'

'Not so hungry,' she said. 'I'm not so hungry either but I still eat something.' She shoved a few plates across with lots of mess on and I stuck my fingers in some bits, dragged them together, and pushed them in my mouth.

It suddenly occurred to her, perhaps for the first time, that I was actually a workman, for she suddenly said, 'Did you have to take the afternoon off to come here? . . . I never thought. . . .'

'No, I was taking it off in any case,' I told her. 'I was playing billiards this afternoon.'

'Billiards,' she said, and raised her eyebrows with a slight interest.

'Yes.'

'I suppose with playing professional football it's not so essential to have a full-time job.'

'Not really, no. One or two don't work at all. They just live off their football money.'

'But what do they do over the summer?'

'Oh. . . . They get some sort of job then.'

'Are you like that, Arthur?'

'No, I usually work.'

'And where's that?'

'I've got a lathe.'

'A lathe.'

She ate a few more of the bits of rich stuff that May had dished out and sucked her fingers. 'Which do you prefer – working or playing football for a living?'

'I prefer football.'

'Oh that's good,' she said. 'I mean you have a gift for football. It raises you above the general level, don't you think?'

'Yes, I think so.' She sounded so out of touch with what she was talking about that I felt sick, and hoped she'd drop it. Johnson was looking up the garden towards the french windows. I doubted if he could see me through the glass, for he went on staring thoughtfully a while before he bent down again to his weeds.

The next thing I knew she was sitting beside me and saying, 'Shall I fill your cup?'

I handed it over to her and she dangled the teapot spout over it but nothing happened. 'Can you hold the lid, Arthur?' she said.

She tipped it right up, with my forefinger on the top. 'It's quite empty,' she complained. 'May can't have put much water in, and she's forgotten to bring in the jug.'

'Shall I go and put some on?' I asked her.

She put the teapot down beside the cup. 'No,' she said. 'That is – unless you want some more tea.'

'No, it's all right.'

I slid my hand into my trouser pocket and started to clean my fingers on my handkerchief.

'It's a shame about the water,' she said.

Then we were face to face.

How long we were like this I don't know. I looked in her eyes and saw BED written in each one. She eased her right breast against my arm. I decided I didn't want to do anything about it.

'We're being watched,' I told her.

She stiffened only slightly, but it was a sign of how she felt. 'Who by?' she asked casually.

'Johnson – he's in the garden, weeding . . . and watching.'

'There are other rooms in the house if you don't like being observed by gardeners.'

'Won't it be a little obvious to Johnson?'

She was a bit impatient. 'I shouldn't have thought that worried you. But it is unfortunate we're right in his view. We can move over to my side of the room, Arthur, if you wish.'

She got up, took my hand, and led me to the other sofa, from where I could see the bonnet and front lamps of my car. It didn't seem to occur to her to shut the other french window. She let go of my hand in time for me to stand up and hear Johnson crunch up the gravel drive and see him glance in sideways.

'It's that man again,' I told her.

'I like you,' she said. 'You're like a cat.'

'I'd like a drink. Do you have anything to drink in the house?'

'Always moving. I've never seen anyone so restless.'

'I don't like seeing that Johnson around so much.'

'He should be going in a few minutes. Then you might cool down. It's extraordinary....'

She went to a cupboard at the side of the gramophone and poured out two drinks. She watched me swallow mine, then sipped half of hers. I'd a feeling Johnson was skulking outside the window. It was whisky. 'Do you want to move?' she said.

I didn't seem to get what she meant. She took another sip and put her glass down.

I moved round to the french windows and glanced out as I passed. There was no one in sight. I was half hoping Johnson might have been there, and have solved the problem.

'I don't know whether I should be here,' I said.

'Oh Arthur.... Don't take *that* silly attitude.' Her voice sounded really kind, sympathetic. She might be talking to a kid.

She came up and just stood in front of me, holding her breath, her mouth slightly open. 'You haven't been upset by anything, have you?' she asked.

'No.'

She put her hand near the top of my arm. 'There's no

need to feel so awkward,' she said with the same sympathy.

She could see me shaking slightly, so she came up so close I had to put an arm round her. She slotted her mouth over mine and slipped her tongue inside.

I made a big effort to pull away, and said, 'I don't know why I came.'

'Don't talk,' she insisted, and put pressure on my arm to turn me towards the doorway. Standing in it I expected to see Weaver.

No one there. I found I didn't mind who came in now. 'I think I ought to go,' I told her.

She cooled down and we let go of each other. 'Why? I thought you were behaving so nicely.'

'I don't think it's fair.'

'Oh, Arthur – fair.' She turned sideways to look at me.

The more I moved the cooler I felt. And I started to walk a few steps across, then round, the room.

'You're not feeling . . . you know – out of your depth, or anything like that?' she asked.

'I probably am.' I stared at the bonnet of the car, and felt safe at the sight of it.

Then she suddenly said, 'It's not Mrs Hammond you're thinking about, is it?'

She was waiting for me to look up quickly. She seemed vaguely concerned.

'Mrs Hammond?'

'The woman you live with. . . . You do live with her, don't you?'

'I lodge there.'

'Well, whatever way you want to put it. I'm not trying to frighten you, Arthur. But is it her?'

'No . . . I was thinking about Mr Weaver.'

'Oh – I see.' She wasn't sure whether she should explain why we needn't worry over him. She came up close again indecisively.

'I think I'll go,' I told her.

It was the wrong thing to say. I had the wrong idea about her, about what she wanted, and I could still change my mind, she seemed to say, but be quick about it, my patience has almost run out. I made a move for the french windows. I hadn't been subtle.

She wasn't sure, now, how angry she should be – or how violent. The way she looked at me I could imagine her picking up the half-ton mahogany table and lugging it after me. 'You're going?'

I'd made it more sordid than it ever could have been. I'd been too clumsy. I was turning down a free sample, and she gave all the appropriate grimaces of the disappointed salesman. She didn't see how disappointed I was myself. She just hadn't a notion of how I felt about jeopardizing my chances with Weaver himself. She just looked on me as the mean frog I felt.

'You are going,' she said again.

I tried to start explaining, telling her what I wanted in life, and how I wanted it. 'But how can I?' I asked her. 'I just can't stand that pace of living.'

'You needn't explain, Arthur. If you feel you must go, you go.'

'You see what I mean? Don't you?'

'Either come in or go, Arthur.'

We both thought for a minute I was coming in.

Then I nipped into the drive, scrambled into the car, and shot off down to the white gate. I left a wide skid mark through the carefully raked gravel. I was sweating freely now, trembling, and blinding everything I could think of. Why hadn't I jumped in with her? She'd be the best sample I ever tasted. She *is* something to sample. And I go and turn it down.

Why? That's too easy . . . I ought to see it all as a joke. It's just not an economic proposition. It's so uneconomical that I've to turn down the best thing that ever happened to me. She may have had a hundred other candidates lined up – I didn't care. She'd asked me. A scrubbing nobody. And I'd gone and turned it down. It was so uneconomical that I'd acted like a decent human being. There was only one thing: If *ever* Weaver showed signs of dropping me. . . .

*

The season started with a bang. We didn't know it then but some had been threatened with dismissal unless a big improvement was made in our League position. George Wade and Dai Willaims, the first team trainer, were at us every minute. Pre-season training was hard and continuous, sweating through the late summer evenings, boxing, sprinting, exercises, seven-a-side, touch-and-pass, and we started the first game with Leeds in high spirits. It came at the right moment for me, a big relief from the growing restlessness. My play was all the better for this; it seemed to have matured over the summer. I was surprised when I found all this coincided with a falling off in Weaver's enthusiasm. It was nothing very noticeable, except I was very noticing on things like that: Maurice seemed to share more of his time. It was also at this time I got my first look at Slomer: a boyish crippled figure shrouded in a rug, sitting in the committee box.

One Sunday morning I made the mistake of driving round to my parent's place. My father was in bed – he was working nights on the railway – but the car woke him and he came down in his underpants and stood in front of the fire.

'I hear you're getting a good start to the season,' he said. His eyes were tired, blurred. He wasn't quite awake.

'Why don't you come and watch a match?' I asked him.

'He does,' my mother said. She was baking, kneeling down in front of the coal fire and kneading the dough. Her face and hands were red with the heat and effort, and her round, aproned figure wheezed and panted in the light from the near flames. 'He goes when he's not on days, don't you love?'

'If you'd have let me know,' I told him, 'I could've got you a season ticket for the stand . . . I still can, I think.'

'Oh,' he said quickly, 'I can pay my own way, can't I, Mother?'

'If Arthur can get you a ticket', she told him, 'you might let him. After all . . .' She saw his warning look, a tight, proud face. 'You wouldn't have to stand so much in the rain.'

'I saw your first match, three weeks ago, is it?' he said, drawing his small, stocky figure up, and turning his back to the fire. 'Seemed to me you were the best player on the field.'

'That's what he always says,' my mother said, and leaned back on her heels to look up at us both.

'It's funny you never played before – when you were younger. I don't remember you as a lad being over keen about rugby.'

'You've to be in touch with people, Dad, for one thing.'

'Aye. . . .' He glanced at my mother. 'We've heard plenty on that.' His voice was tired.

'Don't start off on that on Sunday,' she reminded him, and added to me, 'we don't see you often these days, Arthur. Are you kept very busy?'

She got off her knees and lifted the large bowl of dough on to the table. The smell of it leavening filled the room. She dusted the baking-board with flour and pulled the dough out of the earthenware bowl and began to cut it.

'I've been doing a lot of training after work,' I told her.

'There's a man at work', my father said, 'tells me he sees you often at Stokeley dogs.'

'He could do.'

My mother seemed to wait for an explanation, her back to us. Then she picked up a brown baking tin and began to grease its inside with old margarine paper. 'Where's that?' she said eventually, putting each tin on to a black oven plate beside the baking-board.

'Down the valley,' I told her lamely, and my dad and I watched as she picked up the lumps of dough, shaped them between the flushed cups of her hands, and dropped them into the tins.

'It's got one of the worst reputations,' he said. 'I can't imagine any decent person going anywhere near the place. It's not even affiliated. They dope the wretched animals.'

She carried the black oven plate with the four tins of dough to the hearth. She tilted it on the fender so the tops of the loaves were exposed to the flames, and pricked each lump four times with a fork. The prongs sank in and were pulled out without resistance. 'Do they dope them, Arthur?' she said.

'Sometimes.'

'You don't have anything to do with it, do you?'

'No.'

She bent down and pushed hot cinders under the oven with a long polished poker. She rested a couple more lumps of railway coal on the fire.

'That's all right, then,' she said, 'if you don't have anything to do with it.'

'But why do you go there?' my father said. 'You know they dope them.'

'If they do, it doesn't do the dogs any harm – no more than it does me if I lake football without having had a steak for dinner. The only harm it does is to those folk who back doped dogs. Those are the ones it harms.'

'It's not nice to hear you talk like that . . .' my mother began.

'Nobody ever came to any good on a dog track,' my father broke in. 'Nobody. I'm telling you, Arthur.'

'Are you staying to dinner?' my mother asked. 'If you are I'll start on it now. I can get the meat in straight after the bread while the oven's hot.'

'I told Mrs Hammond I'd be back for dinner. She'll have it ready.'

My father sat down near the fire, his short, muscular legs turned towards it. The skin was pale and knotted with veins. 'You ought to get your trousers on, Dad,' she told him, to distract his growing feeling. 'And how is your Mrs Hammond? I was only thinking yesterday, how many years is it since . . . and it's not a nice district or anything.'

She looked how she felt, flushed and hurt. She moved about a lot, as if all her activity could evaporate anything she or my dad might say in anger about Mrs Hammond.

'It's a cheap place,' I told her, 'and it's near work.'

'But now you've got your motor-car, and you're playing football, can't you get some other place, in the fresh air – up at Primstone, or Sandwood maybe?'

'I don't want to use the car for travelling to work. I doubt if I could afford it every day. And in any case, it causes bad feeling with my mates.'

'You could still use the bus – and live somewhere further out.' Screwing up her eyes to the heat she opened the oven door; then she picked up the oven plate and slid it inside. The dough hadn't risen properly. Some water dropped on the bread. It might have been sweat from her face.

'I've got used to living there now,' I told them.

She straightened up and busied herself with the small chrome ventilator on the oven door.

'I don't know what you're coming to, Arthur,' my dad summed it up, staring into the fire and shaking his head slowly, provocatively. 'I *honestly* don't know.'

'But look at the car,' I told him. 'Look at my suit. You don't get things like that working five and a half days a week on a third-rate lathe. . . . And not only that, people know me. *You* must realize that. Machin's a name that means something in town. It's not just one of the hundred thousand others. I bet people at work talk about me to you. Don't you find that pleasing? That everybody knows about your son?'

'You don't know *what* they're talking about, though, Arthur. That man, all he said about you was he saw you every week at Stokeley dogs. *That's* all he told me.'

'You'll find them like that – the people who don't like to see you successful. They want you to be in the same miserable mess as themselves. Now admit it. You must have heard quite a few pleasing things. Hasn't somebody you never even spoke to before come up to you on Monday morning and said, "Your Arthur played a great game on Saturday. . . ." '

'And that Weaver you seem to mix with,' he went on. 'That crowd were never your sort, Arthur. They're not your kind.'

'I wish you'd be fair about it,' I complained. 'Where there's money there's bound to be dirt. It's up to me to step over the puddles. I want to make some money. I *am* making some money. You don't want me to stop doing that, do you? Look what you've always said about money yourself. Everybody needs some to enjoy any happiness at all. You've told me that since I was little. And now that I've gone out and done exactly what you said ... you throw it right back in my face.'

'Ah, but there's money and money, Arthur,' he said, quietened at seeing me angry.

'Money's money to me. Nobody can cut it up into good money and bad money. Nobody. Look at the Catholics, look at Slomer – they're backing and running lotteries all day long. Ideals don't count where money's concerned. It hasn't got any right and wrong. Ideals! Where do ideals get you? Where have *your* ideals got you?'

'Where?' He stared round him as if it was only too obvious where his ideals had got him, where Mrs Shaw's ideals next door had got her, and Mr Chadwick's beyond her had got him. It was only too obvious.

Then, just for a moment, he saw that through my eyes there was nothing there at all. He saw the neighbourhood without its affections and feelings, but just as a field of broken down ambition. He might have wanted to be a footballer in *his* youth. My mother looked at him as if she'd been turned to stone. He just sat there, the little man with no trousers, his head shaking from side to side in bewilderment, his face screwed up with inadequacy and self-reproach, half-blinded with tiredness and with life-fatigue.

5

I CAN see his face, creased in the darkness, racked with a pain that seems to grow steadily. Between us is a wall of pain that grows and thickens until it absorbs us both. It runs across my face in dull spasms. It wakes me.

My tongue is resting on those empty front sockets, and sending sharp flickers up behind my nose. I feel depressed. Then I think I hear some giggling outside the door.

I get off the bed, shove my feet in my shoes, and shuffle over to the door. I pull the bolt back but the door won't budge. It's locked.

I hear the giggle again outside and I bang on the door.

When I stop there isn't a sound from the landing, though the din downstairs has increased. I put my eye to the keyhole. It could be Tommy Clinton in a funny mood. Or Maurice. I go over to the window but there's no drainpipe in sight. I sit down on the bed and light a cig. Somebody is singing carols downstairs.

A van comes up the drive and stops a few minutes while a lot of bottles clink. Drinks are being replenished, and it must still be early. Maybe ten. The party proper will be just about starting. The van drives off. There are two choirs in the drive singing carols.

I think about Mrs Weaver. With nothing else to do I think about Mr Weaver too. One I don't know any more, the other suddenly doesn't like me. Towards the end of November I had the idea he tried to have me dropped. It was the time things were difficult both on and off the field. And now my front teeth are broken. And by Mellor – though he couldn't have known it was going to be my teeth. Maybe I'm blaming Weaver for too much – what with Mellor being one of his quieter pals. At any rate, I think the only reason I wanted to come tonight was a vague notion I ought to settle up with Mrs Weaver. If I'm going to be had at all I might as well be had properly. Though – at the back of my mind is that other reason. Slomer's due tonight.

A car comes up the drive. I press my face to the window, and find there's a light frost on the glass. The car stops at the porch and into the stream of light steps Ed Philips. He's come in a taxi – lashing out. I shout down at him. He glances in at the front door, waves to somebody, pays the driver, and goes inside.

I feel the need to get out of the room. I have another try at the door, squint through the keyhole, bang and shout, then go back to the window. I open it to realize how cold it is outside. A frost sparkles on the sloping lawn. The sky is clear and full of pale moonlight. Twenty feet or more below is Johnson's scruffy rockery.

I switch off the light and ease myself out on to the sill. I cling there a while like a reluctant window-cleaner. Below I can see the glare from the windows, and those garden rocks. I tug hard and the gutter holds.

Using my feet to climb the window, I pull myself up. A pane breaks and falls quietly into the room. I get my elbows into the gutter and tuck my feet in the open top of the window, and worry about whether I should go on. There's ice and water under my arms; the metal creaks and groans under my weight. The roof is too steep to climb on to, a regular pyramid. Right in front of me a chimney streams out smoke against the pale sky.

To the right is the corner of the house. Round it should be the drainpipe I need. I lower myself until I'm again at full stretch, and push off from the sill. I swing along, grabbing at the gutter. Somewhere the other side of the window, behind me, it cracks, breaks, and suddenly drops a foot. I give a shout and rush hand over hand for the corner.

I reach round but can only feel a bracket where the gutter should be. I test it, and it snaps off.

It's just like Weaver to keep his house in such a rotten state of repair. My shoulders are dropping off and I can't move either way. I haul myself up and slot my elbows back in the gutter. Putting my weight over my left side I free my right arm and start tugging at the tiles on the corner. The first is a bit difficult. It cracks off and I fling it down on to the lawn. The next few prise up more easily, and slowly I'm able to take the corner off Weaver's rotten roof.

Two wooden beams show up, and soon the hole is big enough to pull myself into. I slot my feet between the beams, lie back on the tiles, and light a fag.

Individual voices come up clearly. I listen to the things people are saying, and wonder if I sound as bad as that. There's quite a view over the city. The two big mills, Yarrow's and Sudgeon's, are sailing down the valley like big ships, their windows all alight, moving right into the path of those two power station funnels. Lights flash in the low atmosphere, and glow from thousands of Christmas Eves. It's a party night. I feel cold after my sweat, and start clearing a path through the tiles down the side of the roof. I shove my fingers under the edges and pull up. The tiles snap or come off clean, and I fling them down into the shadows below. Eventually I'm within reach of the only drainpipe I've seen that night, and I slide down.

I've no sooner touched the ground and given a big sigh of relief than a voice snarls over my shoulder, '*What* the hell have you been doing, Arthur?'

It's George Wade. He's leaning forward in the darkness to see my face.

'I've been watching you for the past ten minutes,' he tells me. 'It's a good job I recognized you from down here . . . or you might have fallen into the hands of the police.'

He's sniffing around to smell my breath.

'I got fastened in a room . . . locked in by somebody.'

I smell of soot and stagnant water. Though to George this might mean whisky. He's trembling, and tapping the ground with his stick.

'You must have done a fair amount of damage up yonder,' he says, and bends his head back to look at the skyline. 'I hope you make a point of mentioning it to Mr Weaver. It gave me a great shock that first tile. Very nearly caught me on the head. . . . Did you take all his roof off?'

'There's still the chimney, Mr Wade. I shouldn't worry too much. . . . And what about you? What're you doing out here? You look frozen.'

'Oh . . .' he says, and taps his stick again.

'You're not still looking for the dog?'

'I haven't been able to find the animal, Arthur. All this damn time. I've a mind Maurice let it go on purpose. You know what he's like on these occasions. They go to his head. It's quite like him to do it.'

'Well you won't find *him* looking for it. Anyway – the dog might have gone home.'

'But Mr Weaver assured me it couldn't get out of the garden,' he says as if he's gone over this in his mind many times. 'But if you're impatient to go in, Arthur, don't let me keep you out here. After all, I keep the wretched thing. It's all part of the risks of ownership. If you get cold in those teeth you'll know about it.'

'What's the time?'

He brings out his watch. 'Nearly ten past ten,' he says, and turns, as if that's another reminder, towards the bushes. I watch him go unbelievingly. All over a little pooch.

Round the back of the house, near the kitchen door, is parked Slomer's old and famous Rolls – in the tradesman's drive. I go into the kitchen and have a wash in the sink. I find I've lots of little cuts on my hands. I wipe them clean, brush my clothes down, and start looking round for what's on.

The lounge has been cleared of most of its furniture, though it still has the leaved wallpaper, and it's been taken over by a dancing party. Tommy Clinton stares up at me without recognition, blinking, from a cushion. The other rooms are shared out as bars, buffets, and rest places. In the hall a crowd has collected with the Mayor and Labour Aldermen to sing football songs to carol tunes. 'Put it in – put it in. Pull it out.' They move slowly round the tree which has been hauled into the middle of the floor, half its fairy lights broken like bad fruits.

I recognize Maurice's voice coming from the pantry, singing a line or two behind the party in the hall. I bang on the door and shout his name.

'Is that you, Arthur?' he calls. The lock slides back and he looks out through half-closed eyes. 'What is it, cock?' He's stripped to the waist; his skin is still inflamed from the afternoon's game, and some of the cuts have started bleeding again. 'I thought Tommy'd locked you in upstairs.'

'I've just got out.'

He laughs a minute. Judith, the Mayor's secretary, leans over his shoulder and smiles in a teetering stupor. 'Where's your teeth, Tarzan?' she says. 'Aren't you coming in with the gay young things of 1934?'

'What've you got to offer?'

'Oh, boy. I've got lots of things to offer *you*.'

'Nay, bloody steady on,' Maurice says.

'Have you seen Weaver?' I ask him.

'Not for hours, kiddo.' He shakes his head slowly, trying to clear it. 'Why don't you come in here? I'm coming out

116

soon. It's freezing like a prison, and the bitch's like ice, aren't you, love? Perhaps you could thaw her, Art.' He shuts and bolts the door.

A minute later he shouts. 'You still there, Art?'

'Yes.'

'Why don't you flick off then?' They both have a chuckle.

I go up the stairs, past the second of the aspidistras, which holds a brassière and other clothes in its leaves like sensational fruit. The door of the main front bedroom is slightly open. I'm just getting my eye to the crack when it's pulled right open and Weaver looks down at me with a mild look of surprise, a faint smile, and a blinking of his doll blue eyes. He's in evening dress now, and immediately alters his expression to make me feel scruffy, undistinguished, and unwanted.

'I hope I'm not disturbing you, Arthur?' he says.

I say 'No' and shake my head.

'You surely haven't broken off your celebrations just to come here,' he goes on. 'What is it you want?'

Before I can think of anything bright I hear Mrs Weaver's voice beyond the door. 'Is that Arthur Machin, darling? Why don't you ask him to come in?'

'Come in, Arthur,' Weaver says.

I scrape in past him.

There's one thing – it's comfortable on Mrs Weaver's bed. A chandelier sparkles just above my head and throws the light into every corner of the room.

Behind me, stretching the length of the wall, is an elaborate tapestry of a hunting scene: the dogs have just got their teeth into a small, pale animal, and it's already dripping blood.

Slomer smiles at me, and holds up his glass indicating I should drink. 'You drink up, young man,' he says in a thin dried voice, like rustled paper. 'This only happens once a year.' For him, it seems, it does.

It's the same tone as when he said, 'So this is the young man who had his teeth knocked out today,' as I came into the room.

The glass in my hand is empty. I cover it with my fingers and take a deep drink.

No one seems sure what we are celebrating. As a party, this scene in the bedroom is a flop. Weaver sits in an armchair by the door and stares between his knees at the carpet, where a small pool of the drink he's just spilt darkens the fabric. Mrs Weaver, near the window and me, gazes at the same pool in angry restraint. We sit in silence for a long time because this seems the limit of Slomer's recreational ambitions. I think all the time about how I could get shut of Weaver and Slomer and have a few minutes with Mrs Weaver, who is burning me up from three yards away in a tight dress with a silver sheen.

'They're very noisy downstairs,' she says eventually. I wonder if she has the same idea as me.

Weaver nods moodily. 'It's the last time I turn the house over to this sort of thing,' he says.

'Why?' Slomer asks.

His head turns towards the door, where Weaver is sitting, and reveals a small uneven growth of beard, like down, below his mouth. Even then, in this changed position, I can't see exactly where his deformity is.

'Why?' Weaver says, his eyes queerly distorted as he looks at Slomer. 'Why? . . . Because every scruff in town's crept in. I don't like it.'

'Do they always behave like this?' Slomer asks innocently.

Weaver suspects the slightest thing Slomer says or does, and he concentrates hard before saying 'I suppose they do. The M.P.'s down there, and the Mayor. . . . But I don't suppose those two'll offer any better example.'

Slomer gives a little chuckle, which immediately has Weaver moving in his seat as if one of Slomer's thin white fingers is digging him reproachfully in the ribs.

'Do you think I'm wrong in saying that?' Weaver asks.

'Wrong?' Slomer smilingly examines Weaver.

'After all,' Weaver tells him, 'an M.P. isn't necessarily a better man – it's a question of personal opportunity rather than any distinction of insight or ability.'

'I don't know either man,' Slomer says. 'Their position

means nothing to me. I understand that you were once asked to stand . . . I've forgotten for which party.'

He's satisfied at having committed Weaver to an opinion, and Weaver flushes at having exposed himself.

It doesn't seem I have to say anything. Between taking in Mrs Weaver and wondering how much her dress is reinforced, I've been taking in Slomer – like a drink on a hot day. He finds it amusing, as he does everything in the room. He's fairly interested in the tapestry, though he's said nothing about it. Mrs Weaver keeps glancing from it to him and back again, inviting an opinion. He stares at me and the tapestry background as if he finds the juxtaposition ludicrous or even maybe obscene.

I'm disappointed. To start with, Mrs Weaver's a changed woman. I don't think she's looking at me as I feel I'm looking at her. I'm the court jester, big and dumb, a centre of confidential amusement. I blame this on my teeth, on Mellor, but above all on the cripple in front of me, who seems to suggest his deformity is the only proper shape of the body. I see him as a prematurely aged boy crouching in his chair, his old man's eyes peering out in amusement at the sensations his appearance arouses in those who are prepared to tolerate it. His evening suit's been tailored to fit the distortion. Some kind of tailor that.

'Our young man's growing restless,' Slomer says to Weaver. 'I suppose he feels he should be with people his own age downstairs and not with us old tired dogs.'

'Well I'm sure I don't want to detain him from the brighter attractions elsewhere,' Weaver says. 'He needn't stay up here for me. What about you, darling?'

Before she can tell him, Slomer's saying, 'He'll likely do less damage up here, don't you think?'

'I shouldn't think *he*'d be the one to take the house to pieces,' Mrs Weaver says.

'What's that?' I ask her.

'We thought we heard someone taking the tiles off the roof a while back,' she tells me. 'We had to persuade my husband it was the drinks he'd been mixing.'

'You didn't persuade me,' he says. 'I still think someone

or something was up there. I tell you, I saw something distinctly, like a huge sack dangling from the gutter. . . . How anybody could get up there beats me.' He sounds relieved to have something specific to complain about. 'All the drainpipes are broken at the front.'

'You'd be surprised how industrious people can be', Slomer says, 'when they've a drop of alcohol in their veins. I've often wondered why employers like you, Weaver, don't take advantage of the fact. Controlled alcoholism seems indispensable, I would have thought, to a really proficient industrialist.'

I suddenly get the idea that Slomer is out to cause trouble. He's looking at me, and he's looking at Weaver, trying to fire us into some sort of conflict. I hadn't really measured up his look of relief when I first came into the room. He wanted to be amused.

'Why did you come up here, Mr Slomer?' I ask him. 'To get out of the way of the noise?'

'Well. . . . We *are* celebrating the Eve of Christ's Nativity,' he says slowly.

'That's a good description . . .' Weaver begins.

'The debauchery downstairs is just as much part of it as we are. After all, one of us here has licensed it with his accommodation.'

'Now look here,' Weaver protests reasonably, 'I'm not responsible for their behaviour.'

'I don't know who else is,' Slomer says. 'If they weren't here they wouldn't be behaving like this – least, not in their *own* homes.'

'It's their abuse of a good thing. One expects . . .'

'But surely, Weaver, you're not an idealist where human behaviour's concerned? I've always detected if anything a general lack of faith in your personal dealings with people.'

'What do you mean by that?'

Both of the Weavers flush, and for some reason look at me.

'We don't want to go into that on an occasion like this,' he tells them firmly.

'I'd much rather you would, Slomer,' Weaver says. 'It's not a very pleasant thing to have said about you.'

'Well . . . I withdraw it then.'

'You've already said it,' Weaver tells him. 'And in any case, as a matter of interest, I'd like to know very much what you mean.'

His face is tight and red, like a desperately angry woman, and his blue eyes are full of hate.

'You know what I mean,' Slomer suggests, watching Weaver's sudden display of pettishness with a drawn-out look of mischief.

'I haven't the foggiest notion what you mean. . . . You said I had a general lack of faith where other people are concerned. I've always felt it was otherwise. I've never stinted myself.'

'Well . . . take our young man here, for example,' Slomer says, and looks at me calmly. 'Hasn't he been the cause of a certain lack of faith?'

He watches us all with a healthy slyness.

'Who – Machin?'

Weaver stares at me with the residue of his hate-look to see if I know what's meant by this.

'Machin,' Slomer says.

'What are you talking about?' Weaver asks.

'Oh now look, I don't want to get serious, a night like this,' Slomer says.

'If you want an argument, Slomer, why can't you say so?' Weaver complains. 'If you don't, why do you start things like this?'

'I don't mind arguing,' Mrs Weaver says. 'So long as you make it amusing. It's dry enough up here as it is.'

'And there's the lady herself speaking,' Slomer says. 'But even then, I don't want to rake over things I really don't know that much about.'

'What do you mean', Mrs Weaver asks, 'when you say Machin here is the cause of a lack of faith? What are you suggesting *exactly*, Slomer? Do you know something about the man that we don't?'

'Nothing that you don't know,' he says.

He watches me flush under the strain of his little party game.

'My wife knows about it, too, then?' Weaver asks.

'And you know it,' Slomer answers pettishly.

'Christ, man, what are you trying to say?' Weaver says intensely.

'I know what's he's trying to say,' Mrs Weaver says. She looks straight at Slomer as if to say, 'Come on man, be honest. Out with it.'

'What's that?' Weaver says suspiciously, suddenly not wanting to be hurt.

'He's referring to the story you heard, darling ... about an affair someone imagined I was having with Machin.'

Slomer can't quite control his pleasure, so his attempt to look shocked is slightly overdone.

'No. I wasn't referring to anything like that,' he says, appearing to be subdued. 'If there is such a story it's the first I've heard of it.'

Mrs Weaver is a pricked balloon.

I don't look at Weaver. I listen to Slomer's gasps of embarrassment.

'Oh, come now,' Mrs Weaver says, pulling up courage out of a surprisingly calm voice. 'Don't come with that old trick, Slomer. All this theatrical surprise. Really, man, give us a bit of credit for ...'

'I'm sorry. Very sorry,' he says. 'But I assure you I wasn't expecting anything ... I didn't realize ... You'll have to excuse my silly clumsiness.'

'Well ...' Mrs Weaver says. 'You'd have heard about it sooner or later, I imagine.' She tries to patch the hole now all the air has escaped. 'And you'll understand the natural disgust both I and Mr Weaver feel.'

'Naturally. I have the same sentiments exactly,' Slomer says. 'It seems strange how such a story should have arisen.'

'It does,' Mrs Weaver says. 'Though it has a simple enough explanation which we needn't trouble with now.'

She smiles faintly at me. 'I'm sorry, Machin,' she says. 'Sorry you came overwhelmingly into the conversation just now.'

I tell her about it being all right, and put on a worried look over my stunned bewilderment. I still find it best not to look at Weaver. So *he* knows about that Wednesday visit of mine. Did Johnson tell him? May? I feel like a clay target propped up for pot shots.

'What *were* you referring to, then?' Weaver says quietly.

Slomer shakes his head, slowly. 'I was thinking of that time you were suggesting dropping Machin for that other young feller . . . I forget his name. It was around November.'

They're quiet for a few minutes. Then Weaver says, 'I don't see how that reflects my general lack of faith you mentioned, Slomer.'

'Perhaps not,' Slomer says. 'In anti-climax, Weaver, I doubt if anything now would support my previous opinion. I must have had a little too much of this drink of yours – you go seeing corpses hanging off the end of your tiles, and I see the uncompromising detrimental view of human nature. Let's make our excuse a mutual one.' He looks at me in a way that tells me I should be grateful for the way he's managed things. 'All the same, young man, they were all for dropping you, that selection committee of ours, and I had some job to keep you. Mr Weaver will tell you. He knows. But . . . I can't say I've been disappointed.' He doesn't make it clear whether his satisfaction is with me or the evening. He nods his head once or twice, then slips a large watch between the lapels of his jacket. 'And I see by my onion that it's just after half past eleven. Which means . . . that I should be going. I like to break Christmas in at home.'

He slides off the chair and stands, his eyes tense with the effort. Going up to Mrs Weaver like a small boy he holds up his hand. She shakes it doubtfully, and Weaver does the same. 'Happy Christmas,' they all say to each other.

'You needn't come down,' he tells them. 'I can find my own way to the back door. I brought the car up the rear drive to avoid any possible accident. The young man can come down to see I don't get into trouble with any of your revellers.'

I'm in two minds whether to agree. I'm hoping Weaver will insist on seeing Slomer off the premises, and by accident leave me up here with Diane. But he doesn't say a thing.

'Good-bye again,' Slomer says, 'and my best wishes for Christmas and the New Year.'

I follow him out, closing the bedroom door after me. He stops on the landing to say, 'I didn't want to leave you alone in the room with those two hawks, Machin. You can see me safely down these stairs, if you don't mind.'

The stairs are littered with tired couples in the preliminary stages of party fatigue. As we thread our way through I see that Slomer's deformity comes from his right side, where a swelling bulges his coat beneath his arm at the level of his ribs. I don't think anyone recognizes him – no one seems capable of it. The kitchen's full, but we get outside without hindrance.

As Slomer gets into his special driving seat, he says, 'Tell me, have you been indulging in what I call Mrs Weaver's weakness for the social informalities? In other words, is there any truth in the account I've heard?'

'Is that your business?' I say, standing up to the car as if it was him I was threatening.

'I leave that to you to decide, Machin,' he says in such a way that I see he's put me between two stools.

'No . . . I haven't been to bed with her, or anything like that.'

'And that's the truth,' he states. 'I gather you've been having a good season so far.'

'Until today.'

'Ah, yes . . . I see what you mean. But then false teeth can be a sight better looking than the real thing. What do you think my teeth are?'

He spreads his small lips back and shows two tiny rows of white pegs. 'Yes,' I say, uncertain how he wants me to find them. 'They look very neat.'

'Do you think they're false or real?'

'False . . . well they could be real.'

'They're false,' he says, pleased, and speaking with his lips back so I can go on watching them at work. 'You know you're in an awkward position with Weaver?'

'I know he hasn't liked me for the past few weeks.'

'Now you'll know why. . . . You're not the first one to be

crushed between that husband and wife team, you know.
So you needn't be feeling sorry for yourself . . . You're not
a Catholic, are you?'

'No.'

'You've never thought of becoming one?'

'Not yet, no. . . .'

'It's got a lot of advantages for a young man like you. It
has organization for one thing.' He starts backing the car.
'I'll wish you a Happy Christmas,' he says. His head just
shows above the bottom of the windscreen.

'Happy Christmas,' I tell him.

It only needs a bit of snow falling to make it look like
Santa. I hear him reach the lane and the noise of the engine
fades, and I go into the house.

'You don't mean you're Arthur Machin . . . play second
row?'

'Yeh,' I tell her.

She crosses her legs, easing the fringe of her black sheath
skirt over her knees, and sits back on the cushion in the
middle of the settee. Her knee caps glisten. My shoulder just
touches her when I breathe in.

'I wouldn't have guessed,' she says. 'You look different
on the field.'

'What do I look like?'

'Oh. . . .' She thinks carefully. 'Like a bull.'

The minute I sat down beside her I connected her with a
tobacconist's somewhere. Now I come to think of it she does
look like a carefully wrapped cigarette. I remember that
mechanical shaped chest leaning over a counter.

'It's Arthur Machin,' she calls to her friend across the
room who's mauling Maurice.

'Fancy,' her friend says. 'This is Maurice Braithewaite,
Mag.' They both stop to check the size of their catch.

'Is your name Margaret?' I ask her.

'Oh, yes,' she says, as if it's of enormous benefit to her.
We both gaze across at Maurice, still half-naked and ex-
hibiting his bruises. 'You footballers certainly know the
business,' she says, watching how Maurice places his hands.

When I laugh she twists round sharply. 'What're you laughing at?' she says angrily, but suddenly goes on, 'Hell! ... You've no front teeth!'

She looks across quickly to see if her mate has noticed this deficiency.

'I had them taken out tonight,' I say.

'Are you married?' she asks.

She looks disappointed.

'No, I'm saving up.'

'You want to, dear. Without teeth you're not at a big advantage.'

'You think so? I thought girls liked that bit of difference.'

'Difference,' she says. 'They like a bit of difference. But not a gobful.'

'It's only six.'

'It looks like the lot to me, dear. It's the impression, you see, that counts. Waking up to a face like that you'd think you was living with an old man before your time.'

'I'd not thought of marrying you.'

'Thanks for nothing. That's a compliment.'

'It's a big house,' I say.

'Isn't it.'

'Do you come here often?'

'Do you?'

'Fairly.'

'I don't come often then.'

'How d'you get here, then – by bus?'

'No, dear. My boy friend brings me. Didn't you see his car parked outside when you came in?'

'I must have come before you parked. Who's your boy?'

'Lionel Manners. . . .'

She waits for the effect to take.

'Haven't you heard of him?' she says in surprise. 'Wrestles at the Hippo, and round about.'

'Particularly round about, so I'd heard.'

'Narthen! Just be careful. . . .'

'He used to lake Rugby League at one time, didn't he?'

'You bet,' she says as if this was just one of his minor

accomplishments. 'He packed it up though. Not enough lolly in it, he said.'

She hums a tune of self-approval for a minute, then says, 'Have another drink, sonny. The place's bursting with it.'

She opens a bottle of screw-top beer from the crate her end of the settee and pours it expertly into a couple of used glasses.

'D'you wanna drink, Mavis?' she calls to her friend.

'Naw,' her friend says.

'This Weaver jerk, he must be real mean. It's been beer all night for the men, and cider for the ladies.'

'You're drinking beer,' I tell her.

'Aw . . . yes. I see what you mean. D'you wanna dance?' We listen to the music from next door.

'I don't mind.'

Being sober I feel I'd like to get away from Maurice and his lady across the room.

We push into the room next door and begin a slow, angular move down it as the music changes. We pass one or two items of furniture I'm familiar with. Somebody's pushing a big leggy tart along on the tea tray Mrs Weaver used that Wednesday.

'You're quite a good dancer,' she says.

'You're making the best of a bad job?'

'No, I mean it, sonny. You're a good dancer. You've got style. Most of the other pigs just want to hold you.'

We travel in silence while her mind ticks another revolution. I think about what it must be like to hold a rich sample like Mrs Weaver – the nice smells, the soft mattress, smooth sheets; the understanding it's only a temporary arrangement. No clinging; the knowing of what it is: just a sample, a nice statement between willing people; no slush feelings; decent underwear. I keep my eyes skinned in case she comes down.

'You know what, my friends will be dead jealous when I tell them I've been with you.'

'I'm quite a boy then.'

'What makes you think that?'

'Why will they be jealous?'

'Oh – I get what you mean. . . . Now then, don't get swelled-headed just because I've taken a liking to you. No teeth an' all. They think the City boys are gold, that's all it is. It's funny that, because football's not half as spectacular as wrestling. He's pretty good is Lionel.'

We dance on, and I say, 'Frank Miles, captain of the City, he used to do some wrestling when he was younger.'

'Him! You can't tell me nothing about that big goof. Lionel murdered him. . . . Twice.'

'He had his back broken every other week,' I say.

She thinks about it, leans over a bit to see how her back feels, and says, 'Go on, how could he?'

'The weeks in between he used to win.'

Her laugh comes a couple of steps later.

'How could he mend so quick?' she says.

'He never broke it. I used to wait at the back door of the Hippo in my car, and after they'd carried him out on the stretcher Frank'd grab his clothes and leg it for the car before the crowd got round to see him carried out. They had a man called Johnson who used to ring an ambulance bell they'd rigged up in the changing room.'

'Here,' she tells me, lifting her skirt up high, 'pull my other one, it's got bells on too.' I make to put my hand down. 'No, not here. You're too bloody quick.' She pulls away from me. 'Don't slaver over me, kid.'

When she's quietened down she says, 'Did you say you had a car?'

'A Jaguar.'

'It must be old.'

'Two years.'

'What d'you do when you're not kidding?'

'Talk to you.'

'Where you got it? Outside?'

'No. It's at home.'

'That lets you out pretty square.'

'Ask the man right behind you.'

She turns and sees the M.P. He looks back at her, distantly.

'What, him? I can't ask him. I don't even know him anyway.'

'He won't mind that. You ask him. It's people like you he relies on.'

'All right, all right! Don't preach, sonny. Hey!' she calls to the M.P. 'Hey sonnyjim! What kinda car has Arthur Machin got?'

He peers at her again, over Judith's shoulder. 'It's a Jaguar if I remember properly.'

'How old is it?'

He asks Judith, then says, 'It's almost new, I think.'

We dance in silence again. A faint smell of scented sweat comes from her, and a faint smell of stagnant water from me.

'Where do you work?' she says.

'Weaver's.'

'That's handy. Do all his workers have free run of the house?'

'It depends which worker you are. Where do you work?'

'Does it matter?'

'No – I thought I'd seen you in a shop somewhere, selling fags.'

'I said: does it matter?'

The music stops and starts as somebody lurches against the cabinet. The party's thinning out. The evening people are beginning to leave, and the all-nighters settling in. The Mayor's dancing with Judith now. His railway signalman's eyes twinkle blearily over her back.

'Shall we go next door?' Mag says. 'That Mayor depresses me. He looks so righteous.'

Tommy Clinton's in the hall, swaying under the Christmas tree; a shower of pines covers him. His girl pulls him upright. He sees Mag and says, 'I bet you thought it was a bit of all right. . . . Fastened up yonder all this time with old Arthur. It's just like home from home is that room, I always say. It was me. . . .' he says, digging himself with his finger and swallowing his wind. 'It was me who locked you in. . . . And it was me who just let you out. Just now. . . . Say, say, Arthur! I recognize this floozie. She's the bag old Manners carries around with him.' He puts his hand on her shoulder. 'Did you know it was me that just let you out, Lionel Manners' bag?'

'You mean somebody's just let you out, you crazy sod,' she tells him. 'And it's time they locked you up again.'

Clinton's watering eyes narrow and he laughs.

'Well knock me down. Did you hear that?' he tells his girl. 'She can talk! I wish old Manners was here. He told me if there was one thing his bitch never did it was talk.'

He staggers to the front porch and falls against the side. Broken glass drops into the drive.

'I hope you don't mind me locking you up, Art, old lad. . . . Just a bit of fun you know. Christmas and all that . . . I got blind drunk and forgot, otherwise I'd have let you out sooner. Honest, that's the truth. . . .' He vanishes with a fall of twigs into the drive. His girl goes after him.

'Is he from the City?' Mag says.

'That's Tommy Clinton.'

'Clinton. I'll remember that name. I'll tell Lionel about the way he spoke to me – and we'll see what happens to Mr Clinton. Just you mark my words.'

'He's a friend of your Lionel's.'

'Not much longer he won't be, after I've said my piece.'

She leads the way into the first room but all the seats and most of the floor are taken. Maurice has gone.

'Where's that room he was talking about?' she says moodily. 'Will anybody be there?'

'I should think so. And I haven't got the key either.'

'Is it far to your place?'

'The other side of town. But we couldn't go there.'

A fresh burst of carols comes from upstairs. In the lounge I can hear the M.P. yodelling. He's recently had a holiday in Switzerland. We drift back into the hall. I take a bottle of ale with me and knock it off as we stand there. Then I go back and get another and knock that off too.

Judith suddenly comes out of the lounge. She comes up to me and kisses me hard on the lips. It lasts a few minutes. I open one eye to look at Mag. She's found something interesting the other way. The Mayor's watching, straining himself to look pleased. When Judith lets go she says to Mag,

'Don't fret, darling. He's standing under the mistletoe. Why don't you have a go yourself? Have you seen Maurice, Tarzan?'

'He's on tour.'

'That's a mess. We're going now. The Mayor's decided the party's fallen through, so we're going to his Parlour.'

'What you going to do there you can't get depressed about here?'

'Ring the bells, Tarzan. It's Christmas morning.' She runs off upstairs.

'You can tell what kind she is,' Mag says. She comes up close as if by accident, and spears me with her left breast. 'I'm surprised men fall for it.'

'I'm surprised too.'

'You look pale,' she says suddenly. 'Don't you feel good?'

'No.'

'I feel rather chuffed myself.'

'You go upstairs,' I tell her. 'Find us an empty room, and come and let me know. I'm going to have a sit a while here.'

'Aren't you going to give me some courage to rush up all those stairs on my own?' she says. I bend down and play on her lips. She feels under my shirt and encircles me.

I sit under the Christmas tree till she's out of sight on the landing, then wonder if I ought to go and make a last search for Mrs Weaver. I think about it for a couple of minutes and decide it's all over, particularly at this hour of the morning, so I go and collect an armful of beer from the first room and go outside. I can't get used to the idea she's something I might have had. Even Slomer hadn't put it past me; so people must think I'm up to scratch. Mrs Weaver. My mouth waters.

The Bentley is locked. I try all the doors before I notice the sun-roof is still open. I climb inside and grope around for my overcoat and the carrier with the kids' toys. I sit down while I stuff the beer in the carrier and pull on my coat. Then I get the idea it wouldn't be so bad if I drove the car home. I could tell Mrs Hammond I'd bought it her for Christmas. I feel around the dashboard, but Weaver has collected his keys.

I climb out again on to the drive and knock the top off one of the bottles against the front mudguard. I make for the short cut down the lane to the gate, swallowing the beer as I walk. At the end of the lane I pass Tommy Clinton in a phone booth with his girl. I can't make out whether they're phoning for a taxi or just resting upright for a change.

I'm tired, worried about my teeth, and pouring the ale down my throat as fast as I can. It gives a quiet sort of energy to my brain. I think about Mrs Weaver's legs, and the thick ankles.

Before the road slits into the side of the valley to run into town I can see as far down as Stokeley: the colliery's marked by the crimson and orange glow of its coke ovens, each separate and distinct, and by its lurid flushing of the sky. I imagine Frank lying asleep in his father-of-the-household bed. For a while Stokeley's the only sign of life, then I'm plunged into the blackness of the cutting itself, with the grid cables singing and sighing over my head, and the clopping of my own footsteps. A light flashes through the trees, and straight below me is the orange, stifling glow of the gas lamps at the brick-works.

The lights of the town slowly come into view. Down the valley the panting of a goods engine breaks up the silence. And I break open another bottle.

I drop the carrier as I climb over the wall of the goods yard and smash one of the two last bottles. Both the damn dolls stink of beer. I wipe them down on my handkerchief. Ian's train rattles all right in its cardboard box. I pick up the carrier and scramble down to the short cut across the yard.

The lines cross and curve in every direction. From down the track comes the slow heaving pant of the goods hauling up the valley. The noise echoes, and sounds closer, in the ground mist seeping from the valley bottoms. It's some place I've never been in before. My foot touches a rail and immediately I'm aware of a slow vibration. I have to stop. The sleepers stretch both ways.

I hear a slight whispering behind me, and turning round see this big yellow watery eye. 'What the hell're you doing? I ask it. It hisses, then suddenly jars and spurts towards me

For a second the thing shoots away, grumbling and straining, then it quivers, and comes back to its previous course. The line trembles and quakes. It shudders. Below the watery eye come two bursts of steam. I stumble around in the clinkers between the sleepers.

The eye swings away. I feel a fine spray of water as it spits at me, the heat of its huge black body; for a second I'm lit up by a yellow-red glare, then I'm cool again, and in darkness. The red eye this time disappears into the mist.

I stumble over a lot of rails somebody's just put down. There's the noise of cattle somewhere the other side of the yard. I hear voices and see lamps swinging. Ahead, brakes jar on a wagon, then stutter as a line of low black shapes slide past, rocking and clinking like complaining pigs in procession. I smell for a second the wet coal, the animal grease. I stop to have a last swig from the bottle. A man walks past, swinging a lamp and not seeing me. But he stops when he hears me make a clumsy dash over the last lines and scramble down through the ashes, over the wall, and into the street. Now that I look back I can see the red, orange, and green lights of the signals and the low glow from the shunters' brazier. I haven't met my dad.

There's still a taxi on the all-night rank, and around half-past three I'm in Fairfax Street, which is like a tomb. Mrs Hammond let me have the front door key since I said I'd be in late. Before I go in I unlock the car and take her present out of the back seat. It's heavy. I wrap the paper round it carefully, then slam the car door. But no lights come on. The car is the only thing standing in that long brick alley.

On the table in the kitchen are three cups and saucers, and on the plates the crumbs from the Christmas cake – to show me accidentally she's had visitors. In the fireplace is a saucer of milk and another plate with the Christmas cake almost intact.

She must have been waiting for me – probably she left her bedroom door ajar so's not to miss me coming in. I hear her coming downstairs and I shove the parcel behind the settee. I take the toys out of the carrier as she comes in.

'It's late,' she whispers. 'Have you only just got back?'

She's come down in her bare feet, a coat over her dressing-gown. 'Are you all right?'

'I've had a bloody awful night, if that's what you mean. . . I see you've had a visitor.'

'Two,' she says, pleased. 'Nobody you know.'

'Who's that?'

'Don't get so hoity. Just because you don't know everybody in my life.' She's like a girl. Her eyes sparkle with ready excitement and her secret. 'It was Eric's sister and her husband.'

'I never knew he had one.'

'There! I knew you'd be like this about it. Well, he has. Emma . . . Compton. They'd heard about you.' She rubs her hands together as though they've given her a big thrill by coming. 'Playing football and that. They wanted to know what you were like. Her husband goes to watch you play. And here. . . .' She giggles and picks up a card lying on the mantelpiece. 'Here – just look at this and tell me what you think.'

It's a photograph, already a bit yellow, of three girls, arms round each other, laughing as if the camera's the biggest joke they've ever seen. They're in overalls – wartime overalls – and their hair is covered up by scarves.

'Is that *you*!' I can't stop my surprise. *She*'s there, the middle of the three, leaning back slightly, the sun on her face and mouth, her feelings unlocked and running free. A girl's face, unmarked and spontaneous.

'That's Emma on the right – it was before I met Eric. She introduced us.'

'What were you doing? Where's this. . . .'

'During the war. We worked at the ordnance place at Moyston. Making bombs. You should have seen us!' Her face is still lit up like a kid's. 'We used to have to get up at six, and get on a special train in town. It went all over the place picking people up before it got to Moyston. All women! We had some times! You can just see some of the buildings at the back there – camouflaged. We were even bombed once, during the day. With Emma coming it brought it all back. . . .'

'You weren't married then.'

'No.' Her look slows and darkens. 'I had some chaps. . . . We had some good fun together.'

'When were you married?'

She hasn't been looking at me. She's been flashing her bright look around the room, shyly, remembering. But now she's dampened and she turns back to me.

'After the war.'

'You were a bit late, weren't you?'

'I had my dad to look after. That kept me at home a lot. I suppose that's one of the reasons I enjoyed going to work at Moyston so much.'

'You married, then, when your dad died?'

She shakes her head, and looks doubtful. 'No, I left him. I couldn't stand it . . . I was getting on. He seemed to think I should stay there for . . . well, I don't know how long. So we had a bust-up, and I left him to marry Eric. I've never seen him since – and I don't suppose I ever shall. The last time I heard he'd been moved to some almshouses or something . . . God!' Her girl's face vanishes and she stares at me in horrified amazement. 'You've no front teeth!'

'It's not that bad,' I tell her. I put the photo down and go to the sink and look in the mirror. 'I haven't dared look till now . . . I don't look too good, do I? I've grown ten years. What d'you reckon?'

'I wondered why you spoke funny – with that sort of lisp. I thought you'd been drinking.' She shivers with cold and begins to be worried.

'What's the saucer of milk and the cake in the hearth for?'

'Santa Claus. The milk's for his reindeer. And don't laugh. Because Lynda says he's always glad to have it on a cold night and he'll leave extra presents for the kind thought.'

'Well, I haven't brought the deer tonight, but I appreciate the thought.' I drink some of the milk. It tastes putrid after beer, burning cold. The mice've been at the cake. She watches me put it down and says, 'Have you been fighting?'

'No. I got them broken, and the dentist pulled the bits out. Six bits. Five guineas. I've picked the wrong bloody job.'

She examines my face seriously a minute. 'It spoils your looks.'

'I've been told.'

'By a girl?'

'What other kind worries over me?'

She's quiet as she tries to reconstruct my evening.

'You went to Weaver's after all then?'

'Yes.'

'You look ill. You shouldn't have been out tonight. It said on the wireless after the news that you went off the field but came on again after a few minutes. I didn't think it was serious. . . . If you catch cold in your gums you'll know about it.'

'I've been told that an' all.'

'By another girl? . . . It doesn't seem to put them off very much.'

'I'm not complaining. . . . What shall I do with these toys?'

'I'll take them with me, and put them in the stockings.'

'I've got your present here as well. Do you want it now?'

She glances quickly round the room. 'Where is it? . . . No, don't spoil it now.'

I put the light out and we go upstairs. 'Christ, I'd ne'er have guessed you'd made bombs.' She laughs, and when we reach the landing I ask her, 'Why don't you come to bed with me? It'll be cold, and I need looking after. Tha knows mother alus goes to bed with Santa.'

She holds the door handle of her room, then rubs the paint.

'All right,' she says. 'But just for Christmas, mind.'

Part Two

I

I TOOK my lunch into the stockyard overlooking the river, and sat on the concrete embankment. A barge shuffled low through the dark brown water, throwing up a foam like dead beer. Its wash roared on the pebbles below. The bargee fastened the long handle of the rudder to a loop of rope, and slung a bucket into the wake. He let it drag in the current, then hauled it up, and tipped it along the narrow walk by the hold. He went back to the rudder and tensed it as the barge began to swing.

It was a habit I'd picked up with the New Year, having my dinner in the stockyard. Usually a few others from the shops and the labs came out and sat amongst the steel and pig iron, or played soccer in a space cleared near the yard office. Those of the older ones who hadn't been with the firm long ate their snap and just watched the brown glide of the river sewer as if it was the only familiar thing in sight. But today it was cold and blustery, the spume was being blown into the air off the top of the sluice opposite, and the smell of the works hung low. As far as I could see I was the only one out.

I was surprised to see Weaver threading his way through the rows of metal joists. He was on top of me before he'd time to recognize me.

'Hello . . . Arthur!' he said, automatically.

It was the first time I'd seen him since Christmas Eve. I was relieved to hear him still call me Arthur.

'Do you come out here often to eat?' he said, surprised into conversation.

'Only recently. When it's fine.'

'The works' canteen not good enough for you?' His blue eyes glinted as he dared himself to smile.

'I'm economizing,' I told him pointedly. 'You never know what's around the corner.'

His smile, only half there, vanished. He dusted the concrete decisively with a cupped hand, eased his trousers at the knee, and motioned me to sit down with him. It was something like his old concern.

'I'd been meaning to have a chat with you, Arthur,' he said, and looked down to see if his suit touched my overalls. 'After that rather terrible display . . . by Slomer. At Christmas. I suppose we've all felt a little estranged. He's not really a person to entertain socially. But putting that aside – I'm willing to forget the wretched business, if that's any consolation to you.'

'I'd be glad to forget it.'

He smiled again, seriously. 'I'll take it then we've patched up any ill feeling there was between us?'

He waited steadily for me to confirm it, then brought his hand round the front of his suit. We shook as vigorously as we could sitting down.

'How're your teeth?' he asked. 'Riley showed me the bill we had for them. Quite expensive. I hope they fit all right.'

I smiled for him, and he examined them critically.

'They certainly look all right.'

'People say I look younger,' I told him.

'Do they, Arthur?'

'What do you think?'

'Well . . . I've never thought you looked really old. So any rejuvenating effect is perhaps beyond me. I will say they're not recognizable – as false, I mean.'

He made a circle in the metal dust with his toe cap. Then pulled a line right through it. 'There was another thing.' he said. 'Going back to that not very happy occasion. Perhaps you didn't hear, but the police are trying to find who it was lifted some jewellery from my wife's bedroom that night. Nearly four hundred pounds' worth.'

'I hadn't heard.'

'I mentioned it in case they ask you – purely as routine –

so you won't feel annoyed. You've heard nothing about it?'

'Not a thing. . . . What part of the night was it taken?'

'I'm not sure – we didn't actually discover anything missing until the following morning, Christmas morning, when Mrs Weaver was about to go to church.'

'I'm sorry about it,' I told him unconvincingly.

I realized my attitude to Weaver was rapidly becoming like the way I now thought of Johnson: a withered limb of my ambition. I began to despise Weaver for being so simple, for having his money, his jewellery, his house used by other people. His enemies, in his eyes, were just those people who wouldn't let him be kind to them. 'I want to help everybody' was his motto. It immediately made everybody suspicious: he seemed too good to be true.

'What annoys me most', he was saying, 'isn't the stuff itself going, but the fact that somebody who came to the party must have taken it. You remember what Slomer said about my lack of faith and all that – just how much faith are you supposed to have? They can't be content with taking half the slates off your roof, and breaking things up generally, but they take property away as well. I ask you, Arthur, how are you supposed to treat these people? If you treat them like dogs, the way they treat you, someone of the calibre of Slomer complains you're not human, and if you treat them like people they run all over you.'

'It was me who took your slates off,' I said. 'I'd be glad to pay for the damage. I reckon I ought to have told you earlier.'

'I'm glad you've *told* me, Arthur, because I knew about that myself. The police had the idea the thief forced entry that way, though why they should think anyone needed to force entry that night, God knows. It was old George who explained what had happened – you got fastened in the room, he said.'

I listened carefully while he explained how he was going to overlook the damn fool thing, and how we ought to forget the entire business from beginning to end. He didn't sound well. When I insisted on paying for the tiles he didn't argue.

He mentioned the fact that George Wade came back at two in the morning to look for his dog.

'And did he find it?' I asked him.

'No. Johnson discovered it the next morning when he came to clear up the garden . . . it was like a battlefield. If that dog had died it'd have been the last straw for me. As it was the thing was on its last legs when Johnson found it. You know how attached it is to old George. Still . . . it did *look* funny when Maurice let it go like that. Trust Maurice. He's all action. That boy has never had a thought in his head.'

Another coal barge passed us low in the water, on its way to the power station. The chug of its engine was now the only sound on the river. It pushed the water aside as if it was only a rubber sheet, rippling in thick heavy folds, then collapsing. There were two white gulls swaying over the brown foam.

'You hadn't met Slomer before?' he said casually, suggestive.

'No.'

'He seemed – you know. . . .' He fingered his chin, much like a masculine woman might. 'Very familiar with you, in the way he spoke. I wondered if you hadn't met him some other time.'

He was looking across the river at the different coloured wool bales, yellow, red, blue, stacked and overflowing from their big wooden trolleys. 'What do you think of Slomer, Arthur?' He smiled, but his serious expression didn't change.

'He sounded pretty clever . . . I wasn't sure.'

'You don't like him?'

'I don't suppose he wants you to like him. Maybe he's been hurt into being like that.'

'If he has, then he certainly tries to entertain himself with it.' He rubbed his upper lip with that well-kept forefinger of his. 'I found it odd', he said, 'the way he took to you.'

'I thought he was taking it out of me. I felt like some big rubber dummy stuck up there for him to poke.'

'Did you, Arthur,' he said, relieved, almost smiling.

'But you don't believe that,' I said.

'Let me put it this way, Arthur. There've been times when, I'll admit, I've tried to put a spoke in your wheel – often for your own good, as I saw it, like last November. You might think I had a personal grudge for doing that . . . well, it's very possible something of that sort swayed my judgement. But each time I suggested putting McEwan in your place I was voted down. I was, if you like, persuaded to change my attitude. And you were having a bad patch then. More often than not that persuasion came from Slomer. Not from him personally, you'll understand. But all the same *from* him, from people we all know represent his views on the committee. Now, in my position, what would you be tempted to think?'

'I see what you mean,' I said, and watched the slight shaking of his hands. 'But I still think I've played myself into the team all along.'

'Ah, I'm not saying you haven't.' He held his right hand up, his fingers splayed out like cards. 'Not saying you haven't, at all. I'm not blaming you, Arthur. Don't get me wrong. I was merely pointing out to you the writing on the wall.'

I immediately thought of Ed Philips, and the writing on *his* wall. I couldn't remember exactly what it was.

'What you mean', I said, 'is that you thought you had some ownership over me, as far as that committee was concerned, and you don't like it being taken away.'

He didn't answer. He hadn't perhaps expected it as plain as this, and it pushed him back on his heels.

'Are you trying to tell me you've carried me or something?'

'You *know* you've been carried,' he said bitterly. 'I liked you, Arthur, once. It was my back and nobody else's. Right from the beginning.'

'And you think I'm taking myself away.' I was angry with him, angry that he should allow me to talk to him like this, that he should take all this trouble to expose himself, offer to make up as friends, and, now that he thought Slomer was taking me over, remind me of how much I owed him, and how keen he'd been to give it. Like all effeminate men, he over-emphasized everything. Both Weaver and Slomer seemed worn-out schemes to me: Weaver, maybe through his good nature, was being taken over by other people; Slomer was struggling to keep his religion, his organization, intact. They both seemed due to fall off the branch, and the committee would then take over.

'I don't think you appreciate how much help you've been given, Arthur,' he said. 'I think that's the crux of the matter.'

'I felt I deserved it, and you don't think I do. I reckon that's the crux of the matter if anything is. Am I a good footballer or not?'

'I'm not saying any more,' he told me like a big girl. 'Just don't try to push yourself too far – that's all I've got to say.'

He went away before I could think of anything else. He'd got a short mincing stride. A small backside.

I stayed and talked to the stockyard clerk about his pigeons until the buzzer went.

*

The change wasn't only in Weaver. Mrs Hammond suddenly heeled over. We were out driving one Sunday afternoon when suddenly she came out with, 'Had you thought of buying a TV?'

When I looked surprised she said, 'You've nothing against them, have you?'

'I was shaken at you asking,' I told her.

'I thought you'd say that.' She smiled to herself. 'But if we can afford it, why shouldn't we?'

'You seem to forget – you're sitting in ten TV sets and dressed in another two.'

'You're getting rough. I suppose you mean the car and my fur coat. But I didn't want it to sound I was greedy or something.'

The fur coat I'd bought her at Christmas, cost price from a dealer who was a fan of mine, though he wasn't that close. It'd taken me some time and effort to convince him that knowing me was more important than his profit from one coat. Mrs Hammond's reaction to it on Christmas morning was first surprise and natural greed, then a strict, martyred refusal, and a final reluctant acceptance. There was no doubt she was proud of it, and treated it like a living thing.

Now she suddenly said, 'I'm a kept woman, Arthur. You can't expect me to act otherwise.'

'Oh Christ,' I told her. 'But I know what you mean.'

'Well, then, you shouldn't be surprised at me being straight about it.'

'I reckon not. . . . But I can't see how it helps.'

'You mean how it can help you. What *you* don't see is that if you deal with dirt you mu'n expect to look dirty. People have got eyes, you know.'

I couldn't think why she should say all this, and the shortest way of stopping it I found was to hit her. I cracked her hard across the face, and I wanted to apologize when I saw the mark.

We drove along in the kind of silence that comes after an event like that. The kids were stiff, erect, then Ian began to cry, then Lynda.

'Do you feel like dirt?' I asked.

'What do you think?'

We reached the summit of a hill and coasted down through a leafless wood. I noticed how there'd been a light fall of snow during the night, and how the frost had kept it in place till now. A faint sun was breaking it up into patches: the brown earth and dark grass showed through.

'I don't feel dirty,' I told her. 'I wonder what the difference is.'

'The difference is,' she said after a while, 'I'm still used to being honest. It's one thing somehow I haven't been able to throw off.'

'I said I didn't *feel* dirty. You're talking about seeing – about what other people think from what they see.'

'I'd like to feel clean, that's all,' she said, and added with a queer reluctance, 'I don't want to get at you, Arthur. You've got your own feelings. But I'd just like to be decent.'

'You think I should feel like you? Is that what you mean?'

'You don't need me to tell you how it looks. A car . . . me in a fur coat. Living in the same house as you. You see what I mean now? It's only natural I should feel about it like this.'

'I don't bother about what people feel,' I told her. 'You don't have to take any notice at all, so why bother?'

'You don't mean that. You bother about what your fans feel, about what people tell you, when they tell you how good you are. Look what you're like when you've had a bad match. You break things. You tear about the house like a madman. And just because you dropped a ball or something at the wrong moment. You're always looking at your body in the mirror. Look how you shadow-box in front of that mirror – watching yourself. Don't tell me . . .' She was breathless, hurt; the red mark on her temple and cheek had flushed a deeper, vicious colour that made her face look pale. 'You're not fair to me, Arthur. You just say whatever comes into your head – to make me feel I should be grateful. . . .' Tears hung in her eyes, but she held them back. Her eyes glistened.

'These people who watch – I don't care about them. I don't, honestly. So you're wrong. They're pigs and I don't reckon with them at all. They can go stuff themselves. . . .'

'That's you all over. You just bluster about. Anybody who gets in your way – you just knock them down. Anybody who's stopped being useful – you just throw over on one side. You just *use* people. You use me. You don't treat me like . . . I should be. You don't know what you're like with people. Look how you treat that Johnson now. At one time you couldn't leave him alone.'

'That's good of you to say that. It was you who spoilt anything Johnson and me had between us.'

'Spoilt it! I didn't spoil it. You can't put the blame of things like that on to me. I'd nothing to do with it. I only said I didn't like you bringing him home. I didn't like the man. It was nothing to do with me how you and him found each other.'

'Well, whatever you say now, you set him against me.'

'I didn't do anything,' she said quietly, letting the water at last run from her eyes. She pulled Ian over on to her knee. 'You'll be blaming me next because you're not playing football well.'

We ran out of the wood and accelerated alongside a reservoir. The water had a thin coating of ice, and on a hill the other side a swarm of kids were trying to sledge in the melting snow.

'Why do you carry on like this?' I asked her. 'I've tried to treat you all along as if I cared. You don't seem to appreciate a bloody thing of what I've done.'

'I don't have to tell you why. I'm a mother.'

'If you're going to think this way how can you expect Lyn and Ian to think any different when they're older? Don't you mind what they think about us?'

'Of course I mind,' she said tonelessly. 'But I reckon you'll leave me soon.'

I felt that, in spite of herself, she was always trying to hurt me. Her face seemed to tell me she didn't want to do it, but something prompted her inside, and out these jibes came, almost every day, almost every time we spoke to each other. And here was I, showing all the time how I was growing to rely on her, and she went on doing it. It was as if one side of her wanted me to rely on her, and the other was terrified of the responsibility. She was frightened of committing herself, and so she just went on pushing me off, hurting herself as much as me, and building up a fire and pain between us that neither of us knew how to handle.

The car shook, and something rattled and dropped off as we shot over a hump-backed bridge at the head of the reservoir. The car went on running so I didn't stop. We slowed down to cruise through the village. As we rose up the opposite flank of the valley the kids came into sight again with their sledges. Lynda and Ian stopped crying to watch them. We skirted the foot of their hill. It was an old slag heap; behind it stood the crumbled structure of a disused colliery.

'It's the first I've heard of it,' I said. 'Me leaving.'

'There's always a first time.'

I remember what Weaver had said the night he drove me home after signing on. 'It's amazing how these dead people keep popping up.' Eric, whoever he was, whoever he had been, stood not between us, but behind *her*. 'Don't you see what you're saying?' I asked her. 'Don't you see what you're

145

doing? You're making everything between us cheap – no value. When it could be just the opposite if you'd only let it.'

'I'm not saying it hasn't a value,' she said, thinking clumsily, with difficulty. 'Everything's got a value. But you can always tell a cheap thing. You can always tell when a thing's got cheap value.'

'I never thought any of it was like that.'

We didn't say anything for a while.

Then I told her, 'You sound as if you want to shove me on to some other woman.'

She laughed. 'I don't have to do that, do I? From what I hear you're never short of girls – you and your Maurice.'

'You think I go bedding other women?'

'Think. I don't think. . . . You don't believe I'm that simple?'

'If you think you know that why do you stick with me still?'

'You've never heard me complain.'

'You don't mind me knocking off other women?'

'I might mind.' Her eyes had dried. The mark of my hand still flushed her cheek, and had been joined by two dribbles from her eyes. 'I'm not one to complain.'

'Because you've got nothing to complain about. I've kept clean of other women.'

She gave her funny sort of laugh. Short, and breathless.

'Your Maurice: he wouldn't have the same view, I bet.'

'"Your Maurice" – why is it always "your Maurice", "your Johnson", with you? My mother's the same: "your Mrs Hammond. . . ."'

'I can just hear her saying that. I can just imagine it. I bet your mother was like me when she was younger.'

'I'm not arguing over that. You're so blind wrong about everything that there's not much point me saying anything.'

'Well don't – I don't want to argue about it. Don't say anything else.'

I lowered the window and let cold air stream into the car.

'If I stopped the car,' I asked her, 'you took your fur coat off, and we all got out and walked back, would you feel any cleaner?'

'No. I'd only feel stupid. How could that alter anything? It's just like you: big, swash actions. I've told you, Arthur. In spite of what you say, it's impressions that count more with you than anything else. Make a big impression, and you think everybody will swallow it.'

'But you don't like the idea. You don't like the idea of walking back all those miles.'

''Course I don't. The kids'd freeze to death, even if we didn't.'

'I could wrap them in a blanket. It's getting warmer.'

'And carry them? Being a martyr doesn't alter anything. I've told you. That's what I mean when I say you'll go soon and leave me. You'll find it's the only way you can feel clean.'

'I don't feel dirty!'

'You're all right for another week, then. I don't want to argue about it. The time'll come soon enough for me.'

She calmed down a bit because she started pointing out things we passed to the kids, and we didn't talk till we came over the ridge at Caulsby Castle and in sight of town.

'You don't seem to understand the reason I've done all these things for you,' I told her, and suddenly felt like Weaver making a big-girl complaint.

''Course I do. You do it because it makes you feel good, it makes you feel big – you know how you like to feel big.'

'And that's the reason?'

'I don't know. . . . But you must think: look at me, keeping a widow and two brats thrown in. Aren't I a hero? I must be good if I do that. They depend on me. And I don't *have* to do it.'

'That's how I feel about you?'

'I know how you feel. I've lived with a man before.'

'You'll be glad then when I buy you a TV.'

'I won't grumble. People expect us to live big.' She saw my look and said, 'I've got past being very glad about anything – and more than that – I'm past pitying myself because of it. But I will say this – you've helped me. You've probably helped me as much as the kids. If you hadn't come

147

along I reckon I'd have gone around in a shroud for more than a long time.'

'I thought you were beginning to feel happy.'

'Happy! I could say something there, but I won't.'

'Go ahead. I don't mind. I'd like to hear all of it.'

'You'll hear it soon enough. It's like a disease you can't do anything about. As it is, this's brought it all closer.'

'I'll get the TV then. . . . You'll be able to sell it when I go.'

'Yes,' she said, seriously, as if there was a lot I didn't know, and even more she couldn't tell me.

*

Around March all this coincided with a slight change in her habits. She let herself go a bit. I came home one night from work and found her sitting at the tea table smoking. She laughed at my surprise, and held the cig out for me to have a drag. 'That's one thing I don't like,' I said, 'women smoking.'

'What's the matter with women smoking?' she said, puffing inexpertly and laughing as the smoke drained from her mouth.

'It looks obscene.'

'Oh, obscene. I see. We're getting very classy . . . and you're a right one to talk about that.'

'Maybe I am.'

'Anyway, big boy, I'm only smoking in private. I need the relaxation.'

A week later she was in the backs smoking, and I could see one or two people had noticed. The next day, a Saturday morning, I met her up town when I was with Maurice. She was pulling Lynda and Ian along, and was laden down with a basket and a canvas bag, a cigarette cocked in the corner of her mouth. 'You look bloody awful,' I told her. 'If you feel a slut you shouldn't show it.'

She stared a minute, and didn't look at Maurice. Her look, deep under her eyebrows, seemed to say I'd betrayed her. She bent down and collected the brats, and shuffled off down the street.

'So that's your Mrs Hammond,' Maurice said.

'Is it the first time you've seen her?'

'Yes,' he said, nearly sighing, and nodding his head at me. 'What d'you say that to her for, Art?'

'I don't like seeing her smoke.'

'What's the matter with you, kid? You've never been like that before. I can't think of a bag you know who doesn't.'

'That's what I mean. She's the only one who doesn't. I want her to keep that way.'

'She's not a dog you've trained or bought,' he said. 'You shouldn't say things like that to her. You talk as if you owned the woman.'

'For the moment I do. And she doesn't like it.'

His small, cheeky teeth came out in a smile. He thought I was being funny. We went into the Booth.

Beyond the confectionery counters the British Legion doorman saw us coming and got ready to hold open the smoke-room door. 'Mr Middleton said he wanted to see you, Mr Braithewaite, Mr Machin,' he said.

'What's up?' Maurice said. 'Does he want a new car?'

The doorman half smiled, and looked at me apologetically over Maurice's head.

There were the usual celebrities inside – the Area Manager and the Area Accountant of the Coal Board, the pre- and post-war Conservative nominated candidates, the woodwork master from the grammar school, the Town Clerk. Each had his bunch of confederates and informers. Down the far end of the room were a few old forgotten football heroes, big and fat, a suspect amateur boxer, a selective bunch of fans, all would-be advisers. And the Mayor: Ralph Middleton.

Weaver's group had taken over the tables near the huge coal fire, and he beckoned to Maurice as soon as we came in. Maurice went over; then I saw the Mayor moving to the only empty table and waving me to join him. He must have reserved it. 'Did the doorman tell you?' he said.

'About you wanting to see Maurice and me?'

'I see he did.'

A waiter came up and Middleton ordered a coffee. 'Is he going to be long?' he asked me.

'I couldn't say. He knows you want to see him.'

'Well, I hope he weren't keep us waiting. What I've got to say is of some importance. Even to somebody as important as Maurice Braithewaite.' He was cold and angry, and he kept his eyes on me as if either he didn't want to look across at Maurice or I had something that belonged to him.

I looked round at the oak-panelled walls and timbered ceiling and tried to avoid Middleton's peculiar expression. The fire glowed, through the smoke-stained air, on the coats-of-arms and the pieces of armour decorating the room. The low tone of the conversation, the selectiveness of the people allowed in, the absence of women, made this my favourite meeting place of the week. Only this week it'd been spoilt by Mrs Hammond and now by Middleton, who suddenly changed his look to show he thought I was responsible for Maurice not coming.

'Go an' tell him I want him, Machin,' he said eventually. 'Tell him it's now, not tomorrer.'

I went across and said, 'Excuse me, Mr Weaver, but Middleton's bursting his britches over Maurice not being there to talk to him. He wants us for something important. Right now, he says.'

'Oh?' Weaver looked round the room, ducking and bobbing his head, till he saw the Mayor, who at that moment was signing for his coffee on expenses. 'What's the trouble, Morry?'

'I don't know,' Maurice said, and I immediately knew he did. 'How long do you think I ought to keep him waiting?'

Before Weaver could tell him anything, I said, 'It's up to you, Maurice. I'm going to sit with him. I can't get a seat anywhere else,' and I went back.

'Is he coming?' Middleton said over the steam from his coffee.

'He'll be over in a minute. What's it you want to see us about?'

'You'll know soon enough,' he said, and his cup rattled in the saucer as he lifted it up.

Maurice came across like an innocent breeze, and brought his own coffee. He stirred it while Middleton examined our two faces side by side.

'We've been told we'd make a good picture together,' Maurice told him. He seemed offended by something. I was sure he knew what Middleton wanted.

Middleton answered with a resigned gesture, and said, 'A'm not finding this funny, Braithewaite. Do you mind turning off your schoolboy antics while you're with me.'

'What is it you want?' Maurice said. 'Not to throw this afternoon's game for a fiver?'

'I want to know', he said, looking quickly at us both, 'which of you it is who's responsible for Judith, my secretary, being pregnant.'

'Christ,' Maurice said, stopping a laugh, 'is that all? I thought at first you'd won the pools.'

'It's not news to you,' he said.

'No – I should think everybody in the room knows. . . . As a matter of fact Weaver was just mentioning the secret when I came across.'

'I didn't know about it,' I said, and tried to think of when I'd last seen Judith and what she'd looked like.

'There's innocence for you.' Maurice shovelled his hand at me. 'That lets us two kippers out.'

'I don't see how it does,' Middleton said quietly. 'From all her many friends I still think you two know who I want.'

'Why don't you ask her?' Maurice said. 'I reckon she's likely to know best. Mother always knows, you know.'

'At the moment I find that something I don't want to do. I'd much prefer it if you told me.'

'I don't know her as well as you're trying to make out,' I told him. 'And if it is true, I don't think she'd want you to interfere.'

Middleton looked pained, and he flushed. 'You mayn't understand this, Machin. But the fact is I have a responsibility to that girl. I'm responsible in one way or another for a lot of the people she meets, a lot of the places she goes to. And if that word responsibility means nowt to you, then I'm sorry. I came here this morning with the intention of finding out. And you two are the most likely people.'

'Oh, I understand your position,' Maurice said. 'I mean I can see you thinking people might say it's you.'

Middleton didn't answer for a moment. Then he said, 'It does you no good, that sort of talk. You might think I'm a bit of an ass talking like this, and asking you questions. But Judith's a good girl. I don't want to stick a knife into her – or into the man responsible. I only want to see the situation handled properly from the beginning. Do you see my meaning?' He looked at us both intently.

'I've known Judith since she was a baby,' he went on. 'I've known her parents for as long as I care to remember. They're all people I respect. I think I'm in something of a position to help them now. . . . It's not for nothing I've come to you two first. You both are, to put it simply, number one suspects. I don't go around with my eyes shut, you know. A've seen,' he added confidentially, 'and A've asked.' He propped his forefinger against the side of his nose.

I waited for Maurice to say something, perhaps a vague inquiry about what Middleton intended to do. But he only went on looking at the Mayor with a vacant, ready-smile of a stare.

'How deep are you in this, Middleton?' I said, weakly, wondering if Maurice didn't mind who took the blame. 'Is it a piece of Council politics, or what?'

'If you're reckoning I want to hush it up, then the answer's "yes". I don't want these Primstone–Mecca Saturday maniacs going tearing round with it like a piece of dirt. But if you think I want to use it as a piece of scandal myself, directed against those football 'eroes who strut about town as if they owned it, then you're wrong. It's for everybody and everything concerned that I want to see it taken care of properly, and quietly. Does that show you where I stand, Machin?'

'Yes. . . . All you need now is the bloke.'

'Aye. That's all I need.' He looked at both of us.

Maurice opened his mouth to say something, then closed

it. Then he said, 'Honestly, Middleton, I don't know where you get all this load from.'

Middleton stood up and fingered his Homburg. 'There doesn't seem much need for me to go on asking,' he said. He was still flushed, his eyes anxious and strained. 'I'll say good morning. And good luck for this afternoon.'

He walked out slowly, tipping his hat unconsciously to the uniformed doorman.

Weaver, who'd been watching what was going on over his neighbour's shoulder, got up and came across with all the reluctance and impatience that was supposed to characterize our present relationship.

'What is it, Morry?' he said. 'You don't want to get yourself worked up – or Arthur – before a match. You should leave these arguments for Saturday night, or Sunday.'

He knew what Middleton had been about, and must have thought he'd only to talk a lot to rid us all of worry. 'Why,' he said, 'you don't want to take that man so seriously. He can talk the hind leg off a donkey. If every signalman on the railways is like Middleton it's no bloody wonder the trains are always late. . . .'

'He seems to think', I said, 'that either Maurice or me is a daddy.'

He stared at me sullenly, his blue eyes narrowed. 'This Judith story that's going about? . . . But I don't think that's so serious – for Middleton to cause a commotion about.' He put his arm round Maurice's shoulder, but Maurice, looking both dejected and angry, shook it off. 'Temper, temper,' Weaver said, hurt by this bit of public defiance. He glanced round to see how many were noticing the episode. 'There's no need to act like this, Morry. Christ's sake, pull yourself together.'

'It's that frog Middleton,' Maurice said. 'Shoving his bloody big nose in. I ought to have flattened him.'

Weaver glanced at me to pull Maurice out of his petty mood.

'You want to be careful how you treat Middleton,' he advised him. 'You know what happened to him three years ago?'

'What's that?' Maurice said, looking up and hoping for something particularly damning.

'He separated from his wife. A couple of months later she died.'

Maurice waited, then said, 'What's that got to do with me?'

'Well, you can imagine what people said. No doubt he's been on the lookout ever since for some opportunity to exonerate himself – to show he's not as cold a man as he's made out. I must say I was surprised the way he behaved at my party.'

'Aye, and that's what he may'n be surprised at too,' Maurice said. 'It wasn't only that M.P. that was round her that night. There was him himself.'

'Aw now, Maurice . . .' Weaver began in a whisper, because Maurice's voice was beginning to carry. 'Now look . . .' But when he saw Maurice's face, its tight and bitter look, he stopped. For a moment he looked at me helplessly, then a sudden light came into his eyes. He said, 'The only thing to do, Maurice, is for me to see Middleton. And Judith herself.'

He might even have been jealous of Middleton organizing a crusade, but now that he saw the chance of getting one of his own together all his loose feelings left him. He even looked at me as though a hard word had never crossed between us. It was a wide open opportunity for him to be kind, to be generous, and he put his arm round Maurice's shoulder more firmly this time. 'You just leave this to me, Morry,' he said. 'I'll take care of it. He seemed to be in no doubt that Maurice was responsible.

I fixed up with a dealer in the Booth for the TV to be delivered Monday at cost price. I paid him ten per cent deposit. He seemed glad to do me the service. I signed his kiddy's autograph book. Then we went to the Northern Hotel Grill for a steak lunch.

Maurice had a good game that afternoon. One of his best. I had one worse than bad, and I was met in the changing room by a smiling Weaver. He stood in the clouds of steam, between two piles of mud and jerseys, and said, 'I don't know what *you*'ve got to be worried about, Arthur.' He'd gone back to the easy attitude of our first meeting. He was all smiles. 'Stop worrying. You played terribly today. Thank goodness I for one know the reason why.' He gave me a confidential wink and went over to talk to Maurice.

Judith was at the Mecca that night. She looked a bit strained under the eyes, but she was putting on a show, and no one would have noticed if they hadn't all known she was pregnant. A particular eye was kept on those who danced with her – always a bit apart so's not to touch bellies – and the barman was even careful not to chat too long. She was towing quite a bomb around with her. It took me an hour to get her alone. We shuffled in a tight circle in the middle of the floor. I found myself careful not to press too close.

'You look worried tonight, Tarzan,' she said, perhaps hoping I'd softened. 'I hear you didn't have a good game this afternoon.'

'No.'

'Maurice played well.'

'It's more difficult for him not to. But I'm not worried over that.'

'What is it, Tarzan? Still looking for your ideal lady?'

I thought she nearly said landlady. I told her, 'I saw Weaver up at the ground after the match. I've never seen him looking so happy.'

'What of it?'

'When I see him happy these days it makes me feel uneasy. . . . I wondered what he'd been saying to you this afternoon.'

'Who?' She was astonished. We stopped dancing. 'I haven't seen him since Christmas. You know, the party, Tarzan. You and Mag.'

'Do you often tell lies, Judith?'

'Now what?' She tried to look impatient, and we started moving round the floor once more.

'Everybody here knows you're pregnant by Maurice.

155

What're you trying to act about? Tell me. What did Weaver say this afternoon?'

She slipped from my loose hold, made for the door, and disappeared into the powder-room. Quite a few people stopped to watch her go, then looked back at me. I followed her slowly and waited outside the men's cloakroom, opposite the exit.

Maurice slipped through the crowd on the floor. His bright pink, half-loaded face was angry. 'What've you started?' he said. 'What's the matter with you? Weaver said it was all settled. Now leave her alone.'

'I want to know how it's settled. Don't you?'

'No. If he's arranged things to lie, then let them lie. He knows how to handle these people. You're stupid, Art. You might unfasten all he's done. Christ, you don't want to lake about with her when she's in that condition.'

'I don't like things going on behind my back. You've less to lose than me. I don't want any labels on me, joke or no joke. If Mrs Hammond heard . . .'

He waited for me to go on with this domestic incident. He watched me in bleary half-astonishment.

'If you'd only pull Judith out with you,' I told him. 'And stop all this talking. You've made a mistake . . . why can't you come out with it? You stink, Maurice.'

He waited again, to see if there was any more. Then he said, 'I'd kill you for that, Art, if I hadn't reckoned on you as my mate!' His face was shining and bloated with alcoholic rage. He caught hold of the lapels of my jacket in his hard little fists and tried to pull me towards him.

I gripped his wrists. 'And I'd have done the same for you, Maurice,' I told him. He listened intently as I said it, as if he heard a lot of other voices at the same time. Judith came out of the powder-room with a friend.

We both watched her pass. I thought for a moment Maurice was going after her. He swayed on his toes. Then he rocked back on his heels and flung his fists down from my coat. I lurched back against the wall. 'I'm going to talk to her,' I said. 'Are you coming?'

He stepped aside to see if I would. He didn't follow me.

When I got outside I looked back. He'd disappeared from the entrance.

I caught Judith in Market Street, off City Centre. It was raining hard. 'I'll take you home in the car,' I told her. 'I've got it parked at the Mecca.'

'She doesn't want to talk to you,' said her friend, a clerk from the Education Offices.

'Shove off,' I told her. 'This's private.'

'No. She's staying,' Judith said.

'I said go away, little girl. If you want to see what happens go and stand at the corner.'

'She's staying, Tarzan. I don't want to talk to you.'

'If I can't talk to you,' I told her, 'I might as well go up to your house.'

Her friend brightened up with privileged interest. The bus came and Judith hadn't moved.

'Are we getting on, Judy?' her friend said, rain streaming down her face.

'You're a cad, saying that,' Judith told me.

'Are you coming back to the Mecca, then we can get in the car and talk.'

'No. I'm not going anywhere with you.'

'We can't argue in the street. I'm getting wet. Make your mind up quick. It's either you or your mother.'

I started back across the Bull Ring. After a few minutes I heard her running after me. She'd left her friend at the bus stop. 'Tarzan! Don't run off like that. . . .'

I stepped into a shop doorway and she came in with me. 'I wanted to know what Weaver said to you,' I said.

'Why should it concern you? It doesn't, you know.' Her face was hard, unlike her, and flecked with rain. She was panting after her little run.

'Middleton doesn't seem to think so. He came to see me as well as Maurice today. You know he's having a quiet crusade about it?'

'Yes. I know. But I can't see him getting anywhere.

'What did Weaver say?'

She rubbed her finger against the steamed-up window of the shop; I could just see the vague pyramid outline of piled up tins and packets. 'He said he'd talk to Maurice.' A filter of mist came out with her words. 'He said he'd talk to Maurice for me. Are you satisfied, nosey?'

'And is that all he said?'

'What concern is it of yours, Tarzan? I don't see how anybody should want to drag you in.' She looked back at the empty street, glistening with rain, and her friend waiting at the corner.

'I just don't want people to think it might have been me. At the moment, what with Maurice not coming clean, and all this stupid talking and running about, anything might happen. I don't find this a joke like most people, you know.'

'You're exaggerating,' she said, surprised at my concern and moodiness.

'Well, did Weaver make any arrangement with you . . . or anything like that?'

'You seem to have a grudge against Weaver, as though he's doing something subversive, behind your back all the time. I honestly don't think you're as important as that, Arthur. And Weaver isn't like that. He couldn't be malicious if he tried. . . . And if you must know *everything* he said, then, he offered me money if he couldn't talk Maurice round. That's all he's doing. And he's not buying me off, if that's what you're thinking. You know Maurice on his own'll let things drag. He won't bother to work out what's best for himself, or anybody else. He wants a good time. . . . If we have to get married then I'd rather he did it off his own bat, not because he was dragged into it or because he just dropped into it. Weaver can help him there. If he fails to impress Maurice then he said the baby would never be a financial burden to me – or anybody. God above, I can't think of a finer thing a man could do. . . . And look how you're behaving!'

'You've got your things you're frightened of losing, Judith. And I've got mine.'

'You've no need to be bothered, Tarzan. I can tell you that. So let's all stop this chasing about.'

'And so you said you'd keep quiet about everything till Weaver's had a chance to talk to Maurice?'

She nodded. We both watched a lighted bus fill the street, leaving two furrows on the wet tarmac. Someone walked past the shop doorway. Judith's friend came and stood in a doorway opposite, and peered across at us.

'Let's hope he gets round to it quick,' I said, and stepped out into the rain.

'Knowing Maurice, Tarzan, what exactly would you do in my place?'

There was real appeal in her voice. She pushed past me and ran across the road. She was crying. The two girls met, said a few words, and Judith set off by herself to the Bull Ring. Her friend stepped under a dark shop canopy and watched her go. I pulled up my jacket collar and walked back to the car.

*

I got home from work on Monday to find the TV already in place. The three of them were watching a children's programme in the front room.

'You were quick in getting it,' Mrs Hammond said, standing up smartly. 'I didn't know you'd even ordered one.'

'I said I'd get you one.'

'You're a man of your word,' she said deliberately. '. . . I thought we'd have it in the front room. If it was in the kitchen I'd never stop looking at it. Thank you very much, Arthur.' She kissed me lightly on the cheek and called to the kids, 'Say thank you to Arthur for it.'

'Thank you, Arthur,' Lynda said with a small questioning look at her mother, and turned back to the set.

'Tank Artar,' Ian said. He was beginning to get bored already and rolled about on the floor.

'That's my bloody hero.' I picked him up, and for the first time forgot he was Eric's son. I rubbed my nose on his and he laughed. When I put him down he fell on his head, rolled over, and burbled.

'Be careful with him,' Mrs Hammond said.

'He's all right. We want him to grow into a good forward, don't we?'

She gazed at me critically. Then she nodded and said, 'Yes, if you like.'

I went into the kitchen, she came after me and made my tea.

'We're doing quite well,' I said. 'You'll be able to open a shop when I go.'

'If you've only bought it to boast about you might as well take it back.' She was smiling, and in a good mood.

'I've a good mind to take you upstairs afore I go training,' I said.

'Oh have you. . . . And what makes you so sure I might go?' She laid some plates down and began to margarine the bread.

'I was thinking of the way you kissed me.'

'It shows it can mean something, then. I was trying to show you I was grateful.'

'And can you show me again?'

She put down the knife and smiled cheekily. 'I don't know whether it's worth *two* of what I gave you.'

'But I say it is. And I should know. I bought it.'

I got up and went round the table. She waited for me coming, her head bowed, her eyes on the plate with the knife. I bent down and put my arms round her, my hands over her small breasts. 'Oh, now Arthur,' she whispered.

'Can't I kiss you just once?'

I put my cheek alongside hers, and felt her jaw move as she spoke. 'I don't suppose I could stop you if you tried hard.'

'But won't you give me one without fighting?'

'I don't think I should . . . what if Lynda came in?'

'I bet she'd think I was making up to you.'

I stroked her breast through her dress. She took my hand away and turned her head, her mouth open to say something. I pressed my lips against her mouth, and caught it open, and smoothed my tongue inside. I wanted to tell her how I felt. I ran my hands round her belly and waist and back. Then held her head, like a ball, pressed to mine.

'Aren't you going to say it?' I said, when I pulled back.

She looked weakened and lost, like a kid. 'Say what?' She only whispered when she tried to speak.

'Say you've got some feeling for me . . . that you can feel something.'

'Arthur . . . I can't. Not yet.' She was hot and miserable. She pulled back, and turned to the table again. 'I can't let myself go like that. I'm not sure of you.'

'But you know me.' I tried to touch her, but she stiffened, and my hands fell off her. 'You know how I've been to you.'

'I can't let my feelings go. Not again. Not to have them cut off like Eric . . . and everything gone, in one person, and dead. I want to be sure. You've to give me some time.'

'But we've had all this time. Surely . . .'

'I don't know you mightn't rush away – I don't know what I feel.'

'But Christ, be reasonable. I'd have gone now if I was going to. All that encouragement you've given me.'

'I don't know. You might just want to hear me say it – and see me feel something. Then you might feel that's all you wanted, and go away. How do I know?'

She looked pale and worn. Her good mood had gone quickly, like all her moods, and she was unsure again. Just when for once I'd got close to her, almost too close for her to let go. She picked up the knife, and that hardness came into her face. She'd almost given in, and she regretted it.

'You're always fighting against me,' I said. 'And you know I can't be that bad. When're you going to give us a bit of peace?'

She didn't answer. She went on stroking the fat on to the bread: the grease and the crumbly dough were dirt.

'There mightn't be any of us left by the time you've made up your mind,' I said.

'Don't I go upstairs with you?'

'But that's not the same. I don't feel you mean it. You make me feel I'm buying it off you. I'm just buying. And I'm not.'

'Well, that's me. That's how I am. There's nothing else left for me to do.' She was the angry little woman again. She banged the knife handle on the table. 'I wish you wouldn't work me up like this. I've nothing to give you, Arthur.'

'You don't mean that.'

She stood up and rearranged the table absent-mindedly. 'There you start again,' she said. 'Telling me how I should feel. What I should be like. If you'd only let me alone a bit. But you won't. You're so big. You're so stupid. Arthur. You don't give me a chance.'

I sat with them a while and watched the set. When I went out early to training I already felt it had been the last chance, and I'd never see her happy. I couldn't understand what she wanted from me. She'd never been so close before to saying what she felt, and I thought it was only too plain how I felt, how I wanted to help her out. What else did she want? It'd been her last chance. And it'd been mine. I felt like a big ape given something precious to hold, but only squashing it in my big, clumsy, useless hands. I couldn't even apologize.

I dropped off the bus, and decided I wouldn't go to training. I got off half-way up the hill to Primstone, just when the lights were pricking the valley, making it bleed with its slow night glow. Quite a few people recognized me. They nudged and pointed. They were always doing that. I didn't like Middleton talking about footballers strutting about town as if they owned it. It was the way they were treated that made them like that. The way people looked at me, spoke to me, handled my affairs generally whenever I wanted to buy a suit, a stick of chewing-gum, a gallon of petrol. They *made* me feel I owned the place. Course I strutted about. They expected it. I couldn't help it. I walked in front of these people now, and I felt a hero. They wanted me to be a hero – and I wanted to be a hero. Why didn't *she* see that? It wasn't *me* who was always telling her how she should be, how I wanted her to look, it was *she* who was always on at me. Not so much by words. But in her real woman's way. Keeping her feelings in. Keeping her stinking feelings back so that I felt it was me who was to blame and nobody else. I was always reproaching myself for her, always feeling in the wrong. Never her. She was the bloody martyr with two kids, let loose in the world with nobody to protect them.

So I come along. And she starts to play me about. Was that how it'd been? All along I'd thought of myself as the gallant frog, going out Saturday afternoons to be knocked about, thumped, cut, and treated generally like a piece of mobile refuse, just so I could have that extra load of cash, and help her out. I even used to think of her when I was playing, as if I was playing for her, as if it was all worth it if only to make her happy – with a car, a fur coat, and now a TV.

But I was wrong. She wasn't like that. I knew she wasn't like that because I knew that wasn't the reason I played football, that wasn't the reason I fought for ninety minutes every Saturday as if the world was coming to an end. I knew it wasn't that – because even as I'd been thinking I'd gone on walking up the hill towards the stadium turrets, taking notice of how people noticed me, hooted car horns, and said, 'Good night, Art', even when I'd never seen them before. I was a hero. And I was crazy because she seemed the only person in the world who wouldn't admit it.

She knew that. She really did know that. Perhaps she even thought it was the one thing that held me to her. Because, whatever she said, she needed me. She couldn't manage without me. And she wouldn't admit it. She had her pride. Greater perhaps, because of Eric, than anybody else's pride. She wasn't going to show her need. She had the one hold over me because she knew ; needed *her* to make me feel whole and wanted. I could see her fear now. If she gave me her love, just for a minute, an hour, I might never look at her again.

I couldn't make her feel that wasn't true. I was the big ape again, known and feared for its strength, frightened of showing a bit of soft feeling in case it might be weakness. I might like all these nods and waves and nervous twitches that my passage along the road created, but they were always some distance away. People wouldn't act like that if they were close. I wanted a bit more than a wave. I wanted to have something there for good: I wasn't going to be a footballer for ever. But I was an ape. Big, awe-inspiring, something interesting to see perform. No feelings. It'd always helped to have no feelings. So I had no feelings. I was paid not to have feelings. It paid me to have none. People looked at me as if I was an ape. Walking up the road like this they looked at me exactly as they'd look at an ape walking about without a cage. They liked to see me walking about like this, as if the fact I tried to act and behave like them added just the right touch the next time they saw me perform. 'I saw Arthur Machin last week,' they'd say, 'walking along West Street.' It was just what they needed when they next saw me run on to the field, just the thing to make them stare in awe, and wonder if after all I might be like them. I might be human.

I felt I'd done a night's training already by the time I reached Primstone. The floodlights had been turned on and the stadium bowl was filled with a blue-green glare. A few players ran round the perimeter of the pitch, talking and laughing in the night, filling the empty stands and terraces with their single voices. The people who'd come to watch training were gathered round the tunnel so they could see their particular favourites run out, and maybe catch a word or two of what they were saying, and get a nod or wave in answer to their shouts.

It was cold. I put two jerseys under my track suit and did a couple of laps before Dai came out and started us on exercises in the middle of the pitch. The place was big and bare. We looked like midgets. We bent and strained, twisted and rolled, shadow-boxed in two rows, sprinted up and down the pitch again and again, slowing and spurting according to Dai's whistle. We practised the set moves three times each, then played the 'A' team at touch-and-pass. All this time Maurice hadn't spoken to me. And nobody had mentioned Judith.

In fact nobody would have mentioned any of it hadn't Mellor, when we were all stuffed together in the bath, started off a joke about a pregnant woman. We sat leg to leg, pressed up tight to each other, fighting for a bit of space to

164

duck a head and rinse some hair. The water was its usual grey, with bits of grass floating on the top, but the froth of rinsed soap was slowly hiding the colour underneath. It was the usual smell of body and carbolic, dampened down with steam, broken up by joking bodies. 'Lady,' Mellor finished, 'if I'd known you were in that condition I wouldn't have asked you.'

The bath overflowed with laughter. Mellor's usually stiff face broke up into creases. One or two, who'd waited for the end of the joke, got out of the bath, and Dai, who'd stood by the bath side quietly listening with a ready toothy smile, picked up a towel and started rubbing them down.

Tommy Clinton, who spent most of his life worrying hard how to enjoy it, came to the bath side and said, over everybody's head, 'Have you heard about Arthur, then?'

They looked at him and me, and decided they hadn't.

'What's that, Tommy lad?'

Clinton laughed in preparation. 'He's barn a be a daddy. . . . Aren't I right, Art? And the Mayor's gunna be god-father.'

I pulled a few funny faces, thought about pasting Tommy, and said, 'It's the first I've heard of it.' I looked round for Maurice. He was sitting quietly at the end of the bath, smoking, looking at Clinton through his smoke as if he wasn't sure he'd kill him then or later on outside.

'Nay, Arthur, What about that time last Christmas? Me and the girl friend. . . .' He turned round with a big gesture to everybody, his naked body flushed and trembling with so much laughing. '. . . We was working out, it mu'n've been last Christmas at Weaver's little home from home. Old Art here and Judith were knocking it off in that front bedroom so hard the bloody tiles fell off the roof.'

When the laughing had dropped down again I said, 'You're getting the names mixed up aren't you, Tommy? That was Lionel Manners' sample you're talking about.'

He stopped laughing to think a minute. 'You know, Art, you might be right there. It's surprising how you get things mixed up. Now you mention it I've got a faint reckoning of something like that. Perhaps we can let you off'n it this time. There's alus Maurice to consider.'

'Shut your bloody hole, Clinton,' Maurice said from the far end. So seriously that Clinton almost did.

'Christ. I was only having a joke, Maurice. As far as I'm concerned it's anybody's baby but mine.'...' Clinton risked another joke. 'Even then, if you don't wan' it, Morry,' he said, 'I might tek it o'er.'

Maurice threw his cig across the room, jumped up, and with bodies leaping out of his way in surprise he trampled through the bath. There was a huge swell and cascade of water, out of which Maurice lunged over the side at Clinton.

The reserve had been too surprised himself to move. He thought maybe him and Maurice were going to do a joke together. Maurice caught him with a swinging fist. But they were both wet and badly placed, and Maurice, though he hit him again, didn't hurt him. Dai and some others separated them. They found Clinton had broken the edge of a tooth when he slipped against the concrete bath side.

'Nay, Maurice lad,' Frank said, pushing his great belly against him and fastening him to the wall. 'Just be fair. Clinton's got a big hole. All right. But lay off.'

Maurice told Frank something nobody could hear. He shrugged his huge shoulders, and turned his body away from Maurice. 'Leave the lad alone, Maurice,' he said. 'He won't say owt else about it.'

I got out and dried myself, and put my teeth in.

When Mrs Hammond got the news, as I knew she would, she got hold of the bad end of it, and bit hard. People were always telling her stories about me, on an average one a day. She knew more about me than I did myself, because some days she'd be told how I'd been seen in three different places – all 'bad' places – at the same time the night before. Though she couldn't believe any of them she just took a general impression of what I was like outside. I couldn't blame her doing this, and I couldn't do anything about the impression being a bad one. I was supposed to be 'a bit of a lad' and 'quite a rake on the quiet side': nothing I said or did could alter this. People wanted me that way, and they got it. I suppose my father was treated the same way as Mrs Hammond.

When I got home on Thursday night to change before training, she said, 'I heard about Judith Parkes today.'

'I didn't know you knew her,' I said.

'I didn't. But I do now. She works at the Town Hall. Quite a lady, I was told. A very good reputation, and all that.'

'You've heard about the kid she's having? Taken some time to get this end of town, hasn't it?'

'You don't sound bothered.'

'Should I be? Where did you hear it?'

'I heard it in a shop actually – they all seemed surprised you should be the father.'

'So you've heard that one. You're a bit behind the times. I've been dropped now. Maurice is daddy number two. Who told you about it anyway? I suppose by rights I should go knock their faces in.'

'Does it honestly matter how I heard it?'

'I suppose you believe everything people tell you about me. Like that time you were told I'd raped a little girl. Remember? The woman said she had certain proof.'

'When everybody gets the same idea as this one, though – they can't all be wrong. . . . They said you were seen arguing with her at the Mecca last Saturday night. That you made quite a scene, and they all watched her walking off the floor with you running after her.'

'And you really believe all this pub talk?'

'As I said, when everybody gets the same idea it's not always wrong.'

'No. And it's usually not all right. I thought you'd got past listening to what people told you about me.'

'I'm not saying I do believe it,' she said primly. 'But it's funny that your name should have been connected. There's no smoke without fire.'

'You make me bloody sick,' I told her. I put on my coat and went out. She shouted something after me, but I didn't want to hear.

167

This time I didn't go training. I went up to Primstone, collected my pay, and tried to avoid seeing Maurice. I caught sight of him coming into the ground, and I waited in the tunnel till he'd gone by. I was blaming him – and no doubt he was blaming me and Saturday night far more. As I walked away, taking some trouble to avoid bumping into players going up to the ground, I wondered if I oughtn't to go and see Weaver. What I should see him about I didn't know. I felt all along I'd misjudged him, looked down on him because he wasn't a strong pig like me, just one of those who watched me perform. Yet he was one of the few people who'd treated me as a person – as an oddity, perhaps, but still, an oddity with feelings. I caught a bus through town to Sandwood, and walked up the lane to his house.

Mrs Weaver answered the door. She was completely surprised, almost stunned. I could tell from her look that she was in by herself. 'Hello, Machin. What do you want at this time of day?'

I asked her if Weaver was at home, and she shook her head. 'No, he's out,' she said, and in such a way I felt cheap. She seemed to think I knew he was out and had come up purposely. 'What did you want him for? Anything important?'

'No. It doesn't matter.'

I started thinking we could start where we'd left off, that Wednesday a few months ago. The same idea might have been in her mind. It was dark and misty in the garden, and me standing there – it must have seemed I was offering an open invitation. If her face was anything to go by, she found the idea too sudden to be repulsive.

When she said, 'Do you want to come?' in an unsure voice, I felt she would, after all, be some consolation. Like Weaver himself, she was free to give something without getting or expecting anything back. Maybe, like Weaver, she was getting tired of that role. The last time she'd treated me like an ape. Grabbing hold of an ape was, for some people, better than just watching it perform. She'd been crude, thinking I was crude, and I'd frightened away. This time she looked at me in surprise. She was tired. I must have looked sick, for she was staring at me as if I might be a person.

'If I come in I mightn't behave,' I said.

'That's all right,' she told me. 'I think I can take care of myself.'

I followed her inside and she shut the door. We went into the lounge. Its curtains were drawn, and only a reading-lamp was lit. One or two patches on the leaved wallpaper were all that was left of the Christmas Eve party. I sat down in the chair she showed me to, and she sat opposite, beneath the lamp. She had a wool dress on that made her look stouter than before. Her head had the usual mass of tight curls.

'Shouldn't you be training tonight?' she said. 'Thursday . . . that's one of your nights, I believe.'

'I've skipped it tonight.'

'Why? Aren't you well?'

'I didn't feel like it. I felt like a walk or a talk.'

'And that's what you came to see Mr Weaver about?'

'I suppose so. I don't know what I came to see him about. I just came to see him.'

'Are you in any sort of trouble . . . with the police, or anything?'

'No, it's nothing like that.'

'Well,' she said, getting up, and closing the book she must have been reading. 'Let's see if it's anything a drink won't cure.' She went to the cabinet by the gramophone, and filled up a small glass. She carried it across and stood close while I took it from her hand. She went back to her seat and watched me take a first sip.

'I presume you like whisky,' she said. 'It's all we have in, I'm afraid. Very bad housekeeping.'

I coughed over it, I wondered whether to take my overcoat off, but I'd got my overalls on underneath. She'd already guessed, or seen, and she didn't mention it.

'What's the cause of your sudden lack of enthusiasm for football?' she asked, looking at me as at a patient. 'You've not been taking any more tiles off, I hope.'

'It's probably trouble at home,' I said clumsily, but with enough obvious intention that she found my stare a bit too much and looked away. Her fingers found a strand of wool to pull from the arm of the chair. Then she folded her arms under her breasts and looked back.

'With Mrs Hammond,' she suggested.

'Yeh.'

'I've often wondered about you – and her,' she said. 'If you don't mind me talking about it, Arthur. Mr Weaver used to be very concerned about it. You might remember the night you were signed on at Primstone he took you home. He said then how surprised he'd been to learn you were living there, with a widow and two children. He couldn't understand it. I doubt if he does even now. He appeared to think you were asking for trouble. . . . Do you mind me talking like this? You've only to say. . . .'

'No, I don't mind. I'd like to know what other people think.'

'Well, it certainly isn't every young man's cup of tea. I suppose when you first went there you didn't have much choice. But I'd have thought later on, when you were more secure, you would have moved to a more congenial domestic atmosphere. From what Mr Weaver said, Mrs Hammond's marriage wasn't a very happy one. Her husband was a very sombre, moody man. There was some talk when he was killed that it wasn't all an accident.'

I finished the whisky. I'd never thought why I'd stayed in Fairfax Street. The news about Hammond relieved me. I seemed to see Mrs Hammond there in the room. Not so much see as feel. 'Why have you stayed there?' Mrs Weaver asked.

'I was just trying to think why. I've always felt at home there, if you like. Maybe it was just a habit. I think I felt I had to give a hand . . . I know I first went there because it was cheap, and I thought I was on to a good thing. Then when I'd been there a bit I saw what a load of trouble they were in, and I felt it was only right I should give them a hand. After that . . . it went from one thing to another. The two kids aren't anything I'd look at by choice. At first

I thought they were ugly little . . . kids. I remember, they seemed to be crying and screaming all day. I suppose she was too upset at that time to care. I don't know. But once I'd started helping they all started looking to me for it. Mrs Hammond always tried to refuse . . . you know how a woman's like that. But she needed what I gave her, and the kids weren't so choosy. I reckon I more or less took over from their dad. That's what it looks like now. But I've always thought – you know, that I was independent.'

'And now you've found you're not,' she said.

'Maybe. It's just that she won't *admit* anything. She thinks I'm doing all this for her because it makes me feel good. She doesn't think I care about anything. Except playing football, having crowds after me, and that sort of stuff. She taunts me with it. She tries to make fun of me having no feelings. She drives me off my nut at times, till I've got to hit or something. Like tonight. She thinks I only want to see her give in, to become really . . . relying on me, then I'll go away and find some other mug. That's what she thinks. And to make it seem it really is like me to be like that she comes out with all these stories people tell her about me. You know the sort of muck. She doesn't believe them. She just thinks it's something she can hold over me. It's the carrot I'm chasing, trying to show her I mean what I say, and every time she says she can't believe it, that I've lost. . . . I know this is all talk. I hope you don't mind listening. It's either this . . .'

'No, no, Arthur. I don't mind one bit. I feel quite over-whelmed. I'm glad you've told me. I honestly never thought you felt so much about things.'

'I suppose that's my fault. I'm a natural professional. What I don't get paid to do I don't bother with. If I was paid enough to feel then I'd probably make a big splash that way.'

'Well, that sounds more like the old you. That's the sort of brash thing you usually say. It's the sort of thing which makes people think of you as . . . big. But your feelings about Mrs Hammond. They're a different matter. If you'd *only* get down a while from that great big height you see yourself on. For one thing I'm sure I can understand some of the reasons why Mrs Hammond is frightened of you. You've probably convinced *her* more than you have yourself what a Big Man you are. To you it may all be show. But to her, I should think seeing the money you earn, the things you buy, your photograph in the *City Guardian* every other week – all those things must have convinced her that you *are* big. And she must have asked herself what it is you see in her, and how on earth, once she's admitted some feeling for you, as a person, she's going to keep you. Things like that mightn't occur to you as a man. But I can assure you they do to a woman. She's in a particularly vulnerable position – a widow with two children. You, a young man with the opportunity to go off with almost any girl in town. She must be terrified of showing any feeling for you. Particularly if she knows she has some, if she's committed herself.'

Having both shot our loads we lay back in our chairs. It was very quiet in the dark room. The ship's-wheel clock ticked. But there were no sounds from outside. 'I used to admire you very much,' she said. 'As you know. And in spite of what's happened I think I must still do. I wouldn't have felt this concern if I hadn't. So don't imagine I'm just getting one back at you, Arthur. . . . Taking ordinary people like yourself, and putting them into a sudden limelight can have extraordinary results. You must be aware of that now. Do you think it would help any if I saw Mrs Hammond myself? Perhaps I could smooth things out.'

'I'd thought of that while you were talking. But she'd probably be suspicious. She wouldn't like it, I know. But thanks for the offer.'

'I see. . . .' she said, reading something else into it. 'Then you'd better face it yourself. But a little more gently than you seem to be doing. You both have my sympathy. Mr Weaver and I – we seem to be always patching up people's troubles, including our own. Mr Weaver is up at Judith Parkes's house tonight, I believe. Trying to solve their difficulties, and Maurice's. I hope things work out. Phone me up and let me know how you've gone on.'

She came to the front door to see me out. She gave me her advice again, and offered to drive me into town when she saw I hadn't the car. I said I'd walk or catch a bus. She stood in the lighted doorway till I was out of sight down the drive. I heard the door shut in the stillness of the big garden. I realized I hadn't thanked her.

*

Mrs Hammond had already gone into a gradual decline, looking to me to force the break. She was puzzled why I didn't do this, and particularly why I showed no interest in marrying Judith. 'It's your chance to become respectable,' she told me in the slow voice she'd suddenly adopted.

When I got back from Mrs Weaver's she only stayed up to say this, then went to bed, locking herself in with the kids in the front bedroom. I didn't go to work Friday. I tried to talk to her without getting angry, but it was no go. The more I talked and the more begging I became, the more convinced she was that I'd something to hide. She wouldn't listen. In spite of all she'd heard and all she'd said, she had felt all along that I'd been faithful to her. Now she staggered about the house from one room to another, from one job to another, as if she'd been hit with a hammer. It was a physical affliction: her legs wouldn't straighten as she walked, her head wouldn't lift. She didn't even talk to the kids.

When I told her, after phoning up Mrs Weaver, that Maurice had decided to marry Judith, she was even more shocked. The first thing she asked was, 'Is he doing it for you?'

'No. It's his kid she's having,' I told her for the fifth time.

She seemed hurt it had cleared up this way: she'd used Judith as the last crutch to prop up her own thick pride. She even said, 'You've been let out of this too easy,' as if she still felt I was to blame for Maurice and Judith's behaviour. It was as though she'd been waiting for this Judith affair to come for a long time, and when it had she'd been thankful, in spite of the pain. A part of her wanted it. It meant she could reach a decision. She'd even built up in her own mind the strength to meet the break. And now that it had come, and the cause suddenly taken away, by Maurice, she was left dangling – the ground had disappeared and she couldn't keep her balance. I hadn't been bad after all, and she wasn't in a position to believe it. And I could have killed her for not seeing all the stinking protection I gave her. She seemed determined to carry on as though I was still to blame.

She was watching TV on her own that particular night. The kids had gone to bed, though I could still hear Lynda crying about something upstairs.

She didn't look up when I came in.

'You haven't sold it yet?' I said.

'Not just yet,' she said tonelessly, in a way that could either have meant interest in the screen or just lifelessness.

'I keep coming home expecting to see the brokers carrying thy fur coat and the T.V. out of the door.'

'I'll let you know when it's likely to happen.'

'According to you I won't be here. . . . They wouldn't keep you long. What would you do then? I was wondering only recently why you never pressed for damages from Weaver's when Eric died.'

I waited for her to look up from the play she was watching, but she sat hunched up without moving. 'Even some sort of compensation,' I added. 'Or did you keep that on one side?'

She turned round, already vicious. 'I know you're half drunk, Mr Superman, drowning your sorrows. But just how low can you grovel? Can't you get any smaller than that?'

'If you push me to. You generally do.'

'What have I done to get all this!' she cried out, her eyes turning up to the ceiling where Lynda was already moaning. She picked up a cigarette tray no one had ever used and lugged it at the set. It missed the screen and fractured the woodwork. The faces went on performing unconcernedly. Just above was a mounted press photo of me scoring a try.

'I must want you to notice I'm still around,' I told her.

'I've noticed. Don't worry, I've noticed! I can smell the stench from here when you come in the door.'

'Can you now? Well that's the smell of work,' I told her. 'Perhaps there's not enough of it around here.'

'You've never worked in your life. You live like a spiv, you smell like a spiv . . . and you live with me like one an' all.'

'Because I don't come home grunting, swearing, and sweating like the other pigs round here it doesn't mean I don't work – I do! You bitch! You're always trying to make out I do nothing!'

She got up and came to stand beneath my chin so she could shout what she'd been wanting to shout for weeks. 'Well you can get out right now and join those other pigs because I don't want you in my house any more!'

I stepped back to look at her quietly. 'I'm not going,' I told her, calming down. 'I like living here. I've paid for a lot of the stuff. I like to see you benefit from all I do for you. I like to see these kids get plumper and fitter and a bit more cheerful on the decent living I give them. . . .'

'You'll get out!' she screamed, and ran past me up the stairs. She must have thought of doing this often, because when I reached my room she'd already torn up a couple of shirts. She'd pulled the drawer out, and was standing with one foot in it, straining to rip my best nylon shirt between her hands. The rest of my clothes and some of my paperbacks were in the yard. My first impulse was to kill her. To push her out of the window.

Then I told her, 'Your stuff'll get just as torn when I fling it out of the front.'

She came dragging after me on the landing. She fell on her knees and put her hands together. 'Please, please, Arthur. Leave us alone.'

'I can't. I love you.'

She spat up at my face. But it only reached my shirt. Her face was screwed up like a dried weed. She dribbled on her grey dress. In the bedroom Lynda was screaming, and then Ian. I tried to imagine how it must sound outside.

Lynda opened the door slowly and looked at her mother sobbing on the floor. I felt shy of the kid. She rushed into her arms. 'It's all right, Lyn. I just fell.' They buried their heads in each other's shoulders.

I went downstairs and out at the back to pick up my clothes. Across the back people were standing about like cattle, listening and watching, scratching in the ashes, having a good laugh, pretending nothing had happened. When I went in she was already in the kitchen. The TV screamed through from the other room. Washing powder.

'Are you going now or in the morning?' she said, and watched me dusting down the clothes and shaking the ashes out of the books. She had quietened. Her hands were still flushed from tearing cloth.

'I'm not going at all.'

'What is it you want . . . to make you go? I'll give you anything. Ought we've got.' She pressed herself against the table. 'Do you want to go to bed?'

'I don't want anything you've got. I'm staying.'

'I'll have to fetch the police then,' she said emptily.

'They can't turn me out without a week's notice.'

'*I*'ll go then. I'll take Lyn an' Ian. I'd rather we live in a hole in the backs than stay here with you. You poison us all. Listen at them – scared stiff.' She pulled open the kitchen door so I could hear the kids wailing.

'That's your own bloody fault for screaming round like a maniac. You want to get used to the idea – I'm staying. You'll waste less energy.'

'I can't think of any better way of wasting it. You don't seem to know what you are. What you look like to us.'

'All *I* can see is the food you eat. The clothes you wear, the pleasure you get. When I came here you hadn't a strip of underclothes between you that wasn't in rags.'

'Pleasure, pleasure, pleasure! You say pleasure! You standing over us! Like a bloody lord and master. . . . You *made* us enjoy anything we ever did. You *made* us.'

'You don't seem to appreciate one bloody thing – not one bloody thing I've done for you,' I shouted, crazed by her stinking lack of gratitude. 'I've treated you better than my own parents even. How can you say a thing like that? You've a life better than any other woman on this street.'

'You must be a lunatic. You must be a lunatic if you think I've got any . . . any, any *thing* for what you've done. You're raving! You've done nothing for us that wasn't just your fancy. You've done just what you've liked. You must think you're God Almighty . . . stuck up there in your tin motor-car, with your TV and your cheap fur coat. I'll burn everything! Everything you've touched I'll burn. The minute you leave this house, every stick and every morsel you've touched. . . . You can't *see* yourself. You just can't *see*. A better life than any other woman on this street! My life is hell! I can't lift my head without somebody pointing at me and saying I'm your . . . slut!'

'Who says that?'

'Who says that! Just listen to him. Who? . . .' She choked with laughing, with pulling up laughter, strangled, from her belly. 'Is God hurt because somebody calls me a slut? Is God going to go out there in his big motor-car and knock them down . . . knock them down because they don't say good morning to his kind of dirt? Well – you hit them! *Massacre* them! You smash and tear them up until there isn't two bits of them together! Just you make sure they won't ever do it again. . . . They all laugh at you. Now that's surprising, isn't it? They all point you out. Did you know that? They think you're trying to be different. They all point you out. And they point *me* out. And Lynda. And Ian. We're not proper people now because of you. Because you show off every Sat'day in front of thousands of them. We're like cripples that daren't show ourselves. You've put your stenching mark on all of us.'

'This must sound right good next door.'

'No better . . . no better than it's ever been. They listen every night. Tonight's no different. . . . If it's a week's notice, then you've got it.'

She bent down and screamed into the fireplace – something to the Farrers next door. 'You're my witnesses,' she told them. 'For when the police come. A week's notice to get out from tonight.'

'You must think they've minds like yours. There's no need to go screaming like a lunatic. . . .'

'I don't think they're like me. I know they're not. They're much better. Everybody's much better than me. Before you came here . . . you don't know, but I was respected. Everybody round here, everybody in the street – everybody, they all respected me. They thought well of me – of how I brought up Lynda. . . . But I'm not going to cover myself up now. I don't kid myself. Not like you. I know what I am.'

'You're feeling like this because you're frightened. . . .'

'You don't know me!'

She went round the room, glanced out of the window, looked back at the walls. 'I know you,' I said. 'I ought to. I've been here long enough.'

'You don't know me. Just how do *you* know me? You don't look at anybody but yourself. When I was younger. . . . Before, I felt young. You only make me feel old. I've always been old with you. And I've tried. I've tried to be right. I've tried and I've tried. I wanted . . . I only wanted to be left alone. I didn't want you. I didn't ask you to come here and push yourself in.'

'But you've taken all I've given you. Don't say you didn't want somebody. I've treated you like a queen. Just look at what I've given out here.'

'How you go on! I don't see what you're trying to get out of it.' It looked as though she'd finished, that she was going out. Then she added, 'Can't you get it into your head? We don't need you.'

'The trouble with you is it drives you mad to see somebody who won't crawl about. Isn't that right? You want me to crawl about like the rest – like Eric crawled. Look at the people round here. The people who won't say good morning, tickle me fancy, to you. Just look at them. There's not a bleeding man amongst them. They're all flat out on their backs and anybody can walk over them. They haven't the nerve to stand up and walk about like me. And because of that you try and make out that it's *me* who stinks. Me!'

'How you go on. . . .'

'Shut your hole a minute and listen to me. These people want you to act like this. They don't like you because you're on to a good thing. If we had no cash, no car, and no fur coat you could have a hundred men living here. All they want is to see you in the same miserable dirt as themselves. Can't you see what you're doing? I could tell you some things people have said to me that'd make your toe nails drop off. And just because I'm a Rugby League player. Isn't that right? You *know* that's right. Tell me it's right!'

'You don't know. You don't know what it's like.'

'I know what's it's like. They hate me, they hate *you* . . . they even hate Ian and Lynda. Only you don't want to see it. For some stupid crazy reason you prefer to think like them.'

She twisted against the table, beating it for silence, shaking her head: everything as if I actually had hold of her and she was trying to break away. 'You don't know. You've never gone without a thing in your life!'

Somebody, Mr Farrer, was banging on the wall, then he rooted at the back of the chimney. I banged back with a poker. A piece of plaster fell in the hearth. Kids ran screaming in some game over the ashes.

'The police'll be here any time,' I told her. 'Better get the beer out and the set warmed up.'

'Nothing's clean to you,' she murmured. 'You filthy everything you touch.'

'You're too sentimental. I don't like these arguments either, but I'm not complaining. These people I'm talking about – they're my friends, my fans. I don't mind what they think. If they say anything to me about it I just knock their teeth in. Me – I don't complain about anything. You – you resent me helping.'

She looked at me thoughtfully, dazed, as at some new revelation. 'Thank God there's a part of my life you never touched. There's something that's clean,' she said. 'That's one thing which must reallly hurt you. I can see it, now. You must hate Eric. He's one thing you can't touch. He's what brings me through all this. Him and Lyn and Ian. The one really good thing in all this. . . .'

'Come on, come on – get it over with. You might as well put his bloody boots back in the hearth. Let's all get down and pray for the good soul of Eric – the father of this house.'

'How he must *hurt* you,' she said with all the keenness of at last finding something she thought really did hurt me.

'If I've ever seen a crazy thing, that's it – a pair of dead man's boots in the hearth. Christ, they put people into nut-houses for less than that these days. You even polished them. As if he was going to step into them the next minute. I know enough about you to keep you in a rubber room the rest of your life.'

'What. . . . What do you know about how good Eric was to me – how he treated us? How would you know what a decent father does for his family? How hard he worked? What do you know about Eric?'

'I know he can't have done so bloody much going by what I've seen here. I know he shoved a file in his guts. He was such a good father he virtually killed himself on that lathe. It was no accident. . . .'

She stumbled against the table. 'You want to *kill* me!' she screamed. 'You treat me as if I didn't exist. I'm just nothing, to you. You make me think I'm nothing. Anything I do you knock down. You won't let me live. You make me think I don't exist.'

She got into a chair and wiped her hair aside with her wrist. She was completely exhausted, panting and sobbing.

'I want to live with you. I don't want to squash you.'

'Everything I do you make as if it wasn't important. You make me feel that I'm dead.'

'But I want you!' I shouted.

'I'm one thing you can't have like everything else.'

She seemed a long way off, and disappearing.

'You don't want me to go, do you? *Say* you don't. Say you don't want me to go.'

'I don't want you to stay here,' she said slowly, forced, reciting an idea she'd got too used to to let go. She sat still. Her eyes were glazed. If her mouth hadn't gone on saying it I'd have thought she was dead.

I GOT to Primstone on Saturday afternoon to find my name scrubbed off the team sheet. No one knew why, apart from the fact I hadn't turned up for training Thursday, and the committee men directed me to George Wade who didn't happen to be on the ground. I found I wasn't worried. In fact I felt relieved. I didn't want to play football ever again, and this was the short cut.

I drove back to Mrs Hammond's and packed my things into the car. She'd locked herself in the kitchen wth the kids, as she had on the previous occasions I'd been back that day, so I didn't say good-bye.

I could hear the Primstone crowd as I drove round town. I hadn't realized before how the roar filled the valley: in Market Street, thick with shoppers, the heads turned like pale flowers in the direction of the stadium. I stopped to buy a paper copy of *Somebody Up There Likes Me*.

I got myself a place near the bus depot where I'd stayed years before when I first left home. It was in different hands now. There were two others asleep in the room when Cameron, the latest owner, showed me up. From what was lying around I gathered they were bus conductors. On the window were stuck Eire emblems and a nude. It cost a quid a week, and half a dollar for breakfast. I was back exactly where I'd started.

I paid him and went and sat in the car, which I'd parked on some waste land behind the house. I read the beginning of Graziano's life story, then fell asleep.

It was about midnight when I went back to the room. The other two occupants weren't in. I must have lain awake over an hour before I dropped off. When I did wake in the morning it was to the noise of their heavy breathing. Two bottles of beer and a new alarm clock stood on the cabinet by the beds, and another empty propped up an *English Beauties* on the chest of drawers.

Cameron was sitting in his vest on the front step reading a

Sunday paper. He shielded his eyes against the early morning sun. 'How d'you sleep, whacker,' he said, 'with those two alarm clocks?'

'I never heard them come in.'

'Still got all your money in your pockets?' He suggested I look through. 'Want any breakfast?'

'I'm just going out.'

'That saves a lot of trouble then . . . as long as you don't come back later wanting some. I've fourteen to cook on a morning like this. It's a crying shame, don't you think?'

'You charge enough for it. Why should you worry?'

'Oh, it's no worry,' he decided with a vague stare. 'Unless you'd have wanted yours. That was why I looked at you in that queer way when you came out just now. Perhaps you noticed. I always give that look when I think people might cause trouble. I find it often puts them off.'

'I never noticed it,' I said.

'Didn't you?' His mild stare turned to concern, wondering how it could have gone wrong. 'Is your name Arthur Machin?'

When I nodded he tried to look either serious or interested. 'I thought so, when you came. I thought I recognized your face. I've seen you play at Primstone.' He turned a couple of sheets of his paper. 'What're you down this end of the town for? Come for the fresh air? No trouble involved, is there?'

'No.'

'I'll take your word for it. Remember I've said that. You see, I don't mind who I take, Marilyn Brando, whoever you like, I'm not choosy, but if there's any trouble involved – no thank you. I'm a man who believes in absolute peace. No fights, no trouble, no nothing,' He spread his hands either side of him as he wiped all thought of trouble away. 'I'd rather sleep in the house myself.'

'You don't stay here then?'

'Me and the missis live in the garage at the back. You might drop in sometime when we're not at home and have a look. It's quite cosy. By the way, is that your car at the back?'

'I just left it there for the night.'

'I meant to tell you, whacker. It's a bad place. The nippers round here are mustard. It'll be all spare parts if you leave it too long. You'd do better to park it in the street out here, then we can keep an eye on it. If you want it cleaning let me know. I'll do it for a dollar.'

I waved at him as I drove past, and watched him in the mirror. He stood up, impressed, to see me out of sight.

'If it isn't the man from the Pru!' Frank said, looking up from his digging. 'I'm glad thy's come, Art.' He stepped off the soil, scraping the mud from his boots on the brick path. 'The wife's still i' bed, but she'll be up when she hears thy've come.'

'Hello, Mr Machin,' his twelve-year-old boy said from the back door, then rushed up the stairs to tell his mother.

'Where d'you get to yest'day?' Frank asked. He pointed the way through to the living-room, and stayed in the kitchen to take off his boots. 'They thought thy'd gone away to sulk.'

'They might've been right.'

'Aye. It was a bit of a shock. But then . . . where did you get on Thursday? Riley said you came in for your wage, but apart from him nobody saw you.'

Mrs Miles came in laughing. 'It's right good to see you, Arthur. You're a stranger round here nowadays – apart from the dog track, that is. Go and put the kettle on, Kenny,' she told the boy. 'You can have some tea, Arthur, while you watch me eat my breakfast. I was half up when I heard your car.'

'Mother's day i' bed,' Frank said. 'I had mine at half past six, mind.'

'He can't break the habit . . . getting up for the early shift.'

'It's true.' Frank admitted his fault seriously like a big boy. 'I can't sleep much after half past five on a morning. I'll have a bit of breakfast with you, love. And put in a couple of eggs for Art.'

'Haven't you had no breakfast?' Elsie asked.

'I can tell he hasn't,' Frank said. 'He hasn't even shaved. You do as I say, while him and me go in the front room.'

Elsie nodded significantly. 'I was sorry to hear you were dropped yest'day, Arthur,' she told me.

'Yes, love,' Frank told her.

We went in the front room and he shut the door. He looked immense in this not very large space, his bull neck bowed in fear of the ceiling.

'I see you've come in the motor,' he said, nodding at the window where the top of the car showed over the hedge. 'It was news to me, Art, yest'day. I didn't hear a thing about it until two fifteen. It's not like Wade to cross out a name then run away. I didn't see him at all at the match.'

'I don't suppose you can blame him. He probably feels bad about it himself.'

Frank put himself on to the settee. It buckled and flattened under his weight. 'Why do you think you were dropped?' he asked seriously.

'You should know, Frank – I've played bad for too long. I didn't turn up Thursday, and I never told them why. I'm not blaming anybody for being dropped . . . I didn't really come about that.'

He was full of slow surprise. 'Anything the matter, Art?' He was a big pained dog.

'The little lady's kicked me out at home.'

He waited for the news to be absorbed. I could hear Elsie talking to Kenny next door.

'But you've been with her more'n three year.' He couldn't keep the tone of reproach out of his voice.

'I didn't want to leave. In fact I'm going to try and go back when she's had a chance to calm down. But things have been mounting up. . . . This week they seem to have broke.'

'Well, you'll un'erstand, Art, I never shove my nose into things not my concern, but to be honest – and you'll know why I say this – it comes as no surprise to me. How you've missed it so far is a mystery to me. It beat me how you ever got tangled up wi' Weaver – cos *he's* done you no good. I've been up yonder over twelve year, and I doubt if I've spoke to him more'n that number of times.'

184

'Some people get in the way, Frank. Others don't.'

'Aye. And there were you, straight out of nowhere, and a car and Weaver at your disposal in no time. I told thee then what to be 'ware on.'

He nodded his censure at me with a severe kind of exasperation. 'It rankles me seeing you down in this condition, because it's nowt to do wi' football. And that's all *you* are, Art, socially or any other road. I mean' – he leaned forward and pushed out his huge fist – 'Rugby League's a great game. It's about the only manly game left, and it's only spoilt by people who try and make it something else. Any trouble you're in now, Art, stems from you being too big for your bloody boots. And if anybody encouraged you to that state of mind it's Weaver. I've often wanted to say this, so I hope you won't mind getting it o'er. You rose like the sun at Primstone, and if you're not to set like one you've got some hard thinking to do. What I meant about rankling, about me being rankled, is that George Wade told me they had you in mind for captain when I go. You see, that's how it affects me. A've built that team up o'er the past few years, and all that's chucked away because you had to go sucking up to Weaver, or laking around with that Mrs Hammond. Christ, Arthur, you're on the edge of making a right mess of everything.'

'What do you think I should do? I just don't feel up to playing football again. Do you think I should see Wade, and tell him?'

'It's up to you. I don't know what you should do. I only know how you've stopped yourself from playing. If this Mrs Hammond's at the root of it then I reckon you ought to get that settled. I mean – what is the woman to you? I know she's been hanging around the background all the time, but what's she supposed to be? Did you reckon on marrying her, or was she something you went home to each night? And by the way – I haven't mentioned anything about her to the wife. She doesn't even know Mrs Hammond exists. So don't mention it to her. She thinks you're a right good lad where tarts are concerned.'

Having expected some sort of dumb sympathy from Frank

I found there wasn't much I could say. He listened to a few excuses, and didn't say anything else beyond I should 'put it right with Mrs Hammond.' When Elsie knocked on the door and put her head shyly round we were both standing and looking out of the window in silence.

I spent the day with Frank, digging in the garden, playing with Kenny. I took them out in the car after dinner. In the evening Elsie had her people in: they played with Kenny too, and at cards. Families kill me. When the lad went to bed I made it an excuse to go, and Frank didn't argue. He came out for a last word as the others waved from the window.

The front door was locked when I got back – locked or stuck. There was a light on in one of the upstairs rooms. I banged on the door and nothing happened. It was the same when I threw a pebble against the lighted window.

Round the back there was a light in the garage and one of the large doors was half open. A woman dressed only in a skirt, her breasts folded down like two sacks, put herself behind a curtain. 'Yes?' she said.

'I can't get in. The front door's locked.'

'You don't use the front door at night,' she said. 'Use the back. Push it if it's stuck, there's no latch.'

Her shadow waited on the curtain to hear me go. I climbed up twelve steps at the side of the garage and pushed open the door. There was the sound of celebrating upstairs, and as I passed the door of the lighted room a couple stopped dancing, tripped over a bottle, and stared at me somewhere at the level of my knees. 'Get stuffed, Paddy. Don't look in other people's rooms,' the man said and kicked the door to. Then there was an argument, and when I reached the end of the landing the door opened again and the man put his head out. 'Sorry if I sounded rough, cock,' he called. 'Freda says come in and have a drink.'

'It's all right,' I told him. 'I'm going to bed.'

He went back in. 'He isn't a Pad any rate, so what the hell d'you mean?' he asked the girl, and slammed the door.

There was only one Irishman in the room. He was

dressed in a bus conductor's uniform and looked to be in the middle of a nightmare – he'd got the jacket on but not the trousers, and watched my entry with wide open mouth.

'Hello, Jeepers,' he said. 'You haven't got a better half wid'yew?'

'No, I'm on my own.'

'Tank the lord for that. We tort you had. I can keep my trousers off. . . . You're not Irish?'

'I'm from the town.'

'From the town?' he said swaying immediately with surprise and trying to look like the film Irishman. 'You're one of the natives, by gum an' dall that? What're you doing in this sty, son?'

'I'm on holiday,' I told him, and went and sat on my bed.

'On holiday! But if I don't see a joke there somewhere. Wait till I tell my mate. . . . He's under the bluddy bed. Ay Paddy. D'you can come out now. Comenzee out.'

He bent down and dug under the bed, then unfolded, all in one breath. He'd gone red. 'He's one of the best sort of Irish – a Ukrainian Paddy. Isn't that right?' he said as a fair haired man in his underpants and vest came out holding the trousers of his uniform, smiling and looking nervous. 'He tort he heard you bringing a lady did the boy so he dived under the bed. . . . You'd have tort there were a hundred foot of water the way he went under. Listen at me. He'll brain the daylights out of me in a minute. I meant to say Lithuanian. I get all these orientals mixed up.'

'Does he speak English?' I said.

'Of course I do,' the Lithuanian said with a faint Irish accent on top of his own. 'Pass along please. No more standing. Right down the bus, if you *don't* mind. Any more fares, you bastards.'

'Isn't that as near Irish as ever d'you want?' his friend said proudly. 'I can sit down and listen to him for hours speak my own language better than I can myself. Now you know what they mean when they say Shakespeare was a Russian.'

He finished undressing, and put on a pair of green pyjamas. They were still jabbering when the music had come to an end down the landing and the rest of the house and the street outside were quiet. We all three lay in our beds while the Irishman read out the headings and showed round the pictures in his *English Beauties*.

'I used to be down the pit,' the Lithuanian was telling me over the noise. 'But you English almost work down there. I got out pretty sharp with bad health – I have a chest complaint now. The doctor advises fresh air and the open life.'

'So he stands in the bus doorways on the corners to take in a mouthful of air as they turn,' the Irishman said. 'What d'you think of this – "A star in her eye and the sun in her smile." And this one – "Difficult to approach, but a ladder in her stocking." Gives you quite a beat, don't you think?'

'But my health's improved. There's no doubt of that. I shall soon be strong enough to be a communist and go home.'

'Did I tell you, perhaps I forgot – I'm a republican,' the Irishman told me. 'You see what I mean? – *Re* publican.'

'My family and relatives all live in Vilna, almost on the border of that land next door. I'd like to go back there. Your climate here, it's only weather . . . and this landlord, too, he's not the kind of person I like to live next to. Cameron, and that wife of his. You should see his wife. It's a shame. He could be good. Have you seen them? They live in that garage at the back of the house.'

'I saw it when I came in tonight.'

'You'll know then. He must make twenty pounds a week out of this house, and he lives in the garage. It's not what you expect in an over-civilized country.'

'What the hell you live here for, then?' his friend said. 'Look at this one – "A Heavenly Body arrested in space." D'you think that copper looks a fairy?'

'This country, she's like a car, engine and parts running smoothly, plunging over a . . .'

'Oh shut all that crap off,' the Paddy was saying. 'He tells the same stuff to everybody he meets. Just look at this one. It's pretty pornographic, don't you think? They've tried to tone it down with that lighthouse in the background.'

The Irish–German voices eased a pain somewhere in my

mind, and I slowly drifted into sleep. I finally escaped when the light suddenly went out and I heard the Paddy saying, 'That bastard Cameron – he's turned it off at the mains. I'd just got to that Bride in the Bath one.' I thought a second about the money in my pocket, and the keys to the car, but the effort to wake was too great, and I subsided.

*

The alarm woke me like a blow.

I sat up thinking I was at Mrs Hammond's and the alarm had gone off by mistake. They were already up, buttoning their uniforms. 'The fire's out, every ting's under control, skipper,' the Paddy said.

'Work,' the Lithuanian told me. 'I'm on at five twenty and Ireland's on at five forty-five. Don't you work?'

'I forgot to tell you last night,' the Paddy said. 'He's on holiday.' He turned to me to say, 'Have a nice day on the beach,' and they went next door where they woke someone else, and water gurgled and splashed.

The Lithuanian depressed me – he seemed displaced in every sense. I fell asleep again with his voice in my head. I thought the Paddy came in the door and said, 'I forgot to tell you. Cameron's wife comes round cleaning on a morning. Any money you leave in your pockets she thinks is a tip. So only leave your mess.'

When the sun reached my part of the room I sat up in bed and read some more of *Somebody Up There*. The house was quiet, probably deserted with everybody at work. I thought about going myself, looked at the alarm clock, and changed my mind. When I got up all the loose change had gone from my clothes.

I drove around town and got some money out of the bank. As I came down Market Street I saw Johnson on one of his morning walks. I felt tempted to go and talk, see how he felt, but I drove into a garage instead and had the tank filled up. When I came out he'd disappeared.

From the top of the valley the sight of the town working normally, but without me, made me feel outcast, an outlaw. I wasn't allowed to live there any more. I stopped the car by Caulsby Castle. There was that smell of work in the air. The Road Services' lorries were beginning to move off down and out of the valley: the roads were black and moving, and the City itself was almost a forest with these insects moving amongst the scrubbed undergrowth of the buildings and the stunted trees of the factory stacks. The chemical works' six metal chimneys, joined like bandaged fingers, filtered a thin red mist of nitrous fumes over the river. Alongside Harris's Mill a slim black pipe shot up a vivid bush of white steam, which stuck in the air for several minutes before subsiding to a lazy exhausted trickle. Occasionally one of the stocky chimneys jettisoned a great black termite streamer of smoke across the valley to go curling over the ridge and shroud the gloomy Riding Hospital overlooking Highfield. Close up to the valley side, where the road curved through the trees before ascending to Sandwood, and just below the over-flowing and overgrown cemetery, the frantic panting of the steam boiler at the brickworks echoed like a railway engine dragging a long line of coaches to life. Its rapid puffs of steam mounted into the air in a bulging column, which burst and disappeared in the wind. And sprawling across the valley, down below the town, with its two huge sprout-ing limbs like a dead upturned body, was the power station: the only new brick in sight. It seemed to dam up the town and stop it overflowing down the valley over the small, high-hedged fields to Stokeley. Somewhere beneath all this was the one person I knew: amongst all that mass and detail was a fleck, a speck in the hundred thousand landscape, a smudge on the lattice of all those streets. From up here she didn't count, and I might be God.

During the next few days nobody intensified this feeling of isolation more than the Lithuanian. I probably felt his exile more than he did. Three days on my own were enough to change the whole shape of things. It seemed as if the debt I'd accumulated had suddenly been shoved on me without warning, and I'd been told to pay, or else. The emptiness obliterated every other feeling I had for people or for places. I imagined myself like Mrs Hammond at the time I first knew her – and I found I was glad to feel that. I only felt safe in the car. I'd never been so proud of it. I'd finished *Somebody Up There Likes Me* and had bought *Love Tomorrow*. In it, this tec called Stulton – Cheesy to his pals – had to crack a case in some town I forget, in America. And he falls for the crook's girl friend, and she falls for him. But she's in it so thick with the crooks that it's not unforeseen she gets bumped off. Stulton, driven crazy by this, turns on the crooks and finishes them off in no time. Then he looks round him, and realizes there's nothing left. The girl's dead. He just doesn't want to go·on living any more. At the end he's in his car, driving out of town. He gets on the turnpike and steps on the gas. In no time he's left the place, the people, his memories far behind. The road's clear and open. The car's booming along. He begins to feel better, and he starts thinking about the next town, and the next sample it probably holds.

That touched me. I thought if only I could break things up like this Stulton, and get on to the next place and leave all these wrecks behind. I even tried driving out of town fast. But the roads were crammed. They twisted and ducked about. And I'd only go a couple of miles, hardly leaving town behind, before I was in the next bloody place. One town started where the other left off. There was no place to feel free. I was on a chain, and wherever I went I had to come back the same way.

Early Wednesday evening the Paddy came back helpless. The Lithuanian wasn't a great deal better. They were both sick on the floor; then they fell on the Irishman's bed and lay there a while in each other's arms. I sat wondering whether I ought to clear up or clear out.

Eventually the Lithuanian slipped off the bed and knelt by mine on all fours, his head lolling between his shoulders. He began to bark – low, short barks to start with, then long howls. There was a genuine tone of distress in his voice. The Paddy grunted and belched on his back, and was sheet white – it was obvious his belly was getting ready to bring up another load.

When I got off the bed the Lithuanian bit my leg. I

jumped across to the next bed and dragged the Paddy on to the floor and then to the door. I pulled him along the landing to the lavatory and dumped him with his head on the bowl. The Lithuanian was crawling up and down the room and he greeted me with weird wolf howls but no biting. I told him to get on the bed. He stopped his pacing to look up at me.

'You've been drinking,' he said. 'We met a man tonight who knows you.'

'Did he tell you his name?'

'Of course he did, my friend. Do you think I don't know how to talk to people? He said to remember him.'

'Who was it?'

'Who was it?' He tried to imitate my accent. 'Now don't give me so many names. Let me think – Field. . . . No. Hill, Brook, Dale, Swallow . . . all these names, are you listening? Seal, Fish – they are not names. They're a zoo. We have walked up every hill in the district – did Pad tell you? We walked up *one* side of the valley, then we walked up the other side of the valley. We walked up the valley, then we walked down the valley. Miles and . . . We were in a ladies' lavatory somewhere. Perhaps it was up the valley. It might have been down the valley. You should have seen her face. "What do you think you are doing here, my good woman? Have you got your ticket?" I never realized it until I saw all those – what do you call them? – in a row. Have you ever been in one? It's far more comfortable than the men's – a woman's world, my friend, don't you think? They should label them better. Where's Pad bow wow wow wow?' He slumped on the bed and went on talking into the blankets. All I could hear was his muffled growl.

I pulled my shirts out of the drawer, bundled them up, and got the two books. Paddy was half-way down the stairs when I passed him. I didn't bother telling Cameron I was leaving his sty. I got in the car and drove home automatically, screwing up my guts for all the moralizing I was going to hear. I hoped, on the off chance, my dad might be working nights.

But the first thing I see when I open the living-room door

is neither my mother nor father – I seem to catch the ghost of Mrs Hammond intruding. She got to her feet as I came in, and my mother turned round and looked over her shoulder, pale and startled in the electric light.

We all made a few sounds of surprise, and looked at one another like new, unacquainted people.

'What're you doing here?' I stumbled out. I'd often imagined her here, in this neat living-room, and now that it'd happened it was still in a dream.

'I met your father – on City Road. He asked me to come up.'

I watched my parents performing, as if it'd all been re-hearsed and we were just carrying through with the parts. I started calling Mrs Hammond Val. I said Val this, Val that, or, 'I don't understand, Valerie. What was that again, Valerie?' I wanted to show them, to show her, how she was mine, and there was too much between us for anything or anybody to interrupt. I wasn't talking to Mrs Hammond. She didn't exist any more. Valerie being here proved it.

'We didn't know where you were,' my father was ex-plaining.

'We rang up the football club and they said they didn't know either. We were all worried. Then I met Mrs Ham-mond by chance down City Road, and I asked her to come up, just so she could talk to your mother. Your mother was . . .'

'I think Val's tired,' I told him. 'Do you want to be getting back, Val?'

'And when we heard you'd been dropped we wondered what had happened.'

'Do you want to be going, Val?' I asked her again.

My mother had flushed. She clenched her hands together in her lap, seeming helpless, and staring at the two of us as if we'd planned it all together. 'Mrs Hammond came up here to tell us where you might have gone to,' she said. 'I thought you'd be staying here for the night, Arthur, since you don't seem to have anywhere to go.'

'It'll be more convenient that way for me,' Mrs Ham-mond said. Both the women were putting an accent on, struggling with each other. 'I can get a taxi home.' Valerie, as whenever she wanted to make an impression, was prim. She watched me with that old pleading expression, frightened and uncertain.

'No, I'll come back with you, Val,' I told her.

'It's late,' my father said quietly. 'Let's get it settled quickly. If Mrs Hammond doesn't want you at the moment it's no good you forcing yourself on her. She might have let your room to another lodger.'

He sounded, in this woman's war, too heavy, too crude. His voice seemed to lumber round them and they took little notice.

'I was making arrangements,' she said distantly.

'There you are, then,' he concluded.

'But you can't do that,' I told her. 'That's my room.'

'I don't think it'll be convenient at all if you returned,' Mrs Hammond said in her best professional manner. 'And your mother wants you to stay at home. I wish you could make him see sense, Mr Machin,' she added to my father.

'He'll see all right,' he told her, and looked at me as at some sort of invalid. 'We weren't quite sure . . . we've been a little worried. I'll go and phone a taxi for you myself. It won't take a minute.'

'Val's only trying to be well-mannered,' I told him, angry now that he didn't see how they were using him. 'I'll drive her back.'

She looked at my mother wildly, imprisoned. It was the same maniac-frightened look of the Friday night: a cornered animal. 'I might as well tell you,' she blurted out. 'Arthur and me had a very awful quarrel and I asked him to leave . . . I asked him to leave.'

The two women looked at one another, my mother obviously building up to what she wanted to know, yet not sure of being able to take it.

'I've forgiven Val – Mrs Hammond – ages ago, Mother. She knows that.'

'Forgiven me!' Mrs Hammond reddened with the effort of covering her emotion in front of my parents. She couldn't believe I'd take advantage of the situation. 'I think I should make it clear', she said firmly, 'that it was you who started it. It's wrong of you to twist it like that. I don't know how you can do it.'

She started buttoning her coat. We watched her as though the task involved us all. My mother looked at her as she might at any pro she found me in bed with. Then she said, 'Aren't you going to explain anything at all, Arthur? Don't you think it's time you let your own parents know something of what's been happening? After all, we've supported you through all your troubles before.'

She looked at me directly so she could exclude Mrs Hammond altogether.

'We had an argument – that's all. We lost our heads. It's only natural. We're no strangers, and we've had arguments before. As Val said – it was mostly my fault. I was in a bad mood.'

'You've been at Mrs Hammond's a long time, Arthur.'

'I know. . . . That's why I want to patch it up.'

'Perhaps after all these years Mrs Hammond feels that she should have another lodger.'

We waited to see how this affected the situation – whether it was going to blow us all up. But Mrs Hammond said, 'I'd been thinking of a change. Perhaps a lady this time – or maybe having the house to ourselves for a while.'

'It's the first time you've ever mentioned that,' I told her. 'How can you afford to have it to yourself?'

My mother broke in sharply, 'I'm sure at any rate that Mrs Hammond should not be *bullied* into having you back. If she's been forced to ask you to leave then I don't see that you've any right to demand to be taken back.'

'He *demands* to be taken back', my father repeated, 'as if he owned people.'

They were both prepared to take Mrs Hammond's side if it only meant she'd go away.

'It's for Mrs Hammond and me to decide,' I told him. 'I'll take her home now in the car, and we can talk it over.'

'I'm going home by myself,' she said. 'It's all been settled, if you don't mind.'

'I'll run you home in any case.'

'I'd like your father to ring for a taxi . . . I can pay.'

My mother watched us both with a fierce look, hungry and retching, that sapped all the gentleness and sympathy from her face. It was drained like I'd never seen it. Colourless. 'You can't talk to Mrs Hammond like that!' she cried. 'You talk to people as if they're your slaves just to do your bidding. You *can't* talk to her like that! Dad! go and ring for a taxi, and never mind Arthur.'

He pulled on his railway overcoat, shoving through the silver buttons with his clumsy, curled thumbs, not looking at any of us.

'You're not going with her?' my mother said quietly, as I took Mrs Hammond's arm. She didn't look at her further than where my hand touched her.

'I'm taking her home. I've got all my things in the car.'

My mother finally looked at Mrs Hammond. 'Are you going to let him . . . now?' she appealed to her.

'I'm sick and tired, Mrs Machin! I'm sick of it! I'm sick of him! I'm sick of you! I'm sick of all of you! I don't want to see any of you ever!'

She peered round at us all from deep under her eyebrows, then she was gone out of the front door.

I made a start to follow her, but my mother staggered over to the doorway. 'Leave her!' she cried out, tottering with her rush, holding on to the door frame to keep her balance. 'How could you! How could you, Arthur!'

She was trembling so violently she could hardly stand up. 'How could you! You can't go back.'

'That's what you think of her!'

'I'm not ashamed. You can't go back – not now. Not to what *she* is.'

'Tell me! Have you always felt this way about her?'

'It's for your good, Arthur. Believe me, it's your own good. I can't see you do it. I can't *see* you do something like that.'

'We're trying to help you, son,' my father said, helpless.

'And what of her – mustn't anyone help *her*? What's she going to do?'

'She's no good,' my mother warned.

'I've lived with her too long for you to stop me. You can't stop me going.'

'No good, Arthur,' she moaned. 'She protects her children . . . I protect mine. You can't go back – I've told you. Not now. She's no good. She's no good to you at all.'

'I thought you believed in goodness – in something. Doesn't she count? Hasn't she got any feelings?'

'You saw her feelings. How could you, Arthur? *Crawling* round her like that. Like a filthy little dog. I won't let you go back. You'll have to kill me to get me out of this door.'

Her face had collapsed. All the bone had left it. The skin jolted and folded about like a creased rubber mask. She was nothing I recognized. 'You know I've lived with her!' I shouted at her. 'You know that? Lived with her.'

'We know that – we know how you've been.' It didn't shock her. She'd accepted that a long time ago. But now she could cut it off, and out. I sat down away from the fire.

She knew how easily she could make me feel guilt. My father took his coat off with the drag, the humiliation of wasted effort – a useless uniform. 'You go out of your way to hurt your mother, don't you, son?' he said heavily.

She'd buried her head in her hands and, still in the doorway, was sobbing from shock. 'Leave him,' she mumbled.

'It isn't that, Mother,' he told her, shy and afraid of showing his emotion. 'It's him hurting you I can't stand.' He was trembling too. 'I can't stand that sort of thing. He takes a delight in it.'

'Leave him. Let him be,' she murmured.

'Trying to get yourself a part now?' I asked him.

He stood over me where I was sitting. Then he swung his arm back and smashed me soundly across the face.

'Peter!' she cried at him, and rushed to hold his arm.

But he only intended to hit me once. 'That's for torturing your mother,' he said, his eyes red and teared. 'A woman who's given everything for you.'

They stood across the room to watch, knowing my violent temper. But I couldn't speak for a time. He'd knocked my false teeth into my mouth.

3

ACCORDING to an article by Ed Philips in the *Guardian* there are three kinds of athlete – the animal, the nervous, and the scientific. In Rugby League, a hard game played for money, personal prestige, and an enjoyment composed of these two and other elements, the animal fills most of the ranks.

The nervous athlete, Ed says, is usually seen on the wing – slight build, fast, and very dexterous. He mayn't last long in the game, though he reaches brilliant peaks: a violent injury is often enough to pervert his confidence for good. The scientific athlete is seen most often in the middle, either at stand-off or centre, and succeeds by intelligence rather than sheer physique.

The focus of the three types is found in the scrum-half, for he needs the animal strength of a forward and the nervous agility of his 'backs if he's to succeed at all. He's normally the person who receives most punishment, being, next to the ball, the most important object on the field. For this reason Maurice was tough, he was agile, and he was physically intelligent. He kept his place, Ed said, because, to an observer, he appeared to be impervious to pain. Maurice was the most popular player at Primstone.

His exuberance alone marked him out on the field even to those who couldn't recognize the simple inner mechanism of Rugby League play. This was a big advantage to a player who could never actually produce that final touch of improvisation which distinguishes the great from the good. Also, by reason of his position, he could command most movements on the field and give them his own colouring of either speed, daring, or agility. He could make a player look foolish by the same method, and with that casual inoffensive air which puts the victim alone at fault.

It was this particular device he used on me after, he reckoned, I'd brought him face to face with Judith and her wedding march. I played in the 'A' team a lot after that and whenever I was brought back into the first team he put himself out to make things difficult on the field. The general impression was I'd gone right off form, maybe for good.

I suppose he attached a lot of the blame on to me for having to marry Judith. He wasn't openly angry – we'd probably known each other too intimately for that – so he showed his resentment in the only way he could, without being too petty, by this skilful abuse of the game.

I lived at home now, and my father came down to watch the last home matches, and even travelled like Johnson once had to some of the away fixtures, all the time making a big effort to find them exciting for my benefit. The idea defeated its own ends.

I missed Maurice's company more than I liked to think. I allowed him to make a mess of my play partly because he made me feel I owed him something, partly because I wasn't interested in playing any more. I found more people talked to me now I was off form than ever they did when I was on. They felt I was more approachable. Perhaps I was an even bigger joke.

Maurice didn't invite me to the wedding, which took place at the registry office on the first Saturday after the season finished. Frank and most of the team went along with George Wade. Slomer sent them a telegram and some present or other, and Weaver fixed up a quiet reception. I heard all about it from Frank, to whom I tended to turn more during the close season. By the end of those last few matches I'd lost interest in everything. I just floated along as the wind took me.

Both Judith and Maurice tried to give the appearance it was a natural outcome of events, but Maurice was doubtful how things would work out in the long run. Nobody could believe he wanted to get married. He gave a different impression, however, when he went into a job, in a drawing office, that Mr Parkes, Judith's father, arranged. I wasn't sorry to see him leave Weaver's.

Over the summer, living at home, working at Weaver's, I felt I was slowly drifting back to where I'd been when I first knew Johnson. Maybe for that reason I couldn't even tolerate the sight of him at the distance.

One day, trying to measure my feelings, my mother said, 'Who do you miss most now that you're on your own so much?'

'Maurice,' I told her.

'Were you very good friends?'

'I thought so.'

'Why don't you go up and see him and Judith?' she suggested. 'Isn't her baby due soon?'

'That's one reason I don't go up. Maurice counts me as one of those who pushed him into it.'

'But surely a lot of it was of his own making? You told me Weaver talked him round to it.'

I was tired of the subject. 'Yes,' I said.

'I mean, it was a surprise to you, wasn't it?'

'I was surprised at her parents. They're religious. I was surprised at the way they took it – registry office and all.'

'I can imagine full well how they felt,' she said, suggesting a lot of things. 'Having a belief and church convictions like they have helps you to face up to these defeats, and even helps you turn them into victories.'

'I wonder what Mrs Hammond feels about that. She doesn't seem to believe in anything.'

'Is Judith religious?' she asked.

'I don't think so. At least not like her parents. Maurice'll cure her of any dregs she's got left.'

She nodded absently as if in agreement, probably seeing the case the other way round, with Judith's remnant virtue victorious. 'I've often wondered, since I've been back home,' I said, 'why after a lifetime you still see things as black and white, when you must have discovered nothing is like that. I don't see how you can separate people like you do. I *know* Mrs Hammond isn't evil like you make her out.'

'It may be something *you* can't see,' she answered. 'But that doesn't mean that these divisions don't exist. To *me* things are good or bad. They've got to be. How could you manage if you couldn't tell the difference?'

'But you make her out to be *all* bad. And that's just not

true. She's got good in her. It just doesn't have a chance. . . .'

'You can't expect me to feel like Mrs Hammond.'

'And that's all you can say?'

'I can't see how I can see it any other way. What she's done to you – the way you've behaved – I can't see any good in that if I look all day long.' She thought about it, and suddenly added, 'If you lose someone, through dying, someone you love, surely it's not as bad as finding out that someone you thought loved you in fact doesn't? That's what I mean when I say Mrs Hammond's no good . . . no good for you. She's like something that's left over. You could never be happy.'

These sorts of conversations came up often. I didn't want to impress her with Mrs Hammond. But I was only left in silent rages. There'd be worse moments when I'd be sitting in a chair and she'd go by and unconsciously I'd be thinking it was Mrs Hammond and shove my hand out to touch her. I shook at the thought. I pulled my hand back with an electric pain – except once, I touched the back of her thigh, and gave the impression I was yawning. She knew what it was. I split open and bled.

It was to ease the strain that I dragged myself up to see Maurice and Judith one Saturday afternoon. I knew I was going to see them, but I set off in the car in the opposite direction and gradually, as if I hadn't intended it, worked round to their end of town. They were living in a semi-detached house half-way up the lane between Primstone and Caulsby Castle, the opposite side of the valley from Sandwood. I learned later Weaver had some hand in providing the house, for it wasn't one of the regular City houses. It was only a few years old, post-war, with a bow window at the front and a shallow porch. The garden was fully established, and there was a rough drive of cracked concrete. The area was one normally reserved for lower professional people like married schoolteachers with no kids and accountants without practices.

I made a noise revving the engine at the gate so they'd have plenty of time to bolt the door and barricade the windows. I rang the front door bell thinking they weren't in.

A man in the next garden stopped mowing his lawn to watch. Footsteps ran through the house, and the door was flung open.

Judith was silent with surprise, and flushed. 'Hello, Tarzan!' she said after I'd mumbled a few words. 'Come on in. It's such a surprise seeing you up here. Forgive me if I didn't scream.'

She took me with some pride into a nicely furnished front room, the one with the bow window. It had the surprising appearance of a smaller edition of Weaver's lounge – Maurice's only pattern for the superior way of living. It even had the green-leaved wallpaper and the tea-trolley. 'Isn't Maurice in?' I asked.

She shook her head, smiling. 'Don't tell me it wasn't me you came all the way up here to see . . . Maurice's gone into town. He must have got stuck in the billiard hall. Did you want him for anything special?'

'Not really. I just dropped in to see how you are.'

'You'll have a cup of tea, then. He might be back by the time you've drunk it. Come on in the kitchen while I make it.'

I followed her through the house while she chatted over her shoulder. She was swollen, a different person, and looked a lot more interesting than she'd done before. I'd never seen her so flushed and happy.

'What do you think of the place?' she said. 'It's better even than my mother's house.'

'Quite a palace.'

'It cost us a lot to furnish, although upstairs we've only got the double bed. Look at this.'

We came into the kitchen at the back of the house – it was surrounded on three sides by chromium fittings. 'There're the sink and the taps. A heater. Airing cupboard, ordinary cupboards, shelves, an electric dryer, and bits and pieces. Daddy bought it for us. What d'you think?'

'Some people have nice daddies. It's the best I ever saw. Haven't you got a fridge?'

She took it seriously. 'We'll soon get one. Morry says we need one for the beer. Since I've been in this condition I've been drinking a pint a day. You can tell what the kid'll be like.'

'I see you've got a drive and a garage,' I said, smiling. It seemed too good to be true.

'Oh, now that's a bit *too* ambitious yet. But I'm determined he'll get one, so I can run down into town and not feel so imprisoned up here. The garage isn't very good. . . . Here's the electric cooker.' She turned a switch and put a kettle on to boil.

'How soon is the kid due?'

'Three weeks. But it feels it could come any time the way it kicks.'

'Do you feel it kick?'

'Didn't you know? It's a full back. . . . If it starts moving while you're here I'll let you feel.'

'What're you going to do if it's a girl?'

'It's not a girl. Morry says it's not his if it's a girl.'

She had that intimacy with me which during their pregnancy women usually develop towards other men. She'd plenty of this before, and now it gushed out in an easy friendliness and confidence. It was relaxing. I began to wonder why I hadn't come up before.

We walked down the back garden, which had been freshly dug over, to a low wall at the bottom. Over it was a small field running down to a copse. 'You can see the town from the trees,' she said, leaning her elbows on the stone. 'We went one day for a look. You can see over to Sandwood, too. We're a bit higher up here. You can just see the tip of Weaver's roof and those fir trees in his garden from the back bedroom window.'

As we strolled back, she asked, 'And how are things with you, Tarzan?'

'I'm living at home now. Fairly quiet.'

'You want to get married soon,' she said, carefully. 'We can't have you ending up . . . well, with nothing.'

I told her something about how hard I was trying, and she said, 'It's the best thing that ever happened to me. And to Morry – though of course he wouldn't admit it to anyone. He pulls a face whenever I ask him. You'll be able to imagine.' She laughed, 'Did I tell you I've started going to church? I find it's a big help.'

'How did your parents take it?'

'They've both been bricks. They couldn't have treated us better if we'd been engaged a couple of years. They've still gone on with their Sunday school teaching, *and* they've had to stand some gossip.'

'What did Middleton think to it all? He told Maurice and me he wanted it keeping quiet.'

'Oh, Weaver spoke to him right at the beginning. I don't suppose Middleton could grumble. It hasn't brought him any ill-luck. . . . Morry tells me you're still at Weaver's.'

'Yes. It doesn't look as though I'll budge from there.'

'And you're living at home, you say? What happened to Mrs Hammond?'

'We broke up.'

'What over? . . . I. . . .'

'Nothing – you know, we just lost interest.'

'So you've given up the idea of living in digs?'

'No – I don't think so. I'll wait for things to settle.'

She'd flushed slightly, and looked at me slowly. 'I'm sorry, Tarzan . . . you know, if I had anything to do with it.'

She came across and gave me a strong kiss, and held on to my shoulders tight. 'I truly am.'

'To do with what?'

'With you looking the way you do.'

'You'd nothing to do with it,' I told her, and for some reason kissed her so hard she gave half a moan. We let go and started watching the kettle.

'How are the girls at the Mecca these Saturdays?' she said. 'I don't like putting my nose in now, and they seem to find it a bit of a chuff coming all the way up here to see me.'

'They don't change. One leaves to get married, another comes back from being married.'

'They don't change, do they? I thought *I* never would. I could see myself turning out every week with all those man-hunting women. You know at one time I had my eye on you, Tarzan. Most of the girls did, I suppose. But I thought

I suited you most. We used to discuss it in that powder-room. If you heard the things those women talk about in there! What put me off in the end was the thought of us in bed. Somebody mentioned what a frightful crush it would be. I like to curl up to sleep. With you, there'd be no space.'

'You've got a material mind.'

'But what woman hasn't when she's thinking of getting married? I know, I can laugh at it now. But you don't know what those girls go through every Saturday night at the Mecca. It's more or less an auction sale, and they're terrified of going to the wrong bidder. They all *want* to be bid for – you've got to have *some* prestige. But in most cases they take what they can while they can.'

'I'd have thought the men were in more danger,' I said, thinking one reason I might have taken to Mrs Hammond was because she wasn't a shark of this order.

'Still, you get used to it,' Judith said, her mind wandering off somewhere else. 'I've been surprised myself at the way I've got used to Morry's habits. He's amazing to live with. I often laugh over it when I'm on my own. Last Saturday he was at a loose end and I said, "The garden wants digging. Why don't you do that?" and he *looked* at me. He looked at me and said, "Do you really mean it?" and I said, "Yes. It looks as though it hasn't been dug since the house was first built." You know. And once he was sure I wanted it digging he went out there and dug it all day. He wouldn't come in for a meal or anything until he'd finished it, and then it was dark. He thinks he doesn't know a thing about marriage – he likes to *think* he doesn't – and he likes me to tell him everything he should do. He acts the little innocent, at times. I sometimes think it's only to make me feel guilty.'

I wasn't sure whether she was reassuring herself or just me. It could have been a way of talking about Maurice she'd adopted with her parents. By this time she'd made the tea and we went into the front room again. It was Weaver's habit she'd taken up of calling him Morry.

'If I don't see him today it won't matter,' I told her. 'We start training next Tuesday – I'll see him then.'

'Oh, he isn't going back to Primstone,' she said. 'Didn't

he tell you?' She studied my look of surprise and added, 'He's asked for a transfer and two or three clubs are interested. That's how he hopes to get the car – from the backhander he'll get.'

'I didn't know,' I said. 'What's the reason for him going?'

'Well, I know you two haven't hit it off together. . . .'

'But he's not moving because of me? I might never play again.'

'What he said to me was – he lived so close to Primstone he didn't think he'd enjoy playing there any more. That's all I know.'

'You are staying here, then? You'd not thought of shifting out of here as well?'

'No, of course not. Now don't look so worried, Tarzan. Let's leave football out of it for a while. I'm pretty sick of it myself. No – the only thing he hasn't got used to is my High School accent. He writhes when I say mummy and daddy. Mam and Dad is the way he wants the kid to talk. Doesn't it sound awful? And whenever I try to talk broad he thinks I'm just taking it out on him. He gets really wild at times, you should hear him.'

She gave a cry, jumped to her feet and rushed to the room door. 'He's here! Hide so he can't see you, for a surprise . . . course, I forgot – he can see your car. Let him come in by himself and find us drinking tea, and see what he says.'

Maurice came round the door quietly, pulling off his jacket. 'Hello, Arthur. Never expected to find you at home.' The car had given him time to get over his surprise.

'I thought I'd come up and see how you'd settled.'

He nodded quickly and made a ceremony of going out to hang up his coat. 'Have you been here long?' he said, coming back.

'Long enough for him to have a chat with me, Morry,' Judith said happily. 'I'll pour you a cup of tea. Had your dinner? See – I didn't say lunch.'

'I had a grill in town.'

'Where you been? Billiards?'

'How d'you like the house, Arthur?' he said in the same

quiet voice. 'Does it suit you?' He looked changed, a bit nervous.

'Judith's been showing me. . .'

'He didn't know you were asking for a transfer,' she flung at us before going out to make some fresh tea.

'No,' I told him. 'It's news to me.'

'I've been thinking of moving for a long while,' he said. 'Now I've got this settled and the job, I thought I might as well get it all over with in one go.'

'Get all what over with?'

'Breaking away from the past life.'

We thought about what this meant. 'Are they putting you on transfer?' I asked.

'I've just heard this morning – they've had an offer of three thousand. I might lift a few hundred backhand from that if I try.'

'I can't make out why you're wanting to move now you're settled so close. There'll be all the travelling if you move.'

He worked his tongue thoughtfully inside his mouth, then said, 'I've got tired of playing there, that's all. And Frank Miles is leaving. They'll have to start building up a fresh team very nearly. It's too long. I'll be an old man before they get a seasoned side. I want to get in the Great Britain team this year.'

Judith came back and was pleased we were talking. 'Do you want me to leave you two alone?' she said.

Maurice twisted round sharply. He'd a boil on his neck, covered with plaster. 'What for?' he said.

'So you can have a talk with Tarzan. That's all, Morry.'

'Why should you think you ought to go?' he insisted as if he was suspicious there was some proper rule of behaviour involved. 'You're not a bloody secretary now.'

Judith looked at me to notice this. 'No, dear,' she said, and sat down beside him. 'Anybody would think you were having the baby,' she told him.

'Why?'

'You're so damned nervous.'

'You can see she still acts the lady,' he told me coldly.

'And you're living like a gentleman,' I reminded him, and he pulled a face as though his boil hurt.

We talked, with a cautious interest, for half an hour, then I decided to go. As we stood in the drive Maurice said, 'They didn't send you up here to make me change my mind, did they?'

'No, they didn't!' Judith told him. 'What a way to talk. He was as surprised as I was when I first heard of it.'

'You don't know Arthur like I know him,' he said meanly, 'because there was some talk of him taking over from Frank this season.'

'Yes,' I told him, realizing this might have been one reason for him leaving. 'But I don't think you left much chance of that happening now.'

I got into the car, Judith waved, and I drove off.

*

A lot of trouble was saved at Primstone, when pre-season training started, by Frank's decision to stay on. I knew how he felt about giving up the game, and I wasn't surprised he put it off for another year.

Surprisingly I found myself welcoming training, even enjoying it. I hadn't realized how much on my own I'd been the past few months. Things had settled down now, just as they might before a final and conclusive upheaval.

I even felt confident enough to walk round those parts of City Road I'd been avoiding, and one Sunday I went as far as Fairfax Street. I walked down it and looked at the door a while. I couldn't understand why I hadn't been using it for so long. It was still the same. Still the brown door with the dark greasy handmarks round the knob. The small iron letter-box through which nothing ever came, yet ready to snap your fingers off. I knocked. She wasn't in or she didn't answer. I tried the door and it was locked.

My mother and father had both taken it for granted I'd given up all idea of going back there, and I didn't mean to spoil their illusion until I was once again in my old room. But one day, after my first attempt to see her, my mother bumped into Mrs Hammond in town, and with some bright notion of patronizing her stopped to talk. She'd listened quietly to my mother's gossip, then she'd gone off without having said a word herself. My mother took it as an insult, instead of what it might have been – an emotional necessity – and she told me about it in a confident voice of justifiable anger. 'And another thing,' she added, believing it had worked me up in the same way, 'the clothes she was wearing – the way she was dressed. I didn't recognize her at first. It wasn't until I got opposite her and saw that sly look of recognition in her eyes that I realized it was her. She looked like one of the town poor.'

'Perhaps that's what she is.'

'The way *you* treated her she must have felt a queen.'

'I think she must have at times.'

But I didn't hate my mother for saying this. I'd already seen that she just didn't understand Mrs Hammond. She thought everybody was in most ways responsible for how they were – she applied this rule to everyone, and she always had done. She said, 'I'm granting she does a job few women could do. But I'm sure she could get more assistance than she appears to be getting now if she tried.' But I was so angry I could never answer her.

'Mothers, mothers. Always mothers. Women are never anything but mothers. There's never a wife been born yet. I hate all these bloody mothers and their stinking brats. Can't women ever be anything without kids, kids, all the time? You're not just animals. Mrs Hammond – she's a woman. Somewhere she's a woman.'

She was quiet before she said, almost whispering, 'I'm glad you came away when you did, Arthur. . . . And I'm sure I mean the woman no harm when I say that.'

'Mothers or prostitutes – that's women.'

The second time I walked round Fairfax Street, a Sunday afternoon, I was more determined I would see her, even if I had to beat the front of the house in. I knocked loudly, and could fairly hear the scurrying to windows in the other houses as the sound echoed down the Sunday-dead street.

Knowing she'd take the precaution of looking out of the

front window, I stood flattened against the door until I heard her slow feet the other side. She didn't look surprised, only older.

I had to decide then, at that first glance at her eaten face, whether I was going on.

'I came to talk,' I told her. But the words themselves, no longer intimate, showed the distance that a few months had put between us. They nudged something inside her, gave her a recollection she couldn't quite grasp. She looked just another woman with the weight of the world's dirt on her shoulders. Ian stood behind her and looked round her skirt, much bigger, paler, and more bloated than I could remember. 'Shall I come inside?'

'I'm cleaning. It's untidy.'

'I'm used to that,' I reminded her. 'Or can you put your coat on and we'll go for a walk?'

The idea was beyond her. She could never understand how I liked walking with her. She frowned, and suddenly looked uncertain. 'Is there anything you want?' she said.

I was about to explain it all. Somebody walked past behind me, I said, 'No.'

I looked at her once more to encourage her to make an effort. All that was there seemed a residue of what I'd known. This wasn't Val. It wasn't Mrs Hammond. It wasn't even the woman my mother knew. It was the petered out uniform which Mrs Hammond had once worn. I walked away. Later I began to wonder if she'd recognized me.

Frank Miles made me vice-captain, even though the team didn't usually carry one, and I started playing football harder than I'd ever played before. It was Frank's job to teach me the fundamentals of leadership, though this only meant that at the beginning of each match he'd say, 'Watch me, Art.' But apart from that I was under his care. He lifted me up and put me back on my feet.

I took his gesture seriously. More seriously than I'd done any other. I trained every night, apart from official training Tuesday and Thursday evenings, and would run round the estate in a track suit like a great hooded bear. My mother would have a bath ready when I got back, and afterwards my father rubbed liniment into my legs in front of the fire. The feeling of fitness, as I went through a routine of weight-lifting and exercises each day, was a big consolation. I felt myself changing more and more into the professional athlete, the super ape beyond reproach, the type I'd resented in other players. I drew it on like a welcome disguise. I ran in one or two races at Stokeley Stadium on Sunday mornings against other pros.

I used to see this physical superiority reflected in the eyes of those tigers I was going to tackle or run through. I watched their eyes with a distant interest, as if I wasn't really taking part in the game, and I ran towards them and over-powered them with the same detached satisfaction.

I began to enjoy running with the ball, really to want it, lust for it, like I never had before, moving to openings and breaking through and running with my elbows and knees high so that it really hurt to hold me. Added to this was the agility of all my persistent training, and almost every time Frank served the ball to me he was putting me into a gap and I was doing something spectacular. I developed a good hand-off – I banged each time at the tiger's nose with the base of my wrist, and the sound of that tiny crunch gave me the satisfaction a mechanic gets from the sound of machinery coming into place at the right time. I found when I had to cover I could cross the field running fast yet feeling poised at the same time, and taking most wingers in my stride I'd throw them neatly over the touchline and against the concrete balustrade. This became such a habit and crowd-pleaser that they'd leave all the wingers for me – to turn their heels in the air and crack their nuts against the low wall. It was a sort of professional signature.

By this time, the beginning of spring, I'd moved from home to a flat in the centre of town with which the club suddenly found it necessary to provide me. It was over a small women's department store, just off City Centre – furnished by the club, it must have set them back four or five quid a week. It meant I'd to be always at home to people like George Wade, Riley, occasionally a quickly ageing

Weaver – on Saturday mornings it became something of a meeting place for all the 'sports'. We collected there for a few drinks, a talk, then drifted over, one big happy family, to the Booth. Maurice, who'd moved to another club, came twice. The first time was just after I'd moved in, and he brought Judith, perhaps as a safeguard. They'd left Shirley, their baby girl, with Judy's mother.

The second time he came alone. He was beginning to regret having moved from Primstone. We were third in the League, and I knew he'd have welcomed a move back. Like me, he hadn't made the national, or even county, side.

'I've thirty miles to travel every Thursday for my pay, and thirty miles back, and the same over again Sat'days,' he explained. On Tuesday nights he had leave from his club to train at Primstone.

'You made something like a big mistake ever moving.'

He shrugged his over-padded shoulders. 'What d'you think they'd say now,' he said, 'if I asked to come back?'

'They weren't pleased on you leaving. They thought it had something to do with you getting married . . . and that. Anyway, why don't you ask Weaver?'

'I don't like asking him – I reckon he was upset at me moving and he's done enough for me already. I couldn't ask him. I've to make them give back three thousand quid.'

'It sounds big.'

'You could make them do it, Art,' he said directly.

'How?'

'You and Frank – you're the draw up there these days. You've only to breathe different and they'll fit in.'

'That's why you've come to see me?'

Being Maurice he didn't want to admit it. He shook his head. 'I can't go and ask them straight to their faces. Imagine Riley's face for one. I'll lose money over it as it is.' He frowned and pulled a beaten face.

He didn't say anything when I told him I'd do what I could. He went to the door, nodded his head, and went on out.

I watched him from the window as he jostled in the Saturday crowds, unnoticeable, making his way back home

*

Weaver's announcement of his retirement coincided with Maurice's arrival back at Primstone. Everyone knew his move to have been a failure. They blamed it on him getting married. Young Kelly, the scrum-half who'd taken over Maurice's place, was a long way from first team experience, and had difficulty in learning fast. When he dislocated his shoulder from being too slow and too keen at the same time, Maurice's return was speeded up.

He came too late to be eligible to play in the Cup matches, which meant, with the 'A' team scrum-half, we lost to Widnes and were knocked out of the Cup. It was a big disappointment after a good season, and some people blamed Maurice for arsing around. In the Top-Four play-off we were beaten in the final. We had a collection and gave Weaver a plaque with the club records on and a list of signatures. Neither Maurice nor George Wade could tell me why Weaver had suddenly chosen this moment to retire to Torquay, but George was clearly upset, and turned up twice to training without his dog. When I went to say good-bye to Weaver he gave me a watch.

I saw Mrs Hammond again, one Saturday morning, as I was crossing from the flat to the Booth with Maurice.

I sent him on into the Booth, and waited for her to come up. She was walking near the kerb and looking through the passing crowd at the shop windows.

'Hello, Val,' I said as she was about to bump into me. She swayed as her head swung round sharply. She had Ian with her. Her face was white and bony, though she had some lipstick smeared on which missed the shape of her lips.

'Hello, Arthur,' the boy said as if I'd seen him every day of his life. 'There's Arthur, Mam.'

She grunted and pushed by. I followed her a couple of steps. 'Aren't you going to stop and talk?'

She didn't say anything, and I followed her again. I knew she'd recognized me, knew who and what I was.

'With you in them clothes?' she said. I was in a new lounge suit. Ian put his hand out to touch it and say, 'Suit'.

'Come and have some coffee in the Booth upstairs,' I said.

She laughed and didn't stop moving through the crowd.

'I don't mind,' I told her. 'Why should you?'

'Hello, Artar,' Ian said, his head lolling and bobbing in the wake of his mother. A few people turned to watch our procession.

We were nearly opposite the flat, and when she chose to cross the road it was as if it was the flat she was making for.

I followed her as she dodged between the traffic, scarcely heeding it. She must have thought I'd given up, or just forgotten that she'd met me, for when I grabbed her arm and forced her into the door she seemed more than surprised. 'Do you want to see upstairs?' I said to Ian, and lifting him rushed him up.

He pressed against me, shy and afraid, and when I put him down he looked round for the door. His mother called from the bottom of the stairs, and he made some attempt to go.

I took him to the open window and showed him the Saturday crowd and traffic below. The noise drowned his mother's voice. He watched with his mouth open as the roofs of the double-deckers passed almost within reach.

She stood in the doorway and screamed at him. 'Come and get him,' I told her.

Ian began to struggle and whimper. 'If you don't put him down I'll fetch the police,' she said.

She waited a minute then clattered down the stairs. I let Ian go and he ran after her.

'What did she say?' Maurice said, when I joined him.

'Nothing.'

'She said nothing, kid?'

'She's dead.'

He looked at me a while, and said quietly, 'I shouldn't worry, Art.'

'Worry!' I said.

He must have mentioned this episode to Judith – I'm not

so sure he didn't stop in the Booth doorway and watch me – for it was one of the first things she mentioned when I went up to the Mayor's Parlour, as they now called their house.

'Do you see her much?' she said, half-concerned.

'I don't see her at all,' I told her, and she didn't mention her again.

They had Shirley out on a rug on the back lawn and we spent the Sunday afternoon playing with her. 'Come on you little bastard,' Maurice would say and the kid'd giggle like hell. 'Yes – *you* I mean. You funny little bastard you,' and he tickled his stubby finger into her belly.

'He's always calling her that,' Judith complained to me.

'Well, she nearly was,' Maurice said seriously. He rolled over and over with her, holding her like a precious ball.

'He ought to be in a circus with her,' Judith said. 'Come on, Tarzan, you and me'll go in the house and get some beer.'

When we were alone she said, 'Do you think Morry likes being married? You know – right at bottom. Do you think he's got over it?'

I didn't think she'd have asked me if she wasn't sure herself. 'It's the only way he'd ever have got married. He's the luckiest man to have tumbled with you.'

'But I think he's beginning to find it a bit of a strain. It's only natural for a man like him to be laying a different woman each night.'

'You're soft with him, Judy. You have to treat Maurice hard – to get anywhere.' I was irritated by her for flaunting Maurice like this – showing off her security. She was a different woman from the one I'd known in the shop doorway. Marriage had 'made her'.

'*You*'ve found that?' she said. She opened the fridge door and pulled out the beer. She watched me open it, and we both poured it into glasses. 'What's he like now, with other women?'

'They call him daddy.'

'Do they? Really?' She laughed.

'Don't let him know,' I told her, since it wasn't true. But Maurice was behaving well, and I didn't have the heart to

215

make Judith disbelieve it. We went back with the beer. His small stocky body crouched over the kid.

Later on that evening Maurice and me went for a walk up the lane to Caulsby Castle. He ticked off each house as we passed them, knocking the occupants down into County Hall, Ed Philips-secret-athlete, and teacher types. He liked to keep them that way, then he could make out he was different. We were both laughing when we vaulted the stile, and fell in the long grass in a funny, private hysteria. How long we sat laughing I don't know. We rolled about like a couple of tramps, pushing each other or just pulling faces to start off another peel of screaming. When a couple passed us on their evening stroll, Maurice had only to point to them and say, 'Teachers' and the screams started all over again. We staggered around, pulling each other up, pushing each other down, holding together to keep upright, fighting, and making noises, until, as suddenly as it had begun, it stopped, and we sat cross-legged, exhausted, the laughter dying down in shallow simpers.

We climbed the mound of the castle with our arms wrapped round each other. It was warm. From the top of the hill the valley and city were being swallowed in a low mist, reddened by the dead sun as it dropped in the valley top. Red hot penny in the slot.

'What had you thought of doing after you've finished laking football,' Maurice said, sobered and looking at the sun as if it was a person. 'Still carry on at Weaver's? Open a pub?'

'I hadn't thought. It's a bit early yet.'

'I'd been thinking on starting a business.'

The big red disc seemed to be the right place for him to look.

'When?'

'As soon as I've got enough capital. How d'you feel about joining me?'

He dug at the ground with the toe of his shoe. It was stone dust from the keep. He could never stay still.

'Whose idea is it?'

'The old man's – you know, father-in-law. He's even prepared to come in with us. He thinks I should make a start now, so I can build up something well before I'm due to finish.'

'What sort of business had you got in mind?'

'Locational transport – conveyors, maybe working up to coal screening plant, and that kind of thing.'

I laughed, and he added, 'Parkes has a lot of experience with that sort of thing. He says it's not half as difficult as it sounds. It's something he's always wanted to do himself.'

'He might be right so long as you've a fortune to start off with.'

'You don't need that much, Arthur. Not to begin with. All we need to start with is a good-sized prefabricated building, a bit of transport, and maybe two or three men. It'd be all assembly work at first – contracting, for tenders.'

'But you'd still need *some* money.'

'I've some – you've some. Parkes has a drop.' He looked at me suggestively, but I couldn't see what he was getting at in those dark eyes.

'What about the other thirty or forty thousand?'

'Don't be shy, Art. You've got a bit stacked away – I'm not that badly off. Parkes – he's got a pile, I'm almost sure. While we're still playing we've got a chance to start something like this. Don't you agree? We could live off football to begin with. We wouldn't have to worry about making a living. And that's a big start. Otherwise – it's going to be a pub or oblivion. Look at the way Frank's having to hang on. He daren't stop playing – he's got used to the money, and he finds he won't be able to manage without.'

'If you'd said a sports shop I'd have been ready to believe you.'

'That's no good. A shop's no good. The country's over-flowing with bloody shopkeepers. We want something big, where it's either bust or zoom.'

'Supposing I said all right. You still haven't said where all the money comes from. All we could buy is the desk for the office.'

'Aw now don't be *that* thick, Art.' He looked at me with assumed disappointment.

A long shadow, from the remnant of the castle, curved over the hill we were on. In the air around us a few swallows darted and swayed, and below, in the dark green pool of the small moat, pebbles splashed where a couple of kids were playing.

'You mean Slomer, I bet,' I said.

'He's the money, Art.'

His look of shared confidence only increased and his feet fidgeted in the dust. 'What's the matter? He'd raise a loan. I know for a fact he would. He's done it for all sorts of different people afore.'

'I've sold myself enough, Maurice. Five hundred quid I got. That's all the share I need. He'd want all of you. Don't you know what Slomer's like? You want to ask Ed Philips. Slomer'd want the lot.'

'He'd want to make interest. That's what he's like. He'd want a good investment, and we could give him it. That's the great thing with Slomer. It doesn't matter who you are so long as you work his way. And his way's to make a profit.'

'He's a sick man. He's not like other men. You should see the way he behaves – the way he acts and talks to people.'

'It's his money we want. Not his photograph. . . . Come on, Arthur. I bet you could carry a lot of sway with him. He's a big man. He's the one big string you can pull. I know. And it can take us right out of the ditch.'

I didn't argue with him. We went back, our arms still wrapped round each other, talking about last Saturday's match and the way Mellor played.

He was quiet the rest of the evening, and Judith said to me suspiciously, 'Just what have you been telling him, Tarzan, about me?'

4

JOHNSON had aged quickly in the last year. Whenever he passed below my window – at which he'd give an occasional stare – I'd remind myself how fast the years had caught up and overtaken his appearance. His hair no longer stuck out in a tuft to the left of the neb of his flat cap, and whenever he took the battered thing off a few hairs fluttered out. He'd stopped the rot for a while by gnashing his mouth about in a smart set of false teeth – when they smiled they put his age back maybe five years.

He still came to all the home matches, and had a reserved seat in the stand. When I told him about Maurice's idea he said, 'That's the best thing to do with money. You remember the days when you had none? – and we used to travel up to Primstone on the bus, and to Highfield on the 10. Well, Arthur – we certainly pulled it off. I can't tell you how much I enjoy seeing you run on to the pitch at Primstone and remembering how we first started. You remember the night you signed on? And you kidded me about it? I've laughed many a time at yon. I bet it's a long time since you went up to Primstone on a bus.'

'We used to do a lot together then, Dad.'

'You and that Mrs Hammond, Arthur,' he said, and gave half a laugh. 'She was an old cow – wasn't she a real cow? I could never bear the sight on her.'

'Maurice's asked me to go in with him – in this business,' I told him.

He slotted his pink and white fittings between his thin lips. 'That's you all over, Arthur. Stepped out big all the road up – why should you stop now?'

'There's the question of raising all the money.'

'Money?' he said as though he didn't see what this had to do with it.

'Maurice has the idea I should go to Slomer for it. He thinks I could raise a loan there.'

A small bubble came out of the corner of his mouth, and burst. 'You don't think it's a good idea?' I asked.

'Nay, don't ask me about that. But you know how I feel about people like that.' He wondered what impression he should give me, and why I'd asked him. 'You'd make a big mistake going to Slomer for anything,' he decided.

'I'm glad you said that,' I told him. 'It's what I said to Maurice myself. The whole thing's a washout.'

219

Two weeks before the season started I took a holiday with Maurice, Judith, and the kid, Frank, Elsie, and their Ken. We all went to Scarborough. Frank and his family came in my car and Maurice in his. We raced there through York and Malton in a couple of hours, and stayed at a hotel George Wade had booked for us. He came over himself with his wife on the Sunday to see how we were and to work out the set moves we'd devised during training.

I liked Scarborough. We sat in deck chairs on the beach at South Bay and watched Shirley's first efforts with the sand and Kenny bathing near the shore. It smelt of work. But it was full of the sea. The smell of the sea and the smell of work shrouded the place. The smooth misty curves of the man-cliffs, big and amiable and intimate, the stumpy little harbour curled round the fishing smacks, wallowing in rows, the silver scales of the fish jewelling the pier, the black seaweed rocks and the sand – it was an old comfortable smell. I leaned back in the chair and let it come right in my body, and felt it there. I felt the bay inside me, the rocks and the sand. It was old, and it had been lived in by hard people; they softened each other. Scarborough was a mellowed place.

'I forget to mention it afore,' Frank said suddenly and deliberately, 'we're expecting another.'

Elsie looked up sharply and giggled. 'He meant to keep it a secret,' she said. 'But he's been bursting his buttons to tell you all along. Don't you think he looks a bit shy?'

'He looks a bit out of pocket to me,' Maurice said.

'Congratulations,' George Wade said, and pulled the lead of the dog gently. He leaned round the expanse of his wife's front, who was giggling too as if she already knew. 'What do you want this time, Frank? Another doctor, or a nurse for a change?'

'Oh, it better be a girl this time,' Elsie said. 'I want a bit of company myself in the house.'

'We've to come to the day when we see you married Arthur,' Judith said.

'That'll be the day,' Maurice told her in a murmur. He'd covered Shirley's leg with sand, imitating her gurgle.

'I thought he was the most eligible bachelor in town,' Elsie said. 'I'd have thought. . . .'

'It isn't that they don't like him,' Maurice explained, watching me carefully. 'But Arthur believes in falling in love.'

'I should hope he does,' Elsie said. 'Why else should he get married?' Then she blushed and tried not to look at Judith.

'There you are, then,' Maurice told her. 'All explained.'

'Don't you want to get married, Arthur?' Elsie asked. 'Don't you believe in it or anything like. . . . ?' Her head lolled forward so she could see me along the row.

'Don't be so daft,' Frank told her, lightly. 'Maurice's only having you on, Else.'

'No, but I'd like to know,' she said. 'You do *believe* in marriage, don't you, Arthur?'

'Yes,' I said, blushing for her, and at Maurice's amusement.

'Well then, Maurice,' she said. 'What're you trying to say?'

'I wasn't saying anything no different,' he told her. 'I just said he believed in love.'

Elsie was quiet, thinking how far the joke went.

'Have you thought any more about that offer?' Maurice said to Frank.

'What's that?' I asked him. 'You haven't been asking Frank for money as well?'

Maurice pulled a face. 'How could I do that? I asked him how he'd like to work with us, that's all.'

I looked at Frank, who was watching Shirley intently as she crawled between his feet. 'I hope you haven't been taking him seriously?' I said. 'Because there's no way of raising the money. When it comes down to it's going to be a sweetshop.'

'We'll have the money,' Maurice said, dryly. 'You don't have to worry over that, Frank.'

'You're listening to a magician as far as I'm concerned,' I told him. 'Where he's getting it from I don't know – and I'm supposed to be one of the partners.'

Frank leaned down and picked Shirley up and sat her on the thickness of his thighs. 'It's not that I've anything against the idea,' he said. 'But for me, Maurice, I've got to have a solid sort of security.'

'And so have I!' Maurice pointed fiercely at Shirley.

'I know that, Maurice. But you're just starting. Kenny's well on the way now. We're in it right up to the hilt, and we can't go changing about unless we know we're moving to something pretty definite. I hate the bloody pit, but at least I know where I am with it. With a scheme like yours – I'm not saying you shouldn't go on wi' it – things mightn't turn out as you'd planned.'

'But don't you see, Frank, you've got the chance here to do something different, reaching a position you'll never reach down a pit. You'd never have to work underground again.'

'Aye,' Frank said. He stroked Shirley's legs. Elsie looked at him anxiously. 'I'd give almost ought to get out on the pit. You can see how it all strikes me.'

'He's holding you a carrot,' I told him. 'I don't see why you take it so seriously.'

'Christ! I wish you'd stop saying that!' Maurice said.

Nobody said anything for a while. We watched a couple trying to row a boat through the breakers. Then George said, 'I think you'd be unwise to start anything like that now. You both should wait until you've finished playing football – and I hope that's many years ahead.'

'You'd offer Arthur a job as trainer, then where would we be?' Maurice said.

Judith lifted Shirley off Frank's knees as she began to cry. 'Come on baby, then.'

'He might be better off doing that.'

'You're talking as wet as Arthur, George. The advantage of starting now is that we've got our football money to live on.'

'And that never did any footballer any good – living off his football earnings alone,' George said. 'It's just not a good proposition. Straight after the war – and I'd have said yes. But now – you need a lot of luck.'

'I've got lucky fingers,' Maurice said.

'For football. I don't say for anything else,' George said.

'You see, Elsie,' Maurice suddenly turned to Frank's wife, 'the woman Arthur wanted – well, he couldn't keep her.'

'He couldn't?' she said, unaware of the venom. 'Who was it, Arthur?'

But nobody could tell her.

A couple of days later when the thought struck me I asked Maurice if he'd touched Weaver for a loan. 'He wrote back straight away,' he admitted. 'Said he couldn't stand a strain that size, and in any case he's retired from providing general public assistance. He didn't think the idea was a bad one though.'

'How much did you ask him for?'

'He said when we did get finally started we ought to have a site near Primstone – good publicity and that. He thought we might get cheap labour, maybe volunteer labour, to clear the site and get the building up.'

'But how much did you ask for?'

'You don't like Weaver much, do you, Art?'

'I've never said that. What I don't see is how you can reckon on the faintest chance of anyone backing you. You're not considered to be a reliable person, Maurice. That's what Frank was trying to tell you the other day. You think I'd make a better impression on Slomer so you ask me. But it's still no good. Slomer doesn't have his eyes closed all day. . . .'

'You're a wet rag, Art. Where've you got to? I can't see you any more since that Hammond woman dropped you. Where d'you drop your guts?'

'Don't get me too excited, old dear.'

'You're the big boy, Arthur. Me – I just get pushed about. I drop the job right now. I'll choke if I as much as mention it again.'

It was one of the restrained arguments we had during the holiday. We were both toying with the idea, and Maurice was the only one to admit it. The next couple of days marked out our differences more clearly than ever before. We both knew how much we were considering the scheme, and we were both cut up because I did nothing about it. Something held me back – a memory of already having had my fingers trodden on. But Maurice saw nothing but my dumbness.

It only once developed into a fight, when the two of us and Frank had gone out in a rowing boat with the idea of fishing. Maurice started swimming as soon as we were a couple of hundred yards out, and circled the boat, trying to tip it. When I jumped in after him I caught my foot on the side, and Maurice could scarcely keep afloat with laughing as I threshed around, spouting water. When I caught him we quickly became intense. And Frank, seeing we were seriously concerned with drowning each other, brought the boat over and lifted up the oar. 'I'll crack thee on the skull, Art, if you don't break away,' he said. I strengthened my hold on Maurice, and the next thing I knew something had crashed against my shoulders and numbed my arms. I let go and floated on my back, dazed. 'Now get into the boat, Maurice, and grow up for Christ's sake,' Frank shouted at him. He pulled the bag of muscles on board, then drifted the boat over to me and lifted me under the arms. 'You're like two bloody babies,' he said as he rowed back. We lay breathless on the bottom. He didn't say anything else till the boatman caught the bow and dragged us on to the sand.

'You're a right pair of partners,' he said, and went ahead to join the women. An hour later we were all on Castle Hill finding out who could drain a pint bottle of ale first.

*

We came home determined we'd all go to Scarborough together the next year. I'd just got back from running Frank and his family out to Stokeley when I found George Wade already waiting at the flat. He told me Slomer had died.

'It was on the Sunday I was with you at Scarborough I got to hear of it as soon as I arrived back – I'd thought o sending you a message. Then I thought it might be better to wait until you'd got back. I want you and Frank to represent the team at the funeral, tomorrow.' It was only the second time I remembered seeing George without his dog.

Slomer had pulled a plug out somewhere. I heard myself repeating contracts, orders, details of building construction, questioning employees about the tenders that'd gone out, the contracts we had on hand. George watched it all emptying away and said, 'Naturally, Slomer didn't really mean anything to us personally. There's nothing like that involved, Arthur. It will just be a straightforward appearance by you and Frank. You needn't hang about there afterwards. Well. . . .' He gave a big sigh, and sat down, taking off his homburg. 'It's the hand of Fate, I reckon. That business Maurice was talking about. The hand of Fate sure enough. What do you say?'

'Yes, George.'

'I think this is one of the most important days of my life,' he said pointedly – looking at me with some appeal.

'Why's that?'

'Well – it goes back a long way, Arthur. Some time before you could remember what Primstone was once like. But I've always looked at the club – the ground, the people in it, those who were responsible for running it – as a sort of society. I like to think I've taken a hand in running it. Do you know what I mean? It's been a place I've been partly responsible for governing. I know it sounds a bit of a shut-in attitude. But right from the beginning, over thirty years ago, that's how I've looked on it. And for as long as that it's been dominated by one individual or another. One minute Weaver, the next Slomer, and so on, squabbling and changing about. Now they've both gone. One of them – well, he might just have been disillusioned – the other one has died. You could say Weaver tried to be too kind, and he was abused, and that Slomer didn't have the physical strength. But there it is. They've both gone now. And for the first time we'll have a committee running the club.'

He stared at me to see if this meant anything to me, then he picked his hat up from his side and swivelled it on his hand.

'The way you're talking, George, I'm beginning to think you've been looking forward to this.'

'No. I don't think anybody could say that. I've tried to be fair all along. Naturally, of the two I preferred Weaver. But that was just my personal choice. I can't say I'm very sorry or grieved that Slomer has died. But on the other hand, I've never looked forward to it in the way you're suggesting. If anything, you could say it was something I'd been expecting.'

'It certainly wasn't something I was expecting.'

'I don't know about you, Arthur. You're one of those people who usually keep a tight band round their emotions. I could never tell for instance whether you were relying on that business venture or not.'

'We hadn't a chance, George. You've no need to worry.'

'It's things like this that can ruin a team, particularly at the beginning of a season.'

'Slomer should have left it that bit later?'

'Now lad. . . .' He stared at me thoughtfully, unsure of how I felt. But any observation he wanted to make was thwarted by Maurice's knock and his gay rush into the room. I suddenly realized how brown the week's holiday had made him.

'Well, well, well, what do we find here?' he said. 'Any news?'

'Of what?'

'That's a point,' he told me. I couldn't make out why he was so gay if he'd heard. 'But . . . are you listening to this, Arthur? . . . any moment today, or tomorrow, or – at the very very most – the day after tomorrow, I'm expecting just a teeny message from Slomer to say. . . .'

George's eyes opened wide, then his mouth, and he let out a huge bellow of laughter. He dropped back in his seat and shook like a jelly. I even started smiling myself when I saw Maurice's bewildered face.

'Oh . . . don't let me stop you. . . .' George said between

fits. 'I didn't mean to act like this. It was just you . . . on top of everything else.'

'Where's the drink?' Maurice said, looking quickly round the room. 'Don't tell me you've got George to start drinking?'

'No . . . it's all right, Maurice, really,' George assured him. 'You go on, lad. Take no notice of me.'

'Well, I was going to say – ' Maurice said, discouraged and puzzled.

'Do you mean you got in touch with Slomer before we went away?' I asked him.

'That's what I'm telling you, Art. It's all fixed – all being well. He seems to have the liking for you. When I mentioned you were in with it . . . this's on the phone, I'm telling you about. I wrote him a letter, after laying the whole thing out . . . I didn't tell you while we were away because I wanted it to be a surprise. Then when I got home and found no message I thought he might have dropped it here. . . .' He was looking from George to me with growing bewilderment, thinking his long, breathless explanation should have cleared everything. George, meanwhile, had got control of himself, and sat in jowelled severity, urging me with his look to tell Maurice.

'Slomer's dead, Maurice,' I told him. George was nodding. 'Last Sunday. While we were away.'

There were two things with Maurice – never show any real feeling if it's to do with pain, and if you have to then wrap it up in a smile. He smiled cheerfully. 'Well, that clears it up, Arthur,' he said. 'What d'you say?'

'Yeh.'

'You're sure he's dead – not shamming or ought?' he asked reflectively.

'The funeral's tomorrow, Maurice,' George told him. 'Arthur and Frank are representing the team. I'll be there for the committee.'

'And very nice too,' Maurice said. 'The only trouble is the real people who lose by it won't be there at all.'

'What do you mean?' George tried to sound severe after his laughter.

'Nothing. . . . He picked a good time to drop off the branch.'

'If you want to come,' George said, 'that's perfectly all right by me.'

'You won't find me in church at a time like this. I drown 'em not drip 'em.'

'You'll get over it,' George told him quickly. 'I'll be going Arthur – you two can get over your disappointment together. You might ring me later. We can arrange where to meet tomorrow. I'll let Frank know myself.'

Maurice said, 'It's all right, Doctor. I'm coming too.'

'Aren't you going to stay a bit, Maurice?' I asked him.

'What? . . . ' He waited for George to get out of the door and down a few steps, then said, 'Stay with you, cock? What for? So we can grow old together?'

'We might talk.'

'Talk. Talk. That's all I ever did with you. Arthur. Talk. If it hadn't been for all your talk and hanging around we'd have been set up clean and fine now. As it is. . . . Hell! What am I staying here for? I just don't know you any more.'

He was gone. I heard George's voice talking to him quietly on the stairs. I locked the door.

The funeral was a procession. It seemed the town stood back when Slomer died, and nobody was quite sure what it meant or what should be done. The result was that hardly anything was not done, and all the big businesses sent representatives, and all the taxi firms sent all their cars. The hearse was a solid mass of flowers, from which seemed to protrude only the four wheels below and the driver's head on top. The haphazard and instinctive spectacle brought out large crowds, and the whole thing went off in an atmosphere of awesome bewilderment.

George, Frank, and I shared a taxi with a couple of other men who'd known Slomer slightly, in a business way. One of them, impressed by the number of people who ducked down as we passed to peer in the window, was saying, 'It's the end of a way, you know.'

George lifted his shaggy eyebrows, and looked lost without the dog. 'How do you mean?' he said patiently.

'With Slomer gone,' the man told him, 'you'll find all the big combines finding it easier to move into town. You mark my words. There'll be no king-pin any more. We'll become like all the other big towns – socialist, impersonal, anonymous. The only thing we'll be known by' – he waved his gloved hand at me – 'will be the standard of our football team.'

He stared out at the crowd as the column wound up Market Street towards St Teresa's. It was hot. 'Just look at that,' he said. 'There won't be any more funerals where half the town lines the streets to watch the passing of a man they hardly knew. . . .' He flicked his gloved fingers. 'We'll have a football team.'

George fingered his tight collar. 'And thank God for that,' he said.

5

I DROPPED back into a hole in the ground, and just thought about football. Living was a formality to be got through without looking too closely. I trained more and more each night, running miles, skipping for so long I went dizzy, shadow-boxing till I seemed to beat my own shadow. I was on the move all the time, until I felt I'd driven all feeling out of my body, and it just acted like it'd been trained. I found I'd lost interest in scoring, and was going out of my way to hurt and cause trouble. If I scored, it was all right, but I was taken up completely with running with the ball, and stopping tigers as if they'd run into a cliff. I imitated and didn't play football. It was wrong to be alone, and I reckoned I didn't notice. I told myself I'd been right all along: I had no feelings. It was no good acting any longer as if I had.

When the letter came I took it as just another piece of slush from a schoolgirl. I picked it off the shelf at Primstone where most of the fan mail was left and at first I stuck at the single word written on the top: Sunday. I reminded myself this was Tuesday, and wondered why anybody should put the day on a letter like that. It said Mrs Hammond had been taken to the Riding Hospital. Emma Compton wasn't sure whether I'd be interested in knowing. Those taken to the Riding weren't expected to live.

I told Dai about it and left before training began. I drove straight through town to the Riding which stood on the ridge overlooking Highfield.

I had a glimpse of her. She was either asleep or unconscious. A small amount of argument produced the sister and a lot more brought out the doctor. A small, square Scot, around my own age, he took me into his office when he heard who I was. 'Arthur Machin – you play for the City,' he told me. 'What's your interest in the patient?'

'She used to be my landlady. What's gone wrong?'

'She has a clot of blood on the brain,' he said eventually, after he'd told me how he watched the City now and again. 'There's little we can do about it at the moment,' he added.

'How will it affect her. . . . You know – is it serious?'

'Serious? . . . Yes, it's serious.' He looked at me directly, assessing how much I was involved.

'Will she die?'

I expected him to smile at my naïveté. 'No, of course not,' I expected him to say with a reproving slap on my shoulder. 'I'm afraid I can't say.' He took in a deep breath through his nose, and wondered if it wouldn't be more interesting to talk about football. 'I know what you're thinking,' he said. 'But that's how it is at the moment. You'll appreciate that she's critically ill.'

'How soon will you know what's happening?'

'Let me put it this way. The clot, we believe, is in the more dangerous part of the brain. It might clear up without any effect whatsoever. On the other hand it could be fatal. I'm sorry it has to be like this, but it's better than just an opinion, don't you think? You're no relative of hers?'

'No – she was just my landlady.'

'So you're not emotionally involved.'

'Does that make any difference?'

'It's always useful in a case like this.'

'You can give me an opinion as well as the facts, then?'

'If you want my opinion, I don't think she has much chance of living. That's the face of it. . . .'

'Can I fix a private room for her?'

'Well. . . . It might be possible for you.' He looked me up and down as if my body was directly concerned in this. 'I'll see what I can do. Unofficial, Arthur, as it were.'

'Are you full?'

'We're always full. But we've a pretty rapid turnover of places, so to speak. I think I can arrange it. I'm fairly new here myself.' He smiled slightly, friendly, admiring the fact he knew me and that I played Rugby League the way I did. 'I hear you're scheduled to go on tour to Australia this summer.'

'I stand a chance. I doubt if I'll go. Have you any idea what caused her to be ill?'

He suddenly felt I wasn't appreciating his sympathy and friendliness. I felt I was cheating him: he was decent.

'How long have you known her?' he asked.

'Something like four to five years.'

'And recently?'

'I haven't seen her to speak of for over a year.'

This eased the situation for him.

'The primary cause, I should say, is an exceptionally low morale. If you haven't seen her for the past year you mayn't know anything about it. She's weak all through, and to be frank that's the reason, together with the position of the clot, I don't think she'll live. She hasn't the strength, and more important I doubt if she even has the will.'

There was a long intense silence, in which he didn't seem to have realized he'd stopped speaking. There wasn't a sound in the room. It seemed it was going to last for ever, and I could think of nothing to say, no sound I could make, to break it. Then he added, 'She's the norm here, although we usually deal with older people. You'll understand I'm speaking dispassionately.'

'I wouldn't care to hear you talk about somebody you

didn't like,' I said, and he laughed. I started to try hard to like him. 'But I want the best for her.'

'Okay, Arthur,' he said. 'But I've every reason to believe she wants to die.'

'What about her children? She's got a boy and a girl.'

'They're being taken care of by a relative, if I remember properly. The only one she's got, it seems.'

'Has she any chance at all?'

He paused to assess the tone of my voice. 'Don't let me paint it too black. I've been open about it. There is some hope. How often do you want to come in and see her?'

'I'd like to come every day.'

'Every day,' he said, and made no effort to hide his mild surprise. 'And you say you've no ties with her – emotional or anything. It'd be better for all concerned if you told me right now if there were.'

'I used to live with her . . . you know – close.'

He sighed and tried to look unpleasant. Perhaps he didn't sense how he was the first person outside I'd admitted it to. 'Why didn't you say you were concerned at the beginning? You needn't have explained the circumstances – you could have just told me . . . well, anything. How do you feel about the situation now? I mean, are you wanting to look after her because I've told you she might die? Do you feel guilty – owe her something?'

'You can call it that.'

'I'm not being sentimental about it, Machin, so let's get it straight. Do you feel you owe her something now she's in this condition, something you never gave her before – or does it go deeper than that?'

'I don't know. You might be right. In any case – I feel I owe her *something*.'

He wanted to continue his attack, but he suddenly softened and changed his mind. 'When did you stop living with her?'

'Over a year ago.'

'It was a final break that never mended?'

'I tried to . . . I couldn't get in touch. I don't know where

I went wrong. She didn't want any more. She was frightened.'

'There was some genuine feeling between you, then? You know, affection – something that might have been permanent?'

'I reckon I spoilt all that . . . I don't want to make it sound *all* rubbish.'

'But there was something.'

'There was on my part. There was everything on my part! . . . But I just *couldn't* make her see it.'

'Wouldn't she see you again?'

'No. She wouldn't have anything to do with me.'

'You must have been specially hard,' he said.

'I wasn't hard! . . . Yes, I was. No, I don't know. I just couldn't get through. I was just like an . . . ape with her. I never realized she wasn't as strong as I tried to make her. I must have knocked her about – emotionally – more than I thought.'

He moved round the office, and adjusted three snake-stem reading lamps. 'What do you want me to do, then?' he said.

'I'd like you to get her the room like you said, if it doesn't mean shoving too many people out. And I'll come and see her every day.'

'I'll make you out a card. You'll probably be her only visitor, apart from the relative.'

'When'll you move her out of that ward?' I said as he started writing.

'Tonight if I can arrange it. I'll show you the room I have in mind as we go out. If anything happens I'll ring you.'

I wrote down the phone numbers of Primstone, Weaver's, and the flat.

From the ridge overlooking Highfield I could look down on the lights sparkling in the faint blue mist – the square-set pattern of the estate, curved and quilted by the folds of the broad valley bottom, Fairfax Street, the concertina roofs of Weaver's, the glint of the river between the squat warehouses. I drove up to the moors. There wasn't a sound amongst the great blank folds of heath. The autumn mist was thickened by a low blackish purple. I felt elated – an elation compressed by some bitterness and by self-reproach, as if at last, really at last, I'd got hold of something which before had always slipped my grasp, and which I wasn't too clumsy to hold. Now it was real, and held me. I was no longer alone.

*

I went up to the Riding each night.

Mrs Hammond was in a coma. It seemed only a matter of time before she died.

When I reported for training on Tuesday night, George was waiting for me at the players' entrance. 'There's a message for you, Arthur – from the Riding. They advise you to go up there.' The dog was panting, and George held the car door with fatherly concern.

Everything held me up in town. The car ran out of petrol and I had to run for a can, the lights were fixed to stop me as often as they could, the gears crashed, the clutch slipped – everything as if it was my fault. I left the car – I couldn't drive it – and ran up the hill.

The doctor – a different doctor – and two nurses were just coming out of the room. A room as familiar as my own flat, as Fairfax Street, as Weaver's. The doctor came back in with me to say, 'She seems to be going. How long can you stay?' He left a nurse behind.

I sat beside the bed and held the small hand sticking out from the sheets. It was unbelievable that it had once made great bombs. It was nothing more than a child's. Her large eyes were shut. The skin was stretched tight on her face, dragged into the hollows, gleaming yellow over the bone. Her hand was cold and too still, its fingers clung to mine with an unconscious, lifeless anxiety. A sore hand, stained. She'd been biting her nails and breaking them, and there were thin rinds of dirt. I didn't remember her biting her nails. I thought about it. The vein pumped and pulsed like a wire in her wrist, and the struggle went on in her throat – strings tugging her body to a remembrance of life. Her lips

234

were slightly parted, a tooth gleamed in the tight crevice. Her nostrils were flexed wide to suck in air.

I sat for hours and nothing happened. The doctor came in occasionally. Another nurse took over.

Nothing happened. I kept the hand and stroked it. I'd never had her like this before, and she'd never know it. I pressed my strength into her. I squeezed it through her fingers. I told her not to be mean. Her skin was stained with grease.

She couldn't go, I told her. I told her she couldn't go so she'd believe it. She had to stay and breathe. I told her she mustn't be mean.

In the morning the doctor told me I ought to leave. I noticed how he looked at me – as if there was something there he shouldn't rightly see. But which he'd seen too often.

It was cold outside.

I walked down the hill to the car. It took some time to start it. I drove straight down to Weaver's and waited for the gates to be opened at seven-thirty. It was the first time I'd seen it like that, the first time I'd been so early to work that I was the only person in the shop. It was empty and dead, the lumps of metal lying about the machines like carcasses after a battle.

It came to life with a low vibration of the main loom, then the whine and the shudder as the machines started and belts slipped over the loom, and the floor trembled. Men filtered into the place, their voices, their feet, their blue overalls. A line of sparks curved out as the metal screamed under the grinder; the hiss of hot metal in water. The overhead crane chattered, clanked, groaned, and slowly eased itself forward in a rumble down the shop. The far corner suddenly took fire with a blue light, trembling and sparking as the welders moved their flames over the steel.

It seemed I'd only been out of the room a minute. She was still there, small, rolled up in sheets, her nostrils poised into the air. She looked a thing whose only function was to die.

'She must have a heart of leather,' the doctor said. 'It's

still pumping twenty-four hours after it should have stopped.'

'Does it mean she's still got a chance?'

He pulled his lips together and frowned. 'You should see the end tonight – if you're staying. Her sister-in-law and husband aren't coming.'

'She doesn't look. . . .' I couldn't think of any word to say. He made a grimace with his eyes, sympathetic and resigned.

I fell asleep in the chair. A sleep which was just a struggle to wake up. A large insect appeared on the ceiling, its thin legs spreadeagled from its long plump body. Although it was small I saw every crevice and tiny undulation on its skin. Its two eyes didn't move; expressionless, they stuck out like solid balls, hard and secure. When the legs moved the body arched, the flesh creased, and it shifted rapidly across the ceiling to the wall above the bed. I watched it there a long time as it clung to the smooth paint and made no quiver. Then I suddenly realized how close it was to her: that it was just above her head. I went crazy because I hadn't noticed it before, and I sprang across to the wall to crush it.

And as I moved it dropped quickly down the wall and disappeared behind the bed.

I stood and waited. I watched her to see if it had reached the bed. I began searching, getting slower and slower till I could hardly move at all, and when I finally saw the thing it had grown to twice its size and was standing under the bed watching me. I couldn't move.

I pulled my eyes open thinking I'd heard her whisper. She was still dead except for her breath. Her persistence weakened me. She seemed to grow there like fungus, out of the dead. Persistence of fungus.

The next time I woke a thin trickle of blood was running from her nose. It'd just reached the curve of her lip.

I pressed the bell, and stood back to watch the streak lengthen, and probe its way round the corner of her mouth and edge towards her chin. It received a fresh impetus of darker blood. I opened the door and shouted down the corridor. The nurse was coming at a trot. She put her finger to her lips as she ran. She took one look and was gone.

The doctor arrived, and I was left in the dark waiting-hall. I lay down on a wooden bench and watched the door. I sat up, lay down again, then went out in the cold night air, and looked at all the lights below that no longer meant a thing. I rushed back thinking I heard somebody calling. The hall was empty. I smelt my sweat with the ether.

I wandered into the corridor and down to the wards in the hope of cadging some information, and each time I was turned back by smooth nurses. I started on the wall nearest the door and read all the notices I could find. I worked round the room, reading bulletins, reports, advice, national health regulations, rules for out-patients, no smoking, no spitting, wait on this side of the barrier, ear, nose, and throat. The hall was still empty. I sat in a wheel chair and propelled myself up and down. Somewhere at the back an ambulance arrived and left.

At dawn a nurse came in and asked me what I wanted. She went away and came back with a message that her condition was unchanged. I tried to see the Scots doctor but he wasn't on duty. 'You can wait here, if you wish,' the nurse said. 'But I'm afraid it won't alter anything. It would be much better if you came back later.' She seemed to know me. Below the nurse firmness I seemed to remember a sample at the Mecca. I wondered if she thought I'd changed. I drove to the flat and set the alarm for half-seven. I slept a couple of hours, then went to work.

In the evening I discovered that Mrs Hammond's father was still alive, living in an almshouse at the back of the railway station. I got there the next day just as they were moving him to a home. He didn't understand what I told him and was under the impression I was somebody called Stan. I wondered what would have happened to all of us if his daughter had stayed with him, never done war-work, never gone to Moyston. He must have forgotten all about her: he mumbled on about Stan over the stove as he waited for the car.

They let me see her early Thursday morning. A dressing covered half her face, and though nobody admitted it I felt this was a good indication. I held her hand thinking she might now be able to feel it, but the nurse reckoned to be alarmed when she came in and found the arm exposed.

'Then you think she's a chance of recovering?' I asked her.

'I couldn't tell you, Mr Machin. But we all hope she has, don't we?'

I slept in the chair beside her till morning.

*

The new room was larger than the first – it reflected the difference between the Municipal Hospital and the Riding. And she could see the flowers. Before they'd just lingered there and drooped. Now she saw the freshness as soon as they came into the room. When they showed signs of withering they were taken out. She watched the flowers more than anything – the flowers and the summit of a tree, black with winter, that overlooked her window.

Occasionally she smiled, as if good-naturedly she gave over trying to recall the past, and she just gazed out at me. Her face was small, and smooth, and lay over the sheets like a kid's thinking over the pleasures of the day.

She was back to the girlhood of the photograph she'd shown me – her head leaning back in the sun, her face open to a girl's laugh. For the first time I saw how she had been – without Eric, without me. It was the girl, and the laugh – and in between then and now was emptiness, with everything forgotten.

She'd turn and watch me silently as I came in the door. She never said a word. I sat there – sometimes we swopped a look, inquiring. Every minute passed as a second in the quietness as we made the effort to recognize each other.

One day she laid her hand out of the sheets, cautiously, as if to see what I'd do. I took hold of it. It seemed to confirm our awareness, and mould two pieces into one.

At Christmas I brought Lynda and Ian to see her for the first time. Her eyes widened with pleasure and bewilderment. She didn't recognize but only felt the mutual happiness. As they clung to her on the bed her eyes examined the room in fresh perplexity as she tried to identify their endearment and warmth. Dr MacMahon and the Sister watched the struggle with smiles and a few words of restraint to the kids.

'Why!' she said. 'It's Lynda!'

'And it's me – Ian,' the boy reminded her solemnly. She clung to them with closed eyes.

A week later she died.

6

As I drove in the stream of traffic over New Bridge I had a view of Weaver's over the roof of the next car – the steam from the engine in the stockyard, the metal stocks, the concertina roof with its sooted glass. I had a tune running through my mind, maybe reflecting the assurance my place of work provided in this the most nervous day of the week. I caught the impression of the brown industrial water as it foamed in great arcs over the weir and swirled in slow volutes past the stone embankment and the factory wall. Above the weir, in an apparently still pool, the barges were lying idle, like stubby fingers, roped together below the small cranes and the shiny black coal slip. All this I knew, even if I didn't care to look – the dank smell of the polluted river seeped into the car. But it was all remote.

The man I was giving a lift into town looked across at me, smiling. 'What's it going to be today, Arthur?'

'Easy . . . throw it about a bit.'

'Just the day,' he said.

We both stared up at the low ceiling of grey cloud that obliterated the morning's sun, in view one minute then cut off by the old brick houses of West Street. Once prosperous, the old millowners' houses were now darkened stumps, holding back the refuse of a minor printing works, some houses, a W.M.C., a mill office, and some large irregular shaped shops. They gave a dull, empty response as I watched their flight past the window.

'You'd a shaking last Sat'day,' the man said with the familiarity of the paying spectator.

'One of those days,' I told him bringing the car near the kerb so he could jump out. He took advantage of a general halt of the traffic and opened the door. 'Mind you dispose of them properly today . . . I'll be watching,' he added as if I needed just that incentive. He banged the door and waved.

I parked in front of the Woolpacks. A small figure, shrouded in a large overcoat, emerged from the entrance of the hotel and came and threw a fist at my shoulder.

''Ow do,' Maurice said. 'All right, kid?' He showed his small cheeky teeth.

As we came into the Saloon his dusky face broadened. We joined a small group at the bar, none of whom, with the exception of George Wade, was drinking.

'Hello, Arthur,' he said. 'We were just talking about your new kiddie, Maurice.'

'Is that so,' Maurice said.

'How's Judith?'

'They're both grand. He weighed eight pounds, five ounces – a bloody little tree trunk.'

'That's the way,' George said. 'We'll make a father of you yet.' He murmured some joke in his throat and his small eyes stretched sideways under the hedges of his brows. 'Remember he's to lake at Primstone,' he said. 'Though we've yet to see a father and son lake in the same team.' The others found it fit to laugh a bit – Frank, Maurice, young Arnie, and a couple of nervous 'backs. We moved about restlessly.

Frank, with a slight stoop, watched George through friendly, uninterested, coal-dusted eyes. A white scarf was wrapped tightly round his throat, his face was red, and he showed every sign of having worked the night before. Maurice, looking older and maybe more grotesque than a married man of a few years' standing should, leaned on my shoulder with the same assumed interest. Young Arnie's mouth hung open in a fixed grimace of amusement.

George, supporting himself against the bar counter, knew he was talking froth, but still carried on, fingering the enormous head of his walking stick. Beside him crouched Toby the second like a small seal, its eyes distorted in servility, watching George's neat, polished shoes spread-eagled on the worn carpet.

Crouched round the tables the others in the Saloon were cautious with their own conversation in case they missed any of George's. All of his remarks were passed from mouth to mouth to the far end of the room where a coal fire made a faint, economical glow. The fans, in spite of the heat in there, kept themselves ready to leave should George or any of us give the signal – they were muffled in overcoats and scarves, and I could almost hear them sweating.

Eventually George did look at his watch which he carried below the flap of his sleeve – a recent innovation – and compared it with the clock over the bar which always stood at ten past ten. He excused himself and went to the lavatory. The dog followed him, its lead disappearing into his raincoat pocket. As soon as he'd gone, a bit like a mannequin through an alert audience, Maurice turned on a fresh smile. 'Where're you going tonight, Art?' he said

I told him I didn't know, and he shoved his hand through his short black hair. 'There's a party. Why don't you come and celebrate?'

'Celebrate what?'

He opened his coat and straightened his best suit. 'We'll flatten 'em, cock,' he said. 'I've fifteen quid on – so we better.'

'That's a bit risky, Morry,' young Arnie said seriously after a while. 'Don't let sir know.' He thumbed at the Gents. We laughed thinly at his seriousness.

'I don't know why I wuk down the pit,' Frank said.

George reappeared fastening his buttons absentmindedly, and made Frank's comment suddenly sound bare. He had changed his morning flat cap for his afternoon Homburg.

'I wonder if he made the dog. . . .' Young Arnie began, when George said:

'Time we were moving, lads,' and most of the men in the Saloon stood up. He examined his new watch again. 'Five minutes to two.'

We caught a bus up to Primstone. The car was getting too knocked up to take the hill to the ground, and I didn't bother with it much. I found I was using the bus more and more.

We didn't talk on the way up. The first of the crowd was beginning to thicken either pavement as they trudged up the hill in the thin afternoon drizzle, and the first of the traffic jams was forming.

The grey heavy buildings, stone unlike the brick of the valley bottom, dragged by in procession: the small, varnished wood front of the undertakers' that always made me sure I was going to be killed if I noticed it on the way to a match. I stared at it today as if to dare it. A thick-set, moustached man gazed out from behind the notice in the window at the thickening crowd. The weariness of the climb in the stream of traffic was infectious. I began to yawn a lot.

Maurice was signing autographs by the players' entrance when we caught him up, and we went in single file down the corridor under the main stand. The Visitor's dressing-room was still empty, but everyone seemed to have arrived in the Home changing-room.

They stood about in overcoats, stamping feet, talking quickly, dryly, and passing between the bench and the lavatory. Dai and the masseur were checking equipment in the middle of the room. A groundsman, hunch-backed and immune to the surroundings, was already in the concrete bath scrubbing it out with a stiff sweeping brush, shrouded in a cloud of steam.

I found a place on the bench and absently watched Frank argue with Dai. Maurice was begining to unlace his shoes – apart from Frank he was the only one certain of playing.

But when I had a look at young Arnie again he was taking his coat off too, then his shirt. George must have told him privately he was playing, on the way up. George was beginning to like people who paid him a lot of attention. The boy shoved his hand into the large tin on the floor and brought out a thick string of vaseline. He began to rub the grease into his shoulders, impatiently, then round his ears, already misshapen and inflamed. He had a lot of talk had Arnie – he talked all the time he rubbed the grease in, his abnormally developed muscles quilted with a restrained confidence. Unmarked, they impressed on me a sense of my own maturity. I stood up.

Maurice was naked. He jumped up and down with his customary pre-match excitement, amongst the coated, impatient players. His body, heavily and indifferently scarred, was some consolation. I watched him as if I'd never really noticed him before. His muscles were hard and knotted, fierce little physical intensities. His bowed and prodigiously thickened thighs tucked in to the tight knot of his knees, red and scabbed and about to be bandaged by the masseur.

Three characters came in from the dark passage outside. Well shrouded from the weather, they blinked in the yellow lamplight, and two of them stared benevolently at the players. They'd just been deciding who was to run out there in the rain, the mud, and the cold. The piece of paper that George held drew everybody's attention.

As my name was read out after young Arnie's the kid looked across, his eyes focusing with unmistakable challenge and ambition. I turned away. Why be burnt up about it? Wait a couple of years and see how you feel then. A lot of noise and shouting followed the announcement, and the reserves stood back in the shadows and considered ways of hiding their apparent disappointment by helping. I pulled off my overcoat as George said, 'Thirty-five minutes, lads. Take your time. The other team have just arrived.' He looked about him as if it wasn't odd how he emphasized time so much nowadays. 'I'll bring in their names as soon as I get the list.' He sent one of the committeemen on this errand, then his Homburg bobbed among the busy heads as he elbowed his way over to the masseur's table. He inspected the blue and purple blemishes on Maurice's back. 'Looks like wallpaper, Maurice,' he told him, and leaned down and whispered confidentially in his ear. It was another recent habit of his I resented.

I sat on the bench, took off my shoes, and tucked my socks inside. I tried to think of something to occupy my mind, but as usual nothing came except a vague notion of getting the car fixed sometime. I rubbed some grease over the ankle I'd injured as a schoolboy. I strapped it up thinking it better that Dai didn't see how it'd blown up in the last week or two, then pulled on the blue and red striped stockings and fastened them with tape. I leaned back against the wall and tried to relax before undressing. The water came through my shirt, cool. Young Arnie was almost ready, jumping in a corner, shadow-boxing. He'd only his jersey to put on. I watched, fascinated, the flesh of the kid's heavy shoulders, the lithe muscles sliding across his back. It seemed a greater flexibility than anyone else's, fluid, without hesitation. Had I been like that? I found it better not to look at Arnie for too long. In the opposite corner the two 'backs who'd been with us in the Woolpacks were being strapped up by Dai and one of the reserves. The taller one stood naked, feet astride, chest expanded like a stuffed pigeon, as Dai rolled on several layers of crape and adhesive round his body, covering his ribs and back. By the table, Frank – his belly hanging over his shorts – was rubbing vaseline into his shoulders and neck, and talking to Maurice. George had gone to talk to young Arnie who listened earnestly, diplomatically, to the advice. Toby the second, traced by a lead, was hidden under the bench. The hunchback scrubbing out the bath began to sing a hymn.

I undressed, fastened my shorts, and joined Frank at the table. 'How's it going?' he said with his usual aimlessness, and rubbed his expanded belly with affectionate illustration. 'I'm having to watch this. So's old George. He's bin eyein' me up and down ever sin' I took my vest off.' His coal-dusted eyes blinked, tired. 'Do us me back, cock.' He swung round and I lathered the grease on to the pallid skin, stained by a profusion of blue scars. It was a task I'd reckoned on doing every game since my first.

The familiar smells filled the low room – dry dust and sweat, carbolic, a tang of leather and polish. Above throbbed the steady beat of assembly. I pulled on the number twelve jersey, and as my head came out I caught sight of young Arnie talking to Frank. There were almost twenty years between them. Frank had started playing at

Primstone when Arnie was born. And I knew what occupied Frank most – the fear of letting go of football, of the popularity, the money, and the friendship maybe, and subsiding into the obscurity of his fellow miners, a has-been. This abrupt diminishing of life, just at the point when according to the rules it should be getting larger, was a fear he'd come to recognize too late. It was Frank's first sign of softness. It was something I didn't care over-much to think about.

Feet stamped loudly overhead. A gust of wind and damp air swirled into the heated atmosphere of the room. The committeeman returned with the list of the visiting team's changes, and banged the door authoritatively behind him.

'Still raining?' Frank called. The players collected to see the names. The man's pale face, consumptive, reflected the yellow glow as he lifted his head to the inquiry.

'Aye old lad. It won't ease up now, tha can bet.'

Frank sat back on the bench, his thick hands stretched over his knees, talking to himself. Young Arnie had taken the ball and was throwing it to a player and getting it back in the special way he asked for it. In ten years, I started thinking, he'll be like me. Then it's all over.

'Watch the passing, Arthur,' George Wade whispered the secret. 'It's greasy. They've clever wings out today, both of them – Taylor and Wilki'son, so you'll have to cover fast. Fast!'

'I know, George.'

He must have been hurt. He unbent, and without having looked at me, beyond the edge of my grease-filled ear, he crossed to Frank for a few unnecessary words there.

A knock on the door and the linesman came in. 'Five minutes to go,' he said, and began to inspect the boots and padding. I took my teeth out and put them in my top pocket. 'How's it go, Arthur?' he said, and went on without waiting to find out.

The two 'backs in the corner, their shoulders raised to their ears with pads, chatted in nervous subdued voices, wiping their fingers free from grease, trotting on the spot, chewing George's free gum. They stopped to have their carefully protected bodies examined, then combed their hair in the faded ale mirror. I felt the first aggressive sensation sweep over me as the dexadrin I'd taken at home began to be absorbed.

I joined Maurice at the resin board. He cracked an ammonia phial and we took it in turns to stuff it up our noses. The electric bell rang over the door. Dai began to reel off his last-minute advice.

One or two were a bit frightened – a player had been killed the previous week from a kick on the head. Dai sounded hard, a bit tired. Then he gave the ball to Frank and opened the door. 'Have a good game, lads,' George said paternally, his hands clenched over his stomach. 'No fists remember. But if you hit them – hit them bleeding hard!' It was his weekly concession to swearing. He nodded his head and smiled kindly at one or two.

I followed Frank into the tunnel. A body like his made for some security. A few officials touched his back, then my back, as we turned into the tunnel and broke into a trot. A tremendous roar coincided with the daylight, and grew as we streamed on to the field. The loudspeakers blared the 'Entrance of the Gladiators'.

In spite of the drizzle and the cold, the terraces were black with people. We stood clean and neat in a circle in the middle of the field, passing the ball, conspicuous against the greenery in red and blue arrowed jerseys and white shorts.

A plume of steam, brilliant against the greyness of the sky, detached itself from the lip of the cooling tower and drifted slowly over the field. A man in a white jersey with red horizontal configurations broke from the tunnel mouth. A second roar – rattles, bells, trumpet blasts – a stream of red and white flooded the darker greenery of the lower field. I looked for numbers two and five and at the size of their forwards. They were young.

Frank was standing with the ref and the other captain – bow-legged, small, not unlike Maurice. They shook hands, tossed a coin, and Frank indicated we'd play the way we were already facing.

A fresh burst from the crowd encouraged the line-up

Maurice ran up like he'd done a thousand times before and kicked off. The six forwards ran down the field. I carried on a straight course, knowing I could give the impression of strong attack without having to do anything – the player gathering the ball would run obliquely to the centre of the field and pass to one of the half-backs.

This he did, giving a fast convenient pass to the little captain who'd scarcely collected the ball than he was nearly killed by a short-arm from Maurice coming up in anticipation. The man lay still, covered in mud, his short legs splayed over the grass. The ref went over with a warning glance at Maurice to see how dead the man was. 'That's the way, Maurice,' Frank said.

We made a scrum over the spot, the short piston limbs interlocking, then straining. A movement began across the field and young Arnie ran in with an ankle tap and the player crumbled. The ball rolled free and the boy scooped it up alertly with one hand and side-stepping started to run down the field. He found Frank with a long pass coming up laboriously in support. The great bulk of Frank, his lessened speed, drew the opposing forwards magnetically. They leapt wildly at his slow procession through them. Before he fell under their simultaneous attacks he flicked the ball expertly into the gap he'd deliberately created. Maurice, waiting in receipt, didn't hear the oppressive noise that came from Frank as he hit the ground; he took the ball one-handed and with short precise steps cut his way through to the full-back, and was almost on the line when the winger, coming across with a greater and more famous speed, knocked him over like a stalk.

The two teams shot into position in the thick din of excitement. Frank stood behind Maurice and took the ball as it came between the scrum-half's legs. I started running up from behind, Frank held the ball, then slipped it to me as I passed in full stride. I hit the wall of waiting men like a rock. For a second they yielded, drew together, and held. A dull pain shot from the top of my skull. I struggled into a position I knew would ease the impact and give me more chance with any excited fist. I heard through compressed ears the screams and groans of the crowd, almost the individual voices of agony, before I was flung down.

I rose with the same motion and played the ball. Young Arnie had it. I'd never realized how popular he was with the crowd. When, with an apparently casual blow, he was banged down, I was vaguely satisfied at his indiscretion. I took the ball as he played it and sent it to the centres. It passed straight to the super-protected wingman. He gathered cleanly and bustled up the field only to be shoved into touch. The crowd disapproved.

We folded down to the scrum, panting with the first breathlessness, steam rising from the straining 'backs. I saw the damp shape roll between my legs and Maurice snatched it up impatiently. With an extravagant dummy he shot by the still dazed captain and was caught by the winger. He kicked out, lashed out, contorted, and threw himself over the line.

The crowd screamed and surged like penned animals, like a suddenly disturbed pool. Whistles, bells, and trumpets crashed and soared on the animal roar. I ran to him, banged his back, and we walked back in pleased groups.

The full-back failed at goal. A slight breeze moved across the ground, spraying the drizzle. A spurt of vivid steam swirled over the pitch and drifted in slow ascent. I stared down at the bare patch of earth at my feet, soft and muddy. I bent down and touched it reassuringly, and as the flurry of rain changed direction looked up at the similarly worn patch at the centre. The ball wasn't there. A tiger was running across the spot just after kicking. I narrowed my eyes, and in the thick air, against the dark prominence of the cooling towers, saw the slim oval shape.

'Yours, Art!' Maurice shouted behind me. The wet leather smacked into my crooked arms and I twisted instinctively into the grip of the surrounding men. I fell comfortably and was pressed to the ground. I stopped to watch the ball move from hand to hand across the field.

'Come on, Arthur lad,' somebody shouted either behind me or from the crowd. I followed the ball mechanically, attached to it by an invisible string. Perhaps I didn't need

248

a car now. It was getting too old, too knocked about, and I'd never afford another.

I took the ball and burst down the middle of the field. I avoided two men and passed. The movement petered out.

I took some trouble to stay on the blind side during the play-the-ball. I rested nervously, scarcely tired, slightly puzzled. My ankles ached: I'd bound them too tightly. The drug I'd taken seemed to have been absorbed. My chest was constricted. The dampness went through to the bone, numbing. Black, unknown faces, streaked with skin or blood, slow black limbs, moving continually past, interlocking, swaying, beating, followed by the steam, seeping from the skin, polluted by the mud, vaporizing in the cold air.

I ran in close to a play-the-ball and took the pass. I broke into the oblique long-paced run popular with the crowd.

I chose the right wing, a stretch of field more familiar and where the winger was of a slighter build. He waited for me cautiously, feet astride, nervously crouched, encouraging me to run between him and the touch. I checked my stride and began to run on the outside of my feet, and moved straight towards him. He moved sideways again, still urging me to pass him between the touchline. I hated his mean scheming. I ran at him and shoved out my left fist. I saw his flash of fear, the two arms pushed out protectively, the silly stagger backwards, the two wounds torn in the turf by his sliding heels. I sensed the shape of the full-back running diagonally to intercept. I brought my knees up higher and concentrated on the line.

There was Arnie's boyish supporting shout. I'd only to give it to him for a score. I shoved my hand at the full-back's head as he came in, and felt the slackening of his arms. I threw myself forward, and hit somebody hard. I fell over sideways into touch.

The smell of the earth, and grass – Arnie pulling me to my feet. A brown liquid running down my nose, over my lip, and seeping into my mouth. Arnie watched it with sickened fascination.

'That's great, Art! . . . great!' Maurice was telling me.

I leaned down in the scrum, watched the ball come in, go out. I stood up. The whistle went. Half-time.

The men sprawled and collapsed on to the massage table and the bench. Belching and groaning. There was no gas left. 'Blind that bastard when he comes round the loose head. You go for his legs. Have you got that? Leave the frog's head to me.'

'Did you see how he belted Morgan?'

'Nay, but bloody hell, fair's fair.'

'I got more money playing Union in Wales than I've ever done up here . . . and I tell you, if. . . .'

They calmed down. The warmth, the smell of the hot bath, and Dai's single persistent voice guided the resentment. Frank brought over a bottle of water and rested his steaming carcass beside mine. He tipped the bottle to his lips, swilled his mouth, and spat. When I took the bottle from him I saw the blood oozing from his hair. It dried with the mud over his forehead, round his eyes, and over his swollen nose. 'You all right?' he said. 'I'm stuffed. I'm an arse for wukking last night.'

The room was a stall of steaming cattle. Dai was going at it hard, telling how everything was going wrong. I crunched an ammonia phial in my fingers and shoved it up Frank's nose. He shuddered, choked, and coughed to life.

We walked back on to the field slowly. A milder, impatient cheer met our second appearance, a tired trumpet. We stood and waited in the rain for the other team. With the weather thickening and the light fading early the crowd had thinned slightly either end of the ground. The better part of it was now stuffed in the main stand and in the covered stand opposite. Somewhere amongst the dark mass was my father. And Johnson. 'We're on the radio now,' Maurice said as he ran by. 'Keep your hair parted.'

'See you.'

'That's it, kid.'

The game entered its long drag. With Frank half-dazed I ran about encouraging the side. Everybody wanted a good run with the ball to make sure their names went over the air on the Northern Service. In the scrum I leaned heavily against Arnie, feeling a bated reassurance in holding his back. I began to take advantage of planning the game by not taking part in it. When I actually held the ball and peered out, rain-blinded, at those dim circulating shapes I felt unsure and sent the ball away with a careful movement of the wrists. At one point I turned too slowly and un-balanced, and heard it credited with a noise from the crowd as a dark shape passed me, shooting up mud either side. A roar drew a curtain round the ground. We lined up behind the posts. Overhead, in the low cloud, an aircraft thundered.

'Bad luck, Arthur,' young Arnie said deliberately. I watched the placing of the ball carefully, the meticulous run of the kicker, the swing through of his leg, the small shape spinning silently through the rain and curving between the posts. A crisp eruption by the crowd.

I began to resent the activity around me. An old way of escape. I looked to the life that wasn't absorbed in the futility of the game – to the tall chimney and the two flowering cylinders of the power station, half hidden by cloud, the tops of the buses passing the end of the ground, the lights turned on inside the upper decks, the people sitting uncommitted behind the windows. The houses were lit too, in their slow descent to the valley. I moved back to the centre, imitating the figures whose activity suddenly tired me. I was ashamed of being no longer young.

We were pressed back to our line. Maurice stole the ball and flicked it back to Frank. He stormed into the wall of men and was thrown down in a cloud of dirty steam and spray. Arnie was treated the same. They ran a yard, two yards, from the line and were thrown back as much. Frank tried again, pumping his huge body forward and concealing his grunt of pain as he was flung down. He had another go, and with a cry of frustration and rage, he was seized, lifted, and turned over before being dropped on his head and shoulders. He wheezed like a beaten machine as his skull drove into the earth.

The indignity brought a mixed cry of wonder and amuse-ment from the crowd. I hoped Kenny wasn't there. 'There's nothing on that field that can take punishment like Frank

251

Miles,' George often said to visiting chairmen. 'And I'm including the ball as well.'

To my left the tiger captain watched the struggle of his forwards. 'The ball! The ball!' he was shouting. 'Leave the man. . . . Get the bleeding ball!' He beat himself with impatience.

The leather smacked into my outstretched hands. I ran straight at the man. 'Go on Art! Go on Art!' Maurice screamed behind me. I ran into him, over him. Trampled him and broke free into a gap. A pain thudded in my head in echo to my feet. An arm gripped my waist, slipped, caught again, and a fist sank into my neck. I carried him along. Then another caught me round the nose and eyes, the fingers explored for pain, forcing me to my knees. Arnie took the ball and with his boy's shout of triumph threw himself into the confusion of mud and men, his body searching, like a tentacle, for an opening. He ran ten yards to a scream from the crowd, then fell into the sea of limbs.

I was still kneeling, absorbed in an odd resigned feeling. My back teeth chattered as I pulled myself up, my hands shook with cold, and I despised myself for not feeling hate for the man who'd torn my nostril. I was used to everything now. Ten years of this, ten years of the crowd – I could make one mistake, one slight mistake only, and the whole tragedy of living, of being alive, would come into the crowd's throat and roar its pain like a maimed animal. The cry, the rage of the crowd echoed over and filled the valley – a shape came towards me in the gloom.

I glimpsed the fierce and brilliant whiteness of its eyes and clenched teeth through its mask of mud, flashing with a useless hostility. It avoided my preparations to delay it, veering past out of reach. I put my foot out, and as the man man stumbled took a swing with my fist. I missed, and fell down with a huge sound from the crowd. The man recovered and went on running. He ran between the posts. Frank picked me up, the mud covering my tears. Where's the bleeding full-back? I wanted to shout. But I could only stare unbelievingly at my legs which had betrayed me.

The water rose to my shoulders. It pressed on my chest and I fought for breath, coughing in the steam. Its heat brought my bruises to life. Over on my left Maurice chatted, just his head and a lighted cig above the water. Frank, drawing relief from his fag, turned his bull's back to me. I rubbed the soap over his familiar stained skin. I knew it better than my own.

He submerged and left half the soap on the surface. When he brought his face up again he said, 'Somebody's pissing i' the bath again.' And after looking round with a vacant grin added, 'It'll be Arnie, thy can bet.'

'Who me?' The kid looked hurt and pointed to himself.

Frank lunged through the crowded bath at him. Maurice and me joined him, the others shot out. He screamed for help. We got hold of the wild animal and shoved his obscene head under the cold water tap. Maurice tickled his ribs. Water cascaded into the dressing-room. Everybody joined the shrieking. Arnie was tortured with his own laughter.

Then Dai cleared us out with the hose. We stood in front of the coke fire and were rubbed down. Maurice lay on the table, another cig in his mouth, having his knees dressed. The masseur bent over him, staining his body with orange liniment.

Frank, his belly relaxed and protruding, rubbed his head slowly with the towel, his biceps bunched like rocks. I had my ankles strapped, got dressed, and put my teeth in.

MORE ABOUT PENGUINS
AND PELICANS

Penguinews, which appears every month, contains details of all the new books issued by Penguins as they are published. From time to time it is supplemented by the *Penguin Stock List*, which is our complete list of almost 5,000 titles.

A specimen copy of *Penguinews* will be sent to you free on request. Please write to Dept EP, Penguin Books Ltd, Harmondsworth, Middlesex, for your copy.

In the U.S.A.: For a complete list of books available from Penguins in the United States write to Dept CS, Penguin Books, 625 Madison Avenue, New York, New York 10022.

In Canada: For a complete list of books available from Penguins in Canada write to Penguin Books Canada Ltd, 2801 John Street, Markham, Ontario L3R 1B4.

Also by David Storey

FLIGHT INTO CAMDEN

Acclaimed as a remarkable young writer for his first novel, *This Sporting Life*, David Storey was awarded the 1961 John Llewellyn Rhys Memorial Prize for *Flight into Camden*.

This moving story is recounted by Margaret, the daughter of a Yorkshire miner, who falls in love with a married teacher and goes to live with him in a room in Camden Town, London. Many critics have observed an almost Laurentian fidelity in the descriptions of their love-making and the intricacies of their emotional responses to one another. But in the end family ties prove too strong for an ambiguous relationship which begins to disclose a chasm of emptiness and bitterness.

'An entirely successful *tour de force* ... rises on occasions to a pitch of precise beauty which I can only, however inaccurately, describe as poetry' – *Guardian*

'A love story written with seriousness, sensibility, and intensity' – *Observer*

Also published in Penguins
PASMORE

Published in Penguin Plays
HOME
THE CHANGING ROOM